SAN SALVADOR, El Salvador (UPI)—
Gunmen kidnapped two American businessmen and shot and killed their Salvadoran driver Friday in an ambush near
San Salvador airport, the U.S. Embassy
said.

An Embassy spokesman identified
the two Americans as [Bruce Chapman], 37,
and Fausto Bucheli, both employees of
the U.S. [Hartell Industries] Co.

[Chapman] is the general manager
of the American company's Salvadoran
subsidiary, Aplar, and Bucheli is an
engineer working for the company.

Their hometowns were not immediately
available.

Police, who earlier reported that
only [Chapman] had been kidnapped, identified the dead man as Jose Luis Paz Tratara.

The Embassy spokesman said Paz Tratara, [Chapman's] driver, was shot and
killed when he tried to resist the gunmen.

upi 09-21[-79]   11:23 ped

Hostage!

The true story of an American's
47 days of terrorist captivity
in Latin America

Fausto Bucheli

with

J. Robin Maxson

ZONDERVAN PUBLISHING HOUSE
OF THE ZONDERVAN CORPORATION
GRAND RAPIDS, MICHIGAN 49506.

Edited by James E. Ruark
Designed by Louise Bauer

Library of Congress Cataloging in Publication Data

Bucheli, Fausto.
    Hostage!
        1. Bucheli, Fausto.   2.   Converts—El Salvador—
Biography.   3.   Guerrillas—El Salvador.
4.   Kidnapping—El Salvador.   I.   Maxson, J. Robin,
1947-   .   II.   Title.
BV4935.B83A33   1982   364.1'54'0924 [B]   82-17406
ISBN 0-310-45631-2

Printed in the United States of America

82   83   84   85   86   87   88 — 10   9   8   7   6   5   4   3   2   1

To my faithful and beloved wife
RITA
and our favorite children
HILDA,
FAUSTO,
VERONICA,
HELEN,
TINA
—former hostages,
fellow learners
in the ways of freedom

Contents

Photographs follow page 160.

Preface

HOSTAGE! IS A STORY of intrigue, suspense, and pathos. The events described in this narrative really happened. It has been our intention in the telling of this story to be as accurate as possible in relating *how* things happened.

Of necessity, not all the characters in this drama are presented in the most favorable light. However, *Hostage!* was not written for the purpose of accusing particular individuals of devious behavior. It was written to describe the experiences of a victim of terrorism and the outcome of those experiences for him, his family, and his friends. It is a book of hope, not recrimination.

Accordingly, the name of the company for which Fausto Bucheli was working during the time in question, as well as the names of all other officials and employees of the company, have been changed. While fictitious names are used, the reader should understand that the persons described are real. An exception to the pseudonyms is Fred Rayne, whose true identity is disclosed with permission.

Because the broad facts of this case were covered by the press during the fall of 1979, the identities of the main characters are already a matter of public record. Our decision to use invented names does not reflect an attempt to cover up the truth, but rather to direct the focus of the spotlight.

The primary source for most of the information in this book was Fausto Bucheli. Upon his return from captivity, he made some notes to help him remember both the details and the dates pertaining to his confinement. Then, over a period of several months, he narrated his story through personal interviews, tape recordings, and long-distance telephone calls.

The facts about what was happening in California were provided by Rita, the children, and the friends who were involved. Dave and Pauline Solano, Gert Verhoeven, and Bill Trevan offered invaluable assistance in their willingness to be interviewed.

Information on the negotiations came from a variety of sources. Some was provided at a press conference held by Hartell executives and Fred Rayne the day after Fausto returned to the United States. In addition, both the kidnappers and Fred Rayne gave information to Fausto immediately before and after his release. Interestingly, Rayne's description of the proceedings squared precisely with the data offered by the terrorists.

Other information was obtained from articles and reports published in media throughout the period in question. By sifting through hundreds of news articles, we were able to weed out many of the errors that inevitably crept into news releases, especially the earliest ones.

We also reviewed the letters and telegrams received by the Buchelis from friends all over the world, with the greatest quantity coming from their friends in Berne, Indiana.

Just this past summer Fausto was given access to information collected by those who were directly involved in the negotiations. He spent several hours interviewing one of the team members who was in direct contact with the terrorists from the Sheraton Hotel command post. He listened to many of the recorded conversations between "Juan Ortega" and "Carlos," including the arrangements for delivering the ransom.

Some details, such as the amount of money paid by Hartell, have been omitted at the request of Hartell and the U.S. State Department. There are many other facts that we would like to have been able to include, but they were simply unavailable to us. Mysteries remain that may never be told.

This book contains much dialogue. Obviously, conversations held almost three years before cannot all be recalled verbatim (although Fausto's recall is excellent). Some dialogue, especially the exchanges conducted at the crisis points, is rendered word for word. Some conversations are paraphrases, and some are condensations of several related discussions. All are authentic in that they accurately reflect both the personalities of those involved and the nature of each situation. A few scenes were created to provide continuity in the narration.

It may not greatly matter to anyone else that my wife Louise put in many hours transcribing taped interviews, doing supplementary research at the library, and covering for dad at home with Rachel Beth and Michael Ben for three months—but it matters to me. I am deeply grateful.

I am also grateful to Tim Cone for mowing my lawn all summer, and to Norma Wangeman for helping to get some Spanish material translated into English.

Both Fausto and I want to express our appreciation to the people of Klamath Evangelical Free Church, who shared our commitment to making this story known. They gave me permission to help get it into print and then worked hard during the summer to effectively carry on the work of the church in this community. Without their encouragement and participation, this project would never have been completed.

Finally I want to thank the Lord for the opportunity and the energy to prepare this book. I trust that He will use it constructively in the lives of those who read it.

J. Robin Maxson
Klamath Falls, Oregon

This book represents a partial fulfillment of a promise I made to God in El Salvador: to tell anyone who will listen what He has done, and is doing, in my life. I am pleased for the opportunity to do this, and for the chance to acknowledge the people who helped my family in tangible ways and prayed for our well-being.

In addition, I want to express my gratitude to Paul Landry, my interim pastor, for putting me in touch with Zondervan Publishing House. His initiative and the excellent work by the staff of Zondervan made this book possible.

Fausto Bucheli
Chino, California

Additional Sources

Erdozain, Placido. *Archbishop Romero: Martyr of Salvador*. Maryknoll, N.Y.: Orbis Books, 1981.

Flint, Jerry. "More Cubas in the Making." *Forbes* 125:6 (31 March 1980):41–46.

Fodor, Eugene. *Fodor's Central America*. New York: David McKay Co., 1980.

Gravely, Edmund K., Jr. "Bitterman Slaying Isolates Guerrillas, Bolsters SIL." *Christianity Today* 25 (10 April 1981):70–72.

Haverstock, Nathan A. "El Salvador." *World Book*, vol. 6, 1982.

Kirk, Donald. "Foiling Kidnappers." *New York Times Magazine* (19 February 1978):14–42.

Migdail, Carl J. "Warning Flag Is Up in Central America." *U.S. News & World Report* 87 (20 August 1979):25–26.

Morgenthau, Tom, et al. "Nicaragua's Aftershocks." *Newsweek* 94 (20 August 1979):39.

New York Times. All articles on the political situation and terrorist activity in El Salvador between January 1979 and January 1981.

"No Bargaining for a New Hostage." *Newsweek* 97 (9 February 1981):58.

"SIL Hangs Tough Over Translator Abducted in Colombia." *Christianity Today* 25 (20 February 1981):52, 55.

"Steering a Middle Course." *Time* 114 (3 September 1979):32–33.

Strasser, Steven, with Stryker McGuire. "Black September.'; *Newsweek* 94 (24 September 1979):52.

"The Left Executes a U.S. Missionary." *Newsweek* 97 (16 March 1981):46.

"The Victors Organize." *Time* 114 (13 August 1979):22–23.

The World Book Year Books: 1980, 1981, 1982.

"Undoing the Dynasty." *Time* 114 (6 August 1979):50–51.

APLAR

(EL SALVADOR), S. A.

FAUSTO R: BUCHELI

FULLERTON-CA

Instituto Salvadoreño de Comercio Exterior

ZONA FRANCA INDUSTRIAL Y COMERCIAL

SAN BARTOLO

1
Ready to Erupt

THIS IS REALLY *first class,* I thought as the Pan Am 747 cruised over the mountainous terrain between Guatemala City and San Salvador. *I wish my father could see me. He would approve.*

I admitted to myself that I was enjoying the VIP treatment. Providing the commuter connection from Ontario Airport to the Los Angeles airport was a nice touch. I remembered thinking, as I was checking in at the Golden West counter, how much nicer that fifteen-minute drive from home had been than the hour-and-a-half hassle to LAX would have been. Hartell Industries takes care of their people.

My watch beeped twice, signaling a new hour. I glanced at the digital face: 3:00. I pulled out the canary-colored "Request for Trip Approval and Itinerary" to see when we were scheduled to land: 5:25 P.M. Less than a half-hour. We had lost two hours to time zones. I would have to change my watch later, if I could remember which buttons to push. Five-and-one-half hours from L.A. to San Salvador. Not bad.

I looked again at the yellow carbon copy. There were three signatures at the bottom on the authorization line, and I didn't recognize any of them. *Do they know me any better? I wondered. The secretary had misspelled Guatemala,* typing an *a* instead of the *e*. Did it twice. *It's some comfort that someone else knows less about Central America than I do,* I thought aloud.

13

I looked out the window as the huge jet banked to make its long arcing descent to the runway. From the air, El Salvador is beautiful: Rugged mountains, checkerboard fields, green running right up to the blackened rims of giant volcanoes. Apart from the volcanoes, it reminds me of parts of Ecuador. As one looks down on the farmland below, the narrow ribbon of the Pan-American Highway draws the eye like a magnet to the city of San Salvador itself.

The voice of the pilot crackled over the intercom: "Ladies and gentlemen, we will be landing at Ilopango International Airport in about five minutes, so please fasten your seat belts. As we make our approach you will be able to see the city of San Salvador through the windows on the left. It is situated in the Valley of the Hammocks, over which we have been flying, at an elevation of twenty-two hundred feet. It sits at the base of Volcano San Salvador to the northwest. Nine miles to the east, you can see the blue waters of Lake Ilopango. San Salvador has a population that is rapidly approaching one million people. Their view of the Pacific Ocean is blocked by the Coastal Range immediately to the south. All of these places are easily accessible from San Salvador and you should make every effort to include them on your sightseeing itinerary. Both the temperature and the humidity are at eighty-five on the ground. Thank you for flying with Pan American, and have a nice week."

Douglas Ford, my supervisor, nudged me with his elbow. "He read that real well, didn't he?"

I smiled back. "I think they smuggled on the president of the Chamber of Commerce."

"Well, as nice as it all looks from up here," he replied, "I think this is about as much sightseeing as we're likely to get in on."

"Unless," I countered, "you change the spelling of 'site.'"

Ford laughed. "Not bad, Fausto, not bad!"

We were off to a good start. I just hoped it stayed that way.

On August 6 I had reported for my first day of work at Hartell Industries. I had been hired as a Project Development Engineer to oversee the development of a thick film resistor—an electrical component with a wide range of applications. I had had experience previously in the design and production of similar components.

That morning I met Doug Ford. He showed me around the section of the plant in which I would be working. Then he took me to my desk. He gave me four books to read to get oriented to the company and my work.

The next day Ford stopped by my desk. "Fausto," he said, "we are going to San Salvador."

I didn't understand. "Who is going where?"

He was smiling. "We—you and I—are going to fly to San Salvador. That's the capital of El Salvador, in Central America."

"Right," I said. "Why?"

He explained: "We have a subsidiary down there called APLAR.[1] The less expensive labor was supposed to save us money. But instead, that plant is costing us about two million dollars a year. The general manager, Bruce Chapman, is a bright young man. He's the one who set up that operation for us about five years ago. But production is way off. He apparently needs some help in analyzing and correcting the problems. The company is sending me down there, and I want you to come along."

My mind was still reeling. No one had said anything about this kind of work during my interview. "Why me?"

"You have experience and expertise in the kind of manufacturing they are trying to do." He paused. "And you speak Spanish fluently."

It was starting to make sense.

Ford continued. "Mr. Chapman speaks some Spanish—enough to get by. But frankly, we don't know how much of the problem might be a lack of communication between American management and Salvadoran personnel. You should be able to help us sort that out."

"I see," I replied. "Well, if that's what you want me to do, I'll do the best I can. When do we leave?"

"Our reservations are for Sunday morning. You will catch a commuter flight from Ontario [Airport] to L.A. International. I'll meet you there. You will need to make sure your passport is up to date. The company will make all the other arrangements."

---

[1]APLAR is an acronym for Asian Pacific Latin American Region. The plant employed about five hundred Salvadoran workers.

"O.K.," I said, as Ford turned and walked back to his office.

Incredible! I wasn't even sure how to get from my home in Chino to my job in Fullerton, and my second week of work with Hartell Industries would be spent in El Salvador. El Salvador? What kind of place is that?

† † †

VOLCANOES—SOME twenty-two of them—preside in awesome splendor over the rugged mountain ranges that give El Salvador a spectacular landscape. The occasional puffs of steam seen rising from blackened cones remind the spectator that violent forces that gave this land its present character may be only temporarily banked beneath a fragile crust. Earthquakes that rumble up and down the grand isthmus of Central America underline the atmosphere of uncertainty that pervades these fertile lands.

There are more volcanoes in El Salvador than any other Central American country, though it is the smallest of the seven nations. Given the fact that there are also more people per square mile in El Salvador and that most of them are dirt poor with little prospect for improvement, there could be no more apt symbol for this tiny country than the smoke-plumed volcano. With all the seismic activity in and around the country's political terrain during the first half of 1979, it is little wonder that those with a stake in the nation's stability held their breath through the summer months. Virtually every indicator suggested that a major explosion was inevitable. The only question was, How soon would it come?

Facts and figures, statistics and maps provide the quickest way to orient the unfamiliar to the situation encountered by Fausto Bucheli in August-September 1979. First the map.

The countries of Central America occupy the narrow, roughly funnel-shaped strip of land that runs northwest to southeast linking the rest of North America to South America. El Salvador occupies the bottom side of this isthmus at a point where the Pacific coastline runs virtually east and west, just south of the fifteenth parallel. It is framed on the map by Guatemala on the west and Honduras on the north and east. It is the only Central American nation untouched by the waters of the Caribbean.

By 1979 the region's second-greatest population (4.6 million people compared with Guatemala's 6.5 million) was shoe-horned into a country the size of Massachusetts (8,200 square miles). This gave El Salvador a population density unequaled in most other countries of the world, much less Central America. Jamming more than five hundred people into each square mile would make matters difficult enough if the nation's resources had been more evenly divided. But they weren't.

El Salvador's greatest natural resource is dirt—rich, black volcanic soil. It grows what is arguably the best coffee in the world. It produces so much of it that this tiny country is the fourth-leading exporter of coffee in the Western Hemisphere. *Fincas* (plantations) and farms cover 75 percent of the land. More than half of all workers till the soil, harvest the crops, tend the livestock. But only a handful of people realize any significant return from the agricultural production.

The statistics in 1979 were lopsided:

—One-half of 1 percent of all landowners controlled 38 percent of the arable land;

—2 percent of the people owned 60 percent of the land;

—4 percent of the farms covered almost 70 percent of all agricultural land;

—80 percent of the farms had less than seven acres apiece; 40 percent, less than 2½ acres;

—80 percent of the national income was received by 20 percent of the people;

—Half the population subsisted on less than ten dollars a month;

—16 percent of the work force had year-round employment.

Given such disparities, it offers little consolation to the poor that El Salvador ranked first among Central American countries in percentage of millionaires in 1979. As one Salvadoran businessman put it, "The problem in El Salvador is not that the few have too much—but that too many people have nothing."[2] Statistics don't measure misery, but there may well be more of it per square mile in El Salvador than just about any other country in the Western Hemisphere.

History offers no encouragement. In 1979 it was commonly accepted that, for all intents and purposes, the country is owned and operated by the same handful of families that have controlled the economic structure for nearly half a century. The government, ruled by a succession of military officers since 1931, has been viewed by the masses as an extension of the *Catorce Familias* ("Fourteen Families"). The current president, Gen. Carlos Humberto Romero, appeared to be no more interested in disrupting the feudal status quo than his predecessors had been. Numerous election frauds and the ruthless suppression of opposition parties had squelched any home of accomplishing significant reform by peaceful means.

And so, to those who were desperate, unpeaceful means to bring change became acceptable as the magma of Marxist-Leninist revolution began to flow through the political underground. By the summer of 1979, the ranks of the two-year-old Popular Revolutionary Bloc (BPR), a coalition of workers, peasants, and students, had swollen from two hundred to more than sixty thousand. Resorting to mass demonstrations and the seizure of foreign embassies and cathedrals, the BPR repeatedly provoked confrontations with government security forces. One such clash, when anti-government demonstrators occupied the Metropolitan Cathedral in San Salvador on May 8, resulted in the deaths of twenty-three protesters.

Other groups such as the People's Revolutionary Army and the Armed Forces of National Resistance adopted tactics of outright terrorism. The kidnapping of foreign diplomats and businessmen had the dual effect of undermining the economy (by discouraging investments from international concerns) and raising millions of dollars in ransom payments (variously estimated at from $40 to $72 million).

Not all kidnapping attempts resulted in the payment of ransom. On May 30, four youths attempted to abduct Hugo Wey, a Swiss chargé d'affaires, from his car. When he tried to

---

[2]Jerry Flint, "More Cubas in the Making," *Forbes* 125:6 (31 March 1980):45.

back away from the vehicle blocking his path, the youths shot him through the windows and killed him.

As a means of disrupting the economy and further destabilizing the government, kidnapping was highly effective. Foreign companies began to withdraw their executives. A business community numbering 408 Japanese executives rapidly dwindled to 40 when one of their countrymen was abducted. American firms took out kidnapping insurance to cover the potential costs of ransom payments—with a deductible of $500,000! Businessmen began traveling under false identities. Armored cars and bodyguards were used to protect the people deemed indispensable to company operations. Some multinational firms simply cut their losses and pulled out.

Perhaps the most ominous sign of the summer was the successful overthrow of President Anastasio Somoza of neighboring Nicaragua by the Sandinista National Liberation Front. That turn of events on July 17 understandably struck fear into the hearts of the military rulers of El Salvador, Honduras, and Guatemala. The "Domino Theory" was resurrected by analysts of international affairs, and El Salvador was identified as the domino likely to topple next. Said an American banker in Venezuela, "Nicaragua needed a push, but El Salvador will fall by itself."[3]

† † †

DOUG FORD and I were met at the airport by Bruce Chapman and three of his Salvadoran staff members: Pacho, Raul, and Luis. Bruce drove us into the city in his yellow-and-white Dodge van and registered us in the city's newest and finest hotel, El Camino Real. More first-class accommodations. I was beginning to think I could get used to this kind of treatment.

Ford and I had dinner at El Escorial, the beautiful hotel restaurant, which featured French cuisine and live entertainment. We reviewed our plan of operation for the week ahead. Then we turned in.

The next morning we were met very early by Bruce and

[3]Tom Morgenthau et al., "Nicaragua's Aftershocks," *Newsweek* 94 (20 August 1979):39.

Luis. As we drove to the plant, I recognized that we were driving south on Boulevard del Ejército Nacional, the same four-lane highway we had traveled from the airport. APLAR was located in an attractive industrial area not far from the airport—an ideal location for shipping. Already the road was becoming congested, but the five-mile drive took little more than fifteen minutes.

In fact, the time seemed less than that, thanks to Bruce. He is a very likable, outgoing man with a good deal of energy. He is talkative and has a ready laugh. He gave a running commentary on the countryside, the people, the plant—more things than I can remember.

Luis sat quietly on the passenger's side in the front. He provided quite a contrast to Bruce. Even if Luis could speak English, I don't think he would have tried to get a word in edgewise.

When we arrived at the plant, Bruce called in his three top managers to join us. We had met Pacho and Raul the day before. The third man, José, was the personnel manager. Together we toured the plant, and the managers showed us the layout and the procedures.

Immediately Ford and I could see why APLAR was producing at only 30-to-40 percent of capacity. Equipment was situated wrong, machines were not assembled correctly, people were not operating the machinery properly. It was a motion study engineer's nightmare.

After the initial tour, we told the employees to go about their work as normal. Then Ford took one section of the plant, I another, and we just observed. We spent most of the week writing down the conditions that needed to be changed.

On Thursday he and I spent some time together deciding which changes had to be made immediately and which steps could wait. Then we called the management team together and made another tour of the factory. Because I spoke Spanish, I gave the instructions and pointed out the changes that were necessary. The process consumed the rest of the working week there.

The hours were long, the work intense. Since we knew we had only one week to complete our study, we tried to make good use of our time. We left the hotel early every morning;

when we returned at night, we would eat supper, compare notes, and go straight to bed exhausted.

When I returned home to Chino on Saturday evening and one of my daughters asked me what El Salvador is like, I was stumped. Apart from APLAR, El Camino Real, the highway in between, and what I saw from the airplane, I didn't know much more about the country than I did before the trip. I had not been a very good sightseer. But I hoped Hartell would feel I had been a good site inspector.

† † †

ON THURSDAY, August 16, as Fausto Bucheli and Douglas Ford reviewed their initial findings with the management staff of APLAR, a band of striking union members seized control of a factory of the Apex Textile Company, another American firm operating in San Salvador. Most of the two hundred employees who were working in defiance of the strike fled unharmed. The company manager, William Boorstein, aged sixty, of New Jersey, and a small group of management personnel and office staff were taken hostage. The militant laborers holding Boorstein and the others were demanding wage increases.

The occupation of the plant and confinement of the staff continued through the weekend as negotiations began with government officials and Apex lawyers for Boorstein's release. U.S. embassy officials expressed concern for Boorstein's health, since he had been under treatment for a heart problem and pneumonia.

On Monday the militants permitted a delivery of medicine and food to the factory. They also issued a manifesto to be published in the newspapers of San Salvador as a condition for the release of the American businessman. The proclamation, printed the next day, accused industrialists of "trampling the rights and interests of workers" in El Salvador. Boorstein still was not released.

In the meantime, about 150 Roman Catholic priests, nuns, and supporters continued a fast to register their opposition to alleged human rights violations by the government. They were encouraged in their protest by Archbishop Oscar Arnulfo Romero, who was becoming increasingly outspoken in his criticism of abuses by the military-backed administration.

Apparently responding to the protests of the church and the striking workers, President Romero issued a statement declaring that all political exiles were free to return to El Salvador; the International Red Cross was invited to investigate allegations that political prisoners were being held without due process; and free congressional elections would be held in March.

The occupation of the Apex plant and the captivity of William Boorstein continued.

2
An Italian Hoosier
With a Spanish Accent

FOR MOST AMERICANS the incident that lays undisputed claim to the "Most Memorable Event of 1979" is the seizure of the U.S. embassy in Teheran by some five hundred militant Iranian "students" on November 4. It's not that the final year of the decade was lacking for noteworthy events. Nineteen seventy-nine was also the year that

—The United States established diplomatic relations with the People's Republic of China;

—Teams from Pittsburgh, Pennsylvania, won both the Superbowl and the World Series;

—Egypt and Israel signed a peace treaty ending a thirty-year state of war;

—Margaret Thatcher became the first woman prime minister of Great Britain;

—Pope John Paul II visited Mexico, Poland, and the United States;

—Russia invaded Afghanistan;

—Mother Teresa of India was awarded the Nobel Peace Prize;

—A couple of Central American dictators were overthrown and replaced by military juntas.

But for sheer indelibility, every other national memory is hazy by comparison to the bold-type impressions of American hostages in Iran. We had been intrigued as we watched the political chess match between the Ayatollah (must be some new religion) and the Shah (if he's so rich, why can't he find some place to live?). We had listened uncomprehendingly to reports of an interminable blood bath that seemed to be part and parcel with the Ayatollah Khomeini's rise to power. But no one was prepared for the unthinkable sequence of events that unfolded in November: wild men do not just take over foreign embassies with impunity; madmen do not exercise absolute rule over nations with total disregard for international law; students do not openly flout the benevolence and might of the United States of America!

But they did.

And our fury and disbelief surrendered to frustration and mutual recrimination. It was only a matter of hours before the television anchormen began scratching the marks on the prison walls of our living rooms with the nightly rehearsal of our new identity—"America Held Hostage" (sound of trumpets).

On November 4, 1979, the nation began to experience in some measure the painful emotions that had already racked, then numbed, at least one family for forty-five days. For the loved ones of Fausto Bucheli, the center of the universe was not Teheran. It was the tiny country of El Salvador. And even as television crews were being dispatched to chronicle the outpouring of anti-American wrath outside the embassy gates in Iran, a handful of invisible men were playing out a desperate scene to gain the release of two Americans from terrorists in Central America.

Even in a world where incidents of terrorism have become standard fare in the daily news diet, the thought that Fausto Bucheli would be captured and imprisoned by left-wing Salvadoran revolutionaries remains far-fetched. He didn't belong in El Salvador. He didn't want to be in El Salvador. His awareness of the political situation there was minimal, his involvement nil. Yet, far from being an "innocent bystander" caught in the crossfire of opposing forces, he became the chosen target and victim of a carefully executed kidnapping. No novelist could concoct a more incredible story.

It begins, not in El Salvador or even in the United States,

but in Ecuador, South America. That is where Fausto Bucheli
was born in December 1937. His father, Antonio; a successful
businessman, had emigrated to Ecuador from Italy—which accounts for the name. Antonio married Maria, an Ecuadorian girl
from a prominent and staunchly Roman Catholic family. They
had eight children, of which Fausto is the second, the first son.

† † †

A BOOK about my life, I think, would have five chapters.

The first chapter would concern my childhood and youth. I
was brought up in Quito, the capital city of Ecuador. My family
was prosperous, and I lived a sheltered life. My mother wanted
me to attend parochial school. Though my father was an atheist,
he consented—as long as I didn't take religion too seriously.

After I graduated from high school, I attended the University of Quito. I majored in engineering, which came very easily
for me. I earned my bachelor's degree in record time.

At age twenty I left home to seek my fortune. The second
chapter of my life began when I went to work for an American
crop-dusting company in the seacoast town of Esmeraldas.
Swooping down over banana plantations in a biplane seemed a
lot more exciting than engineering. I made good money, which
I also spent very fast. More importantly, I was gaining confidence in my ability to make it on my own as an adult.

In 1960 my life grew complicated. Her name was Rita, and
she stunned me with her beauty. The complication was religion: Rita was an evangelical Christian. I did not even know
what that meant. But she would not consider marrying someone who did not share her faith. So I went to church with her
and learned how to act and talk like an Evangelical. I did
everything, short of being baptized, to prove to Rita that she
could marry me in good conscience. After five months of
courtship she agreed. We were joined in marriage by Doug
Hodges, an American missionary, on November 19, 1960.

Chapter 3, covering the next seven years, was rough. Almost immediately I stopped pretending to be an Evangelical
and went back to my old ways of living. Rita, of course, was
very disappointed.

In less than a year, our first child, Hilda, was born.

Three things happened one after another in 1963 that put us under a lot of strain: I lost my job in a dispute with another pilot; our second child, Fausto Jr., was born; and Rita was unfairly fired from her teaching post at a Christian school. She was so upset that our nursing baby became violently ill. I was furious with these so-called Christians and their missionary advisers. Rita, too, felt that she had been betrayed by her evangelical brothers and sisters. Though she obtained another teaching position at three times the pay, she carried that hurt for a long time.

When I could not find another job in Esmeraldas, I returned to Quito. I didn't want to leave Rita with the children, but we couldn't afford to have her give up a paying job. I told her, "This will only be temporary." "Temporary" turned out to be a year and a half.

The only thing that turned up in Quito was an opportunity to travel to the United States through an educational exchange program sponsored by the United Nations. Rita didn't even know I had decided to apply for the program until I called her from Los Angeles. Those were difficult days for her—for both of us. I decided to remain in the U.S. and seek permanent employment. Finally I found a job in Detroit as a layout inspector and junior engineer for the Ford Motor Company.

It was a good job with a future. I worked hard to learn English, advance in the field of engineering, and earn enough money to bring Rita and the children to America. Naturally Rita was reluctant to leave her job, her family, and the security of Esmeraldas for the unfamiliar culture of the United States. And I hadn't been such a great husband. But I begged her to come and give it a try—just for three months. She agreed.

Three months stretched into two years. In March 1966, one year after her arrival in Detroit, Rita gave birth to our third child, Veronica. Hilda and Little Fausto were making the transition with ease, as small children do. But for Rita life was difficult. The language was hard, the weather was hard, caring for three preschool children in a foreign land was hard. Since I was involved in the working world, my cultural adaptation was progressing smoothly. But my outgoing Rita felt like a wild bird cooped up in a cage. Eventually she became ill.

Her doctor concluded that Rita's only problem was stress.

He suggested that I devote more time to my family, even if I had to make sacrifices for my career. The diagnosis was painful to me at the time. But it opened the door to the brightest chapter in my story.

The fourth chapter began with the decision to move to Fort Wayne, Indiana. That was the hometown of Paul Erdel, a dear friend of our family who had been a missionary in Ecuador for more than thirty years. He had been appointed Home Secretary of the Missions Department of the Missionary Church. Rita felt that perhaps Paul and other people in the church could help her make the adjustment to living in America. She was right.

Within a month I had taken a position with C.T.S., a company that manufactures electronic components. The firm is located in the rural community of Berne, thirty-four miles south of Fort Wayne. Soon we moved to the place that our family would always consider "home."

Berne didn't seem like home at first. With this move I was the one who had to make the greatest adjustments. I was used to big cities. Not only was Berne not big (population: 2,500), it was not urban. I couldn't believe it when a friend warned me that Berne had dozens of churches but not a single bar. Yet it was true. The Mennonite influence on the community was very strong. Berne is Mid-America—where folks grow corn, play basketball, and go to church.

It's also a great place to raise a family. Ours was completed there with the additions of Helen (June 1968) and Tina (December 1969).

For their part, the townspeople weren't sure what to do with us. We were the only foreigners in a close-knit community, and we had difficulty gaining acceptance. It was a Mennonite missionary, Gerald Stucky, who finally helped to bridge the gap between us and the community. Gerald was home on furlough from his regular assignment in Colombia, a country bordering on our native Ecuador. He spent much extra time and effort to help us feel welcome and comfortable in this new place. His fluency in Spanish and his understanding of our cultural background greatly encouraged Rita. With his help, she began to study English seriously for the first time.

After two years of hard work, we felt as if we had really become a part of the town. The children became involved in their school and enjoyed their participation in church activities. Rita also benefited much from the ministry of First Mennonite Church. She not only became conversant in English but decided she would go to college and get her teaching credentials in America. She enrolled in St. Francis College in Fort Wayne and commuted each week with a friend until she earned her degree.

Rita was the first member of our family to become a naturalized American citizen. In 1972 Hilda, Fausto Jr., and I followed her example. We may not all have been born in Indiana, but we were Hoosiers by adoption. Our whole family was very proud to be citizens of Berne and of the United States of America.

During the late sixties my life revolved around my work at C.T.S. and community affairs. I joined the Jaycees, the Booster Club, and every service organization I could. I was elected to various offices and enjoyed providing leadership in worthwhile community projects.

In 1971 I decided to open my own business—a sporting goods and trophy company. Rita and I had saved $7,000, and I put every penny of it into engraving equipment and stock. The "store" was operated out of our basement for several months. I continued to work full time for C.T.S. But every other waking moment was devoted to that business.

My first breakthrough occurred when I submitted a design for a special trophy solicited by the United States Track and Field Hall of Fame. Even though our operation was relatively small, the organization awarded us the contract. This established us in the trophy business. It brought more customers to our basement. People would come to see The Trophy, and they would buy things—a baseball, bat, a basketball net, some tape.

When boxes of inventory threatened to take over every room in the house, Rita had had enough. I soon accepted a partner, Tom, and opened a real store downtown. Tom's wife ran the store during the day, and we set regular business hours.

In 1975 I organized a buying group and brought together five sporting goods stores in the area. Being able to purchase supplies in quantity boosted sales and profits. Eventually our clientele included thirty-two schools, five colleges, and several community leagues. In 1973 our annual gross sales totaled $150,000; six years later that figure had climbed to more than $500,000.

Chapter 4 of my life looked like the fulfillment of the American Dream. In reality it was turning into the American Nightmare. The price tag for my business success was my family. I was able to give money to my wife and kids, but no time. Often I had only three hours' sleep at night. The children had long since learned to go to Rita for their needs—love, counsel, encouragement, allowance money, permission to do things, whatever. She was The Parent, I was The Bank. Finally Rita issued an ultimatum: "Either quit your job at C.T.S., or sell the store, or I am taking the kids and going back to Ecuador."

She meant it, and she was right. The decision was an agonizing one. But in April 1979 I sold my interest in B & K Enterprises.

I didn't realize how deeply that would affect me. I had started that company from scratch. I had poured my life into making it successful. When I sold it, I experienced grief like someone who has been divorced. It hurt me even to go downtown and see the place.

At the same time, I became dissatisfied with my situation at C.T.S. It didn't seem to offer a great future in opportunities for advancement. Though my family loved Berne, my life there had turned sour. I decided it was time to move.

I sent out resumés and followed up on three offers in Southern California. The most attractive position was offered by Hartell Industries of Fullerton. To the dismay of the three oldest children, I accepted it. That summer, after twelve years, the Indiana chapter drew to a close.

The California segment is the one we are writing now. The contrast between Berne and Chino, our new home, seemed almost as great as the difference between Esmeraldas and Detroit. We didn't have a new language to learn this time, but there were other major adjustments to make.

This transition was hardest on our three teen-agers. Hilda was entering her final year of high school. She was very disappointed that she could not be on the school flag team. Fausto, budding athlete, was worried about whether he could compete successfully in a large California school. Thirteen-year-old Veronica was just beginning to get involved in the youth activities she had anticipated so long.

Transferring from a high school of four hundred to a student body of more than two thousand was scary. Our kids were used to the conservative, close-knit community in Indiana. They were shocked by the attitudes, standards, language, and behavior of teen-agers in California.

Some of our Berne friends might have envied our beautiful ranch-style home with the swimming pool in the backyard. Others might enjoy swapping the moderate Southern California climate for Indiana's hot summers and harsh winters. But if they could, the teen-agers in our family would have taken the next plane back to Berne.

Even now, it is difficult for me to grasp the stresses my family and I were enduring. My desire to become more involved in the lives of my wife and children was what motivated me to sell my business. But that step caused such deep pain to me that I just couldn't keep living in Berne. As a result, all of us were uprooted from the scene of our security and happiness. I have always loved my family dearly. I was trying to make decisions that would be best for all of us. But I don't think everyone saw it that way. In the summer of 1979, the cure seemed worse than the disease.

There were some bright spots. The move itself went smoothly. With thirty days to relocate and report to work, I put our large, three-story house up for sale. It was the only Spanish-style house in Berne, and I thought it might be hard to sell. So I asked Rita to pray about it, and I set a very attractive price on the place. When our real estate agent couldn't talk me into raising my asking price, he bought it himself. Rita's prayers were answered—although I thought I had more to do with it than she did.

We were able to find a lovely home in the attractive Los Angeles suburb of Chino, California. Once I mastered the freeways—a totally new experience—the trip to work would take about twenty minutes. Our home is about a half-hour's drive from Disneyland, Knott's Berry Farm, and any number of amusements for which Southern California is famous. (This is one reason why Helen and Tina were more excited about our move than the other children.) The mountains, beaches, and other recreational sites were also close at hand.

And we were not completely without friends. David and Pauline Solano, who had moved from Berne to nearby Riverside only one month before, were on hand to greet us soon after we arrived at our new home. When they were around, it seemed as if we had a little bit of Berne with us. In the days ahead, the Solanos would become two of the most significant people in our lives.

For chapter 5 was taking a strange turn indeed.

I began my third week at Hartell working with Doug Ford to prepare our report on APLAR. Midweek we reported our findings to a group of department heads, directors of overseas operations, and vice presidents. I chanced to think about the signatures on the bottom of that yellow itinerary I had pondered during my first trip and wondered which of these men had signed them. Our observations about APLAR raised many questions—some of which we could answer, most of which required further investigation.

As the meeting concluded, Ford's immediate supervisor summarized the situation: "You men have done an excellent job. It is obvious that there are serious problems with the APLAR plant. They appear to be correctable, but we need more information.

"Doug tells me that, in his judgment, Fausto is thoroughly qualified to conduct this study. I think we should send him back down to San Salvador for a week to do the follow-up investigation we have been discussing." The others agreed, and the meeting was adjourned.

I gathered the notes I had taken during the meeting. As the others left the conference room, Ford approached.

"Congratulations, Fausto!"

I looked up, surprised. "Congratulations?"

"Absolutely!" He extended his hand and I shook it. "This APLAR thing has been a thorn in our side for months. Now that you have joined the team, we're going to be able to do something about it. These guys really have confidence in you. This could be a major advancement in your career."

I hadn't thought of the situation that way. I had been excited by the challenge, but I was just trying to do a good job. "I appreciate your kind words on my behalf," I acknowledged.

He gave me a pat on the back. "You earned them. You'll do a fine job. Let me know if I can do anything to help."

Doug Ford was a good man to have as a supervisor. After all the heartache of selling my business and making this move, perhaps things were beginning to turn around. Maybe this really was my niche.

"You're going back to El Salvador on Monday?" The tone of Rita's voice told me she wasn't enthusiastic about that idea. My explanation had better be good.

"Rita, I wish you could have been there today! I think my superiors were pleased—impressed, really, with my work! Mr. Ford said that this assignment would really help my career."

"But, Fausto!" she replied, "we aren't even moved in yet!" She pointed to a row of boxes lining the wall of the family room. "This house looks like our place in Berne before you moved the store downtown! And Hartell is flying you all over the world!"

"Not all over the world, Rita! Just to El Salvador!"

"But they didn't say anything about all this travel before you took the job!" she protested. "How many more of these trips are you going to have to make?"

"I don't know," I answered. I put my hands on her shoulders. "They haven't said anything about any other trips beyond this one. Maybe I can take care of everything this next week. We'll just have to wait and see."

I put my arms around her and hugged her. Then I picked up the *Chino Champion* and sat down in the brown-plaid easy-chair. "On my way home from work tonight, I got to thinking about the people down there. I get the idea that they're not very well off. Kind of like the lower classes in Ecuador, you know. If we could correct the problems at the plant and then train the people to use the equipment properly, that could really help the Salvadorans. I would like that very much—to help my fellow Latinos."

Rita was walking into the kitchen. "Just don't forget about your fellow Buchelis!" she reminded. "That is the reason we moved out here!"

I laughed. Rita has a way of making a point with a joke that isn't really a joke.

I scanned the headlines. "One thing I don't like about moving is getting used to new newspapers. This sure isn't the *Berne News*. I can't find the sports page."

"Are you sure the *Champion* has a sports page?" called Rita. "You might have to read the *L. A. Times!*"

"No newspaper calling itself 'the Champion' would dare omit sports coverage!" I replied. I found the sports section. "The *Champion* reports on the local teams. It will take a while to figure out which schools are rivals. I can almost read about these teams without starting to figure out a way to get their equipment account." I glanced over the stories. "But I think you are right about news of the outside world. I've kind of lost track of what's happening in Iran and those other countries in the Middle East."

Rita came back to the family room while drying her hands with a towel. She leaned over the back of my chair and began looking at the paper with me. "Well, Andrew Young resigned while you were gone," she said.

"Andrew Young?" I repeated, trying to place the name. "Oh yeah! At the U.N.! What happened to him this time?"

"Oh, he got into trouble for meeting with someone from the PLO [Palestine Liberation Organization]. I think he quit before President Carter fired him!"

"I think the President's right!" I said. "We shouldn't be doing any business with terrorists."

I turned the page.

"Fausto, are you sure it's safe for you to go to El Salvador? Wasn't there just some kind of a revolution in Nicaragua last month?"

"I wouldn't know about that," I said. "We've been so busy getting moved this summer, there could've been a half-dozen revolutions without my knowledge." Rita was not amused. I put the paper down. She came around and sat on the armrest.

"Listen, Rita! Bruce Chapman has lived down there for five years. He has a wife and two children. They are all Americans. If it was too dangerous, do you think he would stay?"

"No, I suppose not," Rita agreed. "Still, I wish we knew more. I'll feel a lot better when this assignment is all over."

"Rita, I tell you, there's nothing to worry about! This company knows what it's doing." I turned back to my paper. Rita started back into the kitchen.

"I guess I have to agree with you about that," she said.

Her tone of voice was different. "Why do you have to agree with me about that?" I asked.

"Because they hired me today."

I put my paper down again. "What?"

"Hartell Industries hired me today!" She was trying not to laugh.

"To do what?" I asked, incredulous.

She marched back into the family room. "I can do lots of things!" she announced in mock indignation.

"I know that!" I was exasperated. "Of the hundreds and hundreds of things that you can do as well as, if not better than anyone else, what did they hire you to do?"

"Work in the shipping department," she announced triumphantly.

"Shipping department," I mused. "Not a bad place to start. You might work your way up to become company president some day."

She headed back toward the kitchen. "What do you mean might'?"

† † †

THE NEXT day, August 23, William Boorstein escaped from the thirty militant women who had been holding him captive. Left unguarded for a few minutes, he had climbed out the window of his own office and ran to a nearby street. He flagged down a passing motorist who took him to his apartment. He called the U. S. embassy, and the ambassador dispatched a car to transport Boorstein incognito to Guatemala. There he caught a plane to the United States.

On Monday, August 27, as Fausto Bucheli was flying over the west coast of Mexico on Pan Am flight 515, William Boorstein held a press conference in Cherry Hill, New Jersey. Calling his captors "little children," Boorstein maintained that his detention had nothing to do with a labor dispute. "It was a political act," he said. "They have every intention of continuing to do this. The country is going to turn into another Nicaragua."[1]

[1]New York Times, sect. II (27 August 1979):2.

3
A Cloud
in the Silver Lining

MY SECOND TRIP to San Salvador resembled the first in many respects. Yet I was by myself this time, and I was beginning to learn my way around.

The progress APLAR had made during the week I was gone was disappointing. I thought the instructions Doug Ford and I had left were simple enough to put into effect. But apparently, either the managers lacked the training to put the most basic principles of mass-production into practice, or else the communication process within the chain of command had broken down.

I asked Bruce Chapman for a list of the "players" so I could see what the lines of authority were and determine who was responsible for what. By spending time in the plant teaching both the managers and the workers how to perform the various tasks, he and I were able to make good progress toward increasing productivity. One Salvadoran engineer, Mario, really impressed me—with both his aptitude and his desire to learn. We became friends, and he spent as much time with me as he could.

On Wednesday Bruce invited me to have dinner at his home. I gladly accepted; El Camino Real was luxurious, but lonely. I enjoyed meeting Mrs. Chapman and their two children. I had heard someone at the plant refer to the Chapmans' home as a *palacia*. When I saw it, I understood what they meant: It was definitely an upper-class residence, complete with marble floors. The domestic servants who tended the house and grounds, prepared and served the meals reminded me of the days of my own childhood in Ecuador. I could see why Bruce enjoyed living in El Salvador.

The next day José invited me to his home for dinner. I had been up later than usual the night before and was beginning to feel fatigued, so I asked if we could make it Friday night. No problem.

That evening—Thursday—I decided to take a walk before dinner. There was a large, new shopping center called "Metrocenter," just across the Boulevard de los Héroes from El Camino Real. I understood that it had some of the city's finest shops and restaurants there. So I strolled through several little stores and shopped for souvenirs for my family. I ended up at La Tortuga Veloz for supper—a nice restaurant that features native specialties.

Unfortunately, native specialties were not well received by my California stomach, and I left most of my meal on the plate. I decided that a little hike around my 234-room hotel would give me just enough exercise to help me sleep well. It had the opposite effect.

As I came around the corner to the hotel's service entrance in the rear, I was jolted by what I saw: There appeared to be scores of people, pitifully dressed, almost fighting each other to get into the garbage cans. Some were eating whatever they found right on the spot; others were trying to collect enough scraps to take with them—perhaps to share with others. I had seen poor people in Ecuador, but I had never witnessed anything like this. My already revolting stomach turned again, and I retreated to my room via the main entrance. The sight of the luxurious trappings of my accommodations and the memory of the food I had left on my plate plagued my mind. I remembered my daughter's question about what El Salvador is like. I did not sleep well that night.

As we went about our work on Friday morning, I told Mario what I had seen the night before.

"That is how things are in our country, Señor Bucheli!" he remarked. "Right here in San Salvador there are probably forty-five thousand families that live in terrible shacks, or out on the streets. You can see why a company like APLAR is so important to us."

"I'm beginning to see," I replied.

After work José took me home with him, and I had a very enjoyable evening. José and his wife have several children, some the same age as mine. Having a management position with an American company gave José an economic position that in the United States would probably be lower middle class. His home was not as nice as my own, but by Salvadoran standards, he was doing very well. He seemed to be happy with his job. Playing with his children and showing them pictures of my own made me feel very much at home—and a little homesick. I never suspected the role that José would eventually play in my life. I'm sure the same was true of him.

As the week drew to a close, I prepared some "action lists," both for myself at Hartell and for the APLAR staff. I felt that we were making good progress, but I already suspected what Hartell was going to want me to do. I returned to California Saturday, September 1.

When the de Haviland commuter plane taxied up to the Golden West terminal at Ontario Airport, Rita was waiting to meet me. I was very tired and very happy to see her. But when she threw her arms around my neck, I could tell she was troubled.

"O Fausto!" she almost cried. "I'm so glad you're home!"

"I'm glad to be home too!" I pulled back to look at her. "Is anything wrong at home? Is everyone all right?"

"You're all right!" she said, "That's what matters." She held my hand as we walked to the baggage claim area.

"Of course, I'm all right!" I laughed. "Why shouldn't I be?"

"Because they're shooting and killing people in El Salvador, that's why!"

I was incredulous. "Who told you that? I never heard of any shooting and killing!"

"Really, Fausto!" she insisted. "El Salvador has been in the news! There are rebel groups down there, and they are trying to overthrow the government!"

"Well, they must be out in some remote part of the country, because I—"

"No, Fausto, most of the violence is right in San Salvador! I've started checking the newspapers. In May they assassinated the Education Minister and his chauffeur. In June an army officer with the Defense Ministry was ambushed. There have been mass demonstrations and clashes with the police—like the riots in Chicago in nineteen sixty-eight. Those people mean business!"

I wasn't convinced. "Well, they've been leaving me alone! As long as they are fighting each other, I'll just stay out of their way!"

Rita stopped and pulled me around to face her. She spoke deliberately. "While you were down there with Mr. Ford, an American plant manager was taken hostage. He was held captive for a week before he escaped. Before that, a diplomat from Switzerland was killed when he tried to resist a kidnapping attempt. All this week I've wondered, what if that had happened to you?"

I shrugged. "It didn't!"

"Fausto, I don't want you to go back down there! It's too dangerous!"

I walked over to the baggage claim area to pick up my luggage. Rita didn't move. When I came back, I said, "I'm too tired to discuss it now. Could you just take me home and feed me some supper?"

Rita just sighed.

My expectations about Hartell proved to be true. On Wednesday I delivered my report. It was far more detailed than the previous analysis, and it was received with enthusiasm. My recommendations were adopted as the official directives of the company. A copy was immediately forwarded to Bruce Chapman.

One idea that especially appealed to the directors was a plan for expediting the shipment of special equipment needed by APLAR. Materials sent from the California plants invariably got caught in red tape. On my last trip I had to provide a customs official with an early, unrecorded Christmas present just to get a small box of components cleared. If we could find competent tooling companies in neighboring countries, we could service APLAR and eliminate the delays because of the Common Market of Central America. This would bring more business to those countries and make everyone happy.

I knew what was coming. One of the directors said, "Fausto, you are doing such a good job, it looks as if you're going to actually get that plant back on line. I think you should just plan on spending a week at home and a week at APLAR until this mission is accomplished. You can return this weekend."

I took a deep breath. "That will be a problem for me, sir," I said. The room became quiet. "You see, my family has only been in California for a little over a month. And I haven't been here that long." A couple of men smiled. "We're still moving in, and my wife would like me to help." There were some knowing nods.

"Besides," I concluded, "my oldest girl will be eighteen a week from Saturday, and my wife will kill me if I miss that party."

Everyone laughed. The director said, "Stay here for another week then. You can return to San Salvador after the party. Meeting adjourned." Everyone rose to leave.

My "thank you" was drowned out by shuffling papers and sliding chairs. I hadn't even voiced my main concern.

That evening, with fear and trembling, I broke the news to Rita. I tried to be positive. "Well, Rita, guess what? I get to be here for Hilda's birthday."

It didn't work. "They're sending you down there again, aren't they?" she snapped.

I nodded. "They are really pleased with the job I've been doing! They want me to finish it! I don't have to move down there or anything like that. Just a week at a time until things are straightened out.

Rita was not happy to hear this at all. "Haven't they said anything to you about what's happening in that country?" she asked.

"No," I said. "In fact, on the next trip I'm going to take along another engineer. He's going to look around down there for some suitable tooling plants. I'm sure they wouldn't be sending people down there if it was really dangerous."

Rita didn't say another word. Not for a long time.

On Friday afternoon, September 7, Rita and I were intercepted by John Pike in the parking lot. "Mind if I catch a ride home with you?" he called. "Karen's car is in the garage, and she had to use mine to pick up the kids after school."

"Come right along," invited Rita. John was in the personnel office and lived just a few blocks from our home. He had helped us with our move to California.

"Are you folks all moved in yet?" John asked, making conversation.

Rita seized the opportunity. "We would be if Fausto would stay at home where he belongs!" I winced and John laughed.

"I've been hearing good things about your work in San Salvador. The Brass must be really impressed!"

"That's nice to hear," I acknowledged. "It is a little hard on the family."

"Well, if it would make things any easier, we could carpool to work," suggested John. "Then I could drive Rita when you have to be away."

This sounded to me like a good idea. "What do you think, Rita?"

"I like the car-pooling idea just fine," she replied. "And I would be happy to let John take his turn at driving." She didn't bother to say the rest.

We dropped John off at his place and drove on home. Rita went into the family room, kicked off her shoes, stretched out on the sofa, and picked up the paper. I pulled off my tie, hung up my jacket, and took a pitcher of tea from the refrigerator. I had just finished filling a glass when I heard Rita shriek.

"Fausto!"

What could be wrong?

"Fausto, look at this!" Rita was already in the kitchen with the paper. She slammed it down on the counter, jammed her finger on an article, and demanded, "Read that!"

The day before, four masked gunmen had blasted their way into the home of President Romero's older brother, retired Professor José Javier Romero, and shot him to death as he watched television.

"All right!" I said. "On Monday I will talk to the company about this situation!" Rita glared at me. "I promise!" Rita stormed down the hall to the bedroom.

On Monday morning, as I promised, I went to see Doug Ford. I showed him the article about the assassination of the president's brother. "Does Hartell know about what is going on down there?" I asked.

"I'm sure the company directors are keeping tabs on the situation," he replied. "This sort of thing goes on in Latin America all the time. We wouldn't have put a plant down there if we thought the risk was too great."

"But that was five years ago!" I said. "Things are changing! My wife has been checking out the news stories coming out of El Salvador, and this incident is not an isolated case. She is very upset!"

"Well, let's go find out what is going on."

We spent the next hour talking with a series of executives. We would enter an office, present my concerns, ask questions, and get referred to the next higher level. Finally we arrived in the office of Carl Reynolds, vice-president for legal affairs.

Again I explained the situation and expressed my doubts about the wisdom of going to El Salvador at this time. Reynolds was very attentive.

"You know, Fausto," he said when I had finished, "the further away you get from a place, the more serious the news sounds. Why don't we call Bruce Chapman and find out from him how things really are? He lives there, as you know, and I'm sure he's as concerned for his own safety and that of his family as you are for yours."

"Fine," I said.

He pushed the button on his intercom. "Mary, would you put through a call to APLAR and get Bruce Chapman on the phone?" Turning back to us, he said, "It may take awhile to get through, so why don't you fellows go on back to work and I will let you know when I hear something."

Rita was far from convinced. "How do we know whether he knows anything?" she challenged. "You were right there when that Apex plant was seized and you didn't even find out about it until you got home!"

"But Bruce lives there!" I countered. "And he gets out and around. All I ever saw was the plant, the hotel, a couple of houses, and the streets in between. He said that the American press always blows things all out of proportion. I've seen that happen plenty of times! He may be right!"

"But Fausto!" she protested. "It was the *president's brother*. How can you blow *that* out of proportion? It still sounds serious to me!"

"Perhaps it was," I replied, "but maybe things have settled down again. I'll have them contact Bruce again on Friday, and I will talk to him myself. Also, I will give him our home telephone number so he can call me during the weekend if it looks too dangerous for me to come."

"It's already too dangerous!" said Rita, getting in the last word again.

I spent the rest of the week preparing for my third trip to San Salvador. Mostly I followed up on my personal "action list" from the previous trip. This included drafting production guidelines and procedures in Spanish. I also collected more equipment parts to take with me.

The other thing I remember about the week is that I sat down with my family in the evenings and watched television. I hadn't done that since we left Indiana.

The reason I remember this is that the mini-series "Holocaust" was on each night. It really got to Rita, and I kidded her about crying over a television program. "It's just a story," I chided.

"But those things really happened," she sniffed, "to real people. And it's sad that human beings do such terrible things to other people."

"That was long ago and far away," I said.

"Not so long and not so far," she replied. "It could happen again."

"You're too sensitive," I teased, "but then that's why I love you!" I gave her a squeeze.

"You're not sensitive enough," she countered, snuggling against me, "but I love you anyway."

† † †

THE BRUTAL assassination of Professor Romero was the first of a series of violent acts that had been promised by leftist leaders.

With El Salvador's Independence Day approaching on September 15, militant opponents of the Romero regime vowed that the month would be recorded in history as "Black September." They made good on that pledge.

On the Monday that Fausto went to his superiors for assurances of his safety in El Salvador, eleven people were killed in the escalating conflict between the forces of the political left and right. Seven of the victims were students, ambushed en route to a beach by masked members of a right-wing vigilante squad. The attack was apparently retaliation for the execution of Professor Romero.

Even moderate voices from the business and religious sectors began to call on the government to introduce extensive economic and political reforms. The Carter administration in the United States "suggested" that President Romero move up the date of national elections. The possibility of a coup d'état had become a topic of public conversation.

On September 14, three days before Fausto was scheduled to make his third trip to El Salvador, government forces opened fire on several hundred students and teachers taking part in an anti-government protest march in San Salvador. Two high school teachers were killed; about thirty other persons, including American reporter Kathy Barber Hersh, were wounded.

The next day, Independence Day, as Fausto, Rita, and their family celebrated Hilda's eighteenth birthday, some twenty-five hundred people marched through the streets of San Salvador in a funeral procession for the two slain teachers. The march was conducted in defiance of a government order forbidding public demonstrations.

Recognizing that volatile forces were pushing his country to the brink of disaster, President Humberto Romero summarily canceled all scheduled Independence Day ceremonies. If Fausto Bucheli had known a tenth of what President Romero knew, he likely would have canceled his trip. A telephone call from El Salvador could have told him all he needed to know.

But the phone never rang.

4
Kidnapped!

ON SUNDAY MORNING, September 16, Rita and I visited Faith Missionary Church for the second time. Dave and Pauline Solano had belonged to the Missionary Church in Berne and had attended this one a few times. Rita had grown up in that denomination in Ecuador. Because Faith was close to our home, it just made sense to attend. The pastor, the Rev. Donald Crocker, was a quiet-spoken man who was easy to like. He had already made one attempt to visit us, but we were not at home.

Faith Missionary Church was much smaller than First Mennonite Church in Berne—the opposite condition from most of our changes. So getting used to the church became one more adjustment for our family to make.

But the biggest difference in the Bucheli worship experience was my participation. I had attended church very little in Berne. Here I thought the church might provide a kind of steadying influence amid so much that was new and different. And this was something I could do consistently with the whole family.

On this Sunday, I stayed only long enough for Sunday School because I had to take a visiting friend to the airport. But between the services, on my way to the car, I talked with Pastor Crocker. "I am going back to El Salvador tomorrow," I told him. "But when I return, Rita and I would like to talk with you about joining this church."

"I'll look forward to that, Mr. Bucheli," he replied.

That was the most encouraging conversation Rita had heard in a long time.

Monday morning was overcast, outside the house and in. There had been no call from El Salvador, so I prepared to leave. I woke up the girls and kissed them good-by. The atmosphere was thick with apprehension.

Rita would have no part of taking me to the airport, so I asked Fausto Jr. if he would drive. He had had his license for almost four months, so driving was still something of an adventure. He readily agreed.

Saying good-by to Rita was not pleasant. I didn't want to have a big argument just before I left; but she was intent on making a last stand. "Please, don't go! I really don't want you to go!"

"Rita, I'm not going to argue with you now! This company moved us out here. I owe it to them to do what they tell me. If I don't, I could lose my job!"

"Then lose your job!" she said. "What good will it have done for us to move to California if something happens to you down there? What good will your job be to you then?" There were tears in her eyes.

"I've made up my mind, Rita. And I have to leave now. I will see you on Saturday afternoon." I moved toward her to kiss her good-by, but she turned her head and backed away. Then she retreated to the bedroom and slammed the door.

I picked up my briefcase and suitcase and walked out the front door. Fausto Jr. followed, closing the door behind us.

There was silence during most of the trip to the airport. The route had become so familiar that I was no longer entranced by the rows of eucalyptus trees lining the roadway or by the orange groves interspersed among the housing developments. As I tried to recover from the scene with Rita, I looked over at my sixteen-year-old chauffeur in the striped rugby shirt. I was struck again by his resemblance to that movie actor, Sylvester Stallone. To tease him, the girls sometimes called him "Rocky." That boy was going to make his father proud.

I finally broke the silence. "Fausto!"

"Yes, daddy."

"You know, when I'm away, you have to be the man of the house. You take care of your mom—and the girls."

He nodded as he pulled the car up to the ticket meter at the airport parking lot.

"I'm going to tell you what my father used to tell me," I continued. "You are the one who will carry on the family name. You must live in a way that will bring honor to that name." We pulled into a parking place.

"I'll do my best, dad," he replied.

"I know you will, son. Your sisters all look up to you. You take good care of them and have a good week at school."

"Right," he said, getting out of the car. He took my suitcase out of the trunk. "I'll carry this in for you," he volunteered.

We crossed the street to the square, red brick terminal. We checked the suitcase through to San Salvador, and I received my boarding pass. he looked at his watch and announced, "I'd better get going or Hilda and I will be late for school."

I looked at my itinerary. "O.K. You'll need to be here at four o'clock Saturday afternoon." I set down my briefcase and gave him a hug and kiss, Latin-style. "See you, son!"

"Bye, dad!"

I met Tom Elliott at L.A. International and we flew together to El Salvador. Tom, an engineer, was going to try to locate some tool-and-die shops in Central America that could serve APLAR with manufacturing and repair facilities. He had heard about the troubles in El Salvador, too, so he was nervous about the trip.

It didn't help matters that our luggage got lost. Mine turned up three hours after we arrived, and someone from Pan Am delivered it to the hotel. But Tom had to spend the night without his personal belongings.

The next morning, Bruce Chapman came for us with the ever-present, ever-silent Luis. "Fausto, I'll drop you off at the plant," he explained. "Then I'll run Tom over to the airport and we'll try to track down that luggage."

This trip to APLAR was a different experience. Tom was not treated to the friendly banter from Bruce that I had promised. Nor did we follow the normal route. Instead, Bruce drove with a walkie-talkie in one hand and the steering wheel in the other. The voice that crackled through the speaker was giving directions, and we were led by this invisible guide down side streets and avenues that I had never seen before. Tom looked at me, wide-eyed. I just shrugged. Occasionally Bruce would speak into his transmitter and the voice would answer. Eventually we arrived at the plant.

I was greeted warmly by my friend, Mario, who began to show me around the factory so I could see the changes that had been made. Before we had gone very far, I stopped him and said, "Mario, I need to talk to you about something important."

"*Sí*, Señor Bucheli. What is it?"

"Who is Luis? What does he do?"

"He is Señor Chapman's bodyguard," Mario replied. "He watches over his home at night and goes with him wherever he goes during the day. I understand he used to be a sergeant on the police force."

"Why does Bruce need a bodyguard?" I asked.

Mario hesitated, then spoke softly. "We have big problems in our country. Most of our people are very poor." I remembered the scene behind the hotel. "The government does little or nothing to help the poor. The president seems to help the rich get richer. So the people are banding together in resistance groups, and they are using force to fight against the government."

"Would they try to hurt us Americans, Mario?" I asked. "We're trying to help the people by giving them jobs, bringing in money."

Mario shook his head. "Most of the money goes to the factory owners. There aren't enough jobs, and the pay is low. Many Salvadorans view Americans as part of the problem. Most American businessmen ride to and from their offices in armored cars. All of them have bodyguards."

"Why hasn't anybody told me about these problems before?" I almost shouted.

"Please, Señor Bucheli!" Mario raised his hand to quiet me down. "We were told not to tell any of these things to visiting American executives. We were afraid that if you found out what was happening here, you might shut down the plant and we would lose our jobs."

"Who told you not to tell us anything?" I asked.

Mario just shrugged.

"Then why are you telling me this now?"

Mario smiled. "I have watched you very closely, *señor*. You have been working hard to fix our problems. You have taught me many things. I can see that you are not here to hurt us. You are our friend—a Latino like us!"

I relaxed a bit. "Thank you, friend, for talking to me. Now, why don't you show me what you've done?"

After about an hour, Tom Elliott and Bruce Chapman returned to the plant. "We finally located that luggage," Bruce announced. "Why don't you show Tom around, Fausto? Then we can coordinate our schedules for the week."

When we were alone, Tom practically exploded. "We shouldn't have come down here! This place has me scared to death! I think I heard gunshots out there!"

I tried to calm him down. "I think we're safe here, Tom! Today I'll show you the equipment they're working with so you can record the specifications. Then tomorrow you will go with Bruce to Guatemala or Costa Rica to see if you can locate the tooling plants we need. You won't even be here most of the week."

"That's fine by me!" he allowed. "I just hope we can get back to the hotel in one piece."

"I guess as long as we stick with Bruce, we'll be safe. He seems to have a system worked out."

"Yeah," he answered. "I just hope that Luis is on our side."

Bruce and Tom flew out of San Salvador the next morning, and I had the run of the plant for the next two days. The bulk of my time was invested in training. I distributed the manuals I had prepared and worked through each of them with the management team and the production people. The two days proved to be well spent.

Another activity was taking notes—not about APLAR, but about El Salvador. I wrote down everything Mario had told me. I collected all the newspaper articles I could find. Hartell was going to get a piece of my mind when I returned, and this report was going to be documented. As things turned out, it was a report Hartell never saw.

Tom returned to the hotel Thursday evening. He and Bruce had found nothing in Guatemala, and there wasn't enough time to explore other countries.

"Well, you've done what you were sent to do," I told Tom. "How would you like to fly back to the States in the morning instead of waiting 'til Saturday?"

"That suits me fine!" he replied. "The sooner I get out of this place, the better!"

A call to the airport took care of the change in the reservation. Come the next morning, there would be one less *gringo* to worry about.

I went to bed thinking about Rita and wishing that it was my flight that had been changed.

† † †

WHEN I awoke on Friday morning, September 21, I thought to myself, *Well, this day has finally arrived! Today I will finish this nerve-wracking project, and tomorrow I'm gone!*

Though my room in El Camino Real was air-conditioned, a glance out the window told me this would be another hot, muggy day. I was glad that suits and ties were not the required uniform at APLAR. I put on a pair of black, lightweight slacks and a white, short-sleeve sportshirt—the same one I had worn for the I.D. photo I clipped to my pocket. The designer had scattered tiny tick-tack-toe patches of red and blue across the fabric to give it some color. It was a present from Rita.

I met Tom Elliott in the coffee shop for a roll and coffee before Bruce came for us. The trip to the airport was another tension-filled exercise in evasive driving. Tom was clearly relieved to arrive at Ilopango Terminal without incident.

When his flight was announced, I said to him, "Will you do me a favor, Tom?"

"Sure! What do you want?"

"When you get home tonight, will you give Rita a call and let her know I'm all right. And tell her I'll see her at Ontario Airport at 4:00 P.M. tomorrow."

"I'll tell her that," he promised. He turned to walk down the runway.

"And tell her I love her!" I called.

He turned and waved. "I sure will! Bye!"

When Tom was out of sight, I asked Bruce, "How long have you been using the walkie-talkies and taking the scenic route?"

"We only do that when we catch wind of trouble some place in town," he replied. "It's a system that keeps us from wandering into some 'hot spot.'"

"Are there that many hot spots?" I questioned.

"I guess you could say things have heated up a little," he answered. "But it's nothing to worry about!"

We returned to the van. "Well, I guess as long as I stay with you I'll be all right," I said as much to myself as to Bruce.

He laughed. "You worry too much, Fausto! If you lived down here, you would get used to it."

The rest of the day passed quickly. During the afternoon rest break, I searched out Mario. "I've noticed some beautiful towels in some of the shops in town."

"Oh yes," he beamed, "those towels are a Salvadoran specialty, a work of art."

"I would like to pick up a set for my wife," I said. "I was wondering if you could give me a ride into town this evening and take me to a shop that sells them."

"Oh sure," he replied. "I know just the place. You'll love it. Do you want to leave around five?"

"Five o'clock will be perfect. I just have one more meeting with the management staff and then I'm through."

The meeting ended, and I began to gather up my notes and collect the inventory lists of materials that Hartell would need to ship immediately. Bruce came to me and said, "Fausto, I'll give you a ride back to the hotel. We'll leave at five."

"You don't need to do that," I said. "Mario has agreed to take me and help me shop for some towels for Rita."

"Well, you tell Mario that I'm going to take you!" he insisted. "I want to talk to you some more about those production quotas."

I shrugged. "We may as well. I don't know when I'll be coming back again. I'm sure not planning to return until things settle down more." I had been hoping I was through with Bruce. But it would probably be better if we tried to work out our disagreements before I made my report. The ride to the hotel wouldn't take long.

I put my reports and notes in my briefcase and carried it across the room to a desk where I had left a small suitcase filled with samples of APLAR's products. I was taking them back to Fullerton for analysis. I opened the suitcase and took one final inventory of the contents. As I closed it and locked the latches, Mario appeard. "Are you ready to go, Fausto?"

"Oh, I'm sorry, Mario," I said. "Bruce wants to go over some more things with me, so he's going to take me to the hotel. Is that all right with you?"

"That's O.K.," he smiled. "Have a nice trip back to your family."

"Fausto!" Bruce was standing by the main entrance to the building. He called out across the plant, "I'll give you a ride to your hotel. Are you about ready to go?" Everyone looked toward me. I nodded to Bruce and picked up the suitcase. Out of the corner of my eye, I saw José pick up a telephone and place a call. He spoke very briefly and hung up. I tried to catch his attention to wave good-by, but when our eyes met, he turned away. *Have I done something to upset him?* I wondered. *Oh well, I can't worry about that now. I guess everybody is on edge these days.*

When I climbed into Bruce's van, Luis was already sitting in his customary place in the front. Bruce got behind the wheel. I slid over to the middle of the second seat so I could look between the two men to see out the windshield. The briefcase was on the floor in front of my knees, the box of components on the seat next to my right elbow. It was about 5:15 P.M.

Bruce turned and said, "You'd better put on your seat belt. The traffic around here can get really wild!"

When we pulled out onto the four-lane highway, the traffic had not yet become congested. I noticed that Bruce wasn't using his walkie-talkie or taking the back roads. "I take it that things have cooled down in town," I said.

"Yep!" he acknowledged. "The coast is clear!"

As we drove along, Bruce and I talked about APLAR. As usual, the English conversation was of no interest to Luis. I tried to remember if I had ever heard him speak—maybe he was mute. In our discussion, Bruce was of the opinion that I was expecting too much change too soon—that my expectations were unrealistic, my target quotas too high.

We were going past a women's penitentiary on our right as we came up behind a bus. Bruce steered the van into the left lane to pass it. Suddenly, from out of nowhere, an American military jeep shot between our van and the bus. It was overflowing with people—they looked like teen-agers. No sooner were they in front of us than the driver jammed on his brakes. Bruce could not avoid them, and the van rammed into the back of the jeep and stopped abruptly. My seat belt did its job, but my knees banged into the briefcase. As I reached down to rub my shin, another vehicle hit us from behind. I looked around to see a red truck. We were pinned between it and the jeep.

Bruce swore.

I asked, "What did you say?"

He said, "They got us!"

"They got us?" I didn't have a chance to ask what he meant. The young people poured out of the jeep with submachine guns in their hands. They pointed them at our van. I heard the rapid burst of gunfire. The windows exploded, and shattered glass flew about our heads. Instinctively I ducked. *My God!* I thought. *This can't be happening!*

Luis tried to reach for his pistol, but he never even got it out. Someone jerked open his door, lifted a gun, and fired at point-blank range. Blood spattered over the front of the van. All I heard from Luis was a quiet groan. I had just watched a man die.

Two more youths, standing behind the executioner, aimed their weapons in our direction. Already I smelled the acrid odor of burnt powder. I closed my eyes: I was about to die. "O God!" I prayed. "Help me!"

The submachine guns erupted simultaneously. The two seconds it took those young men to empty their chambers seemed like an eternity. In slow motion the body of Luis Paz jerked violently across the front seat under the impact of the bullets. Then the shooting stopped. Not only was I still alive, but I hadn't even been hit! Every bullet had been discharged into the already lifeless form of the bodyguard.

My heart was pounding so hard I thought it would explode. I was paralyzed with terror, my mind unable to comprehend what was happening. The first cold waves of shock and nausea swept over me as I stared at the mutilated corpse of what only moments before had been a living man.

The sliding door to my right screeched open. I covered my face with my hands and closed my eyes. *This is it!* I thought. *Now it's my turn!* But there were no shots, no guns, no death. Instead two hands gripped me. One grabbed my shoulder, the other had a handful of hair. They tried to pull me out of the van, but my seat belt held me in place. "Wait!" I screamed. "I'm tied in!" The pain in my scalp was agonizing. I unlatched the seat belt, and they pulled me out. The box of components crashed to the ground.

"*Es un sequestro!*" barked one of the teen-agers. "This is a kidnapping!"

A young man with a dark complexion, black hair, and fierce, deep-set eyes slapped a pair of handcuffs on me. They were much too tight. Someone behind me began wrapping wide adhesive tape around my head. He wound it right around my glasses, ears, and hair.

"*Muevete!* Move!" they ordered. "*Apurate!* Hurry!"

The jeep was already moving when they hoisted me into the back seat, thrown in head first. For a time my legs dangled over the side. Finally someone pulled me all the way in and managed to set me upright in the seat. "Do what you're told and you won't be hurt!" a voice commanded.

The tape didn't completely shut out my field of vision, as there was a slight gap between a strip of tape and the bottom of my glasses. I could tell that Bruce was sitting next to me. They didn't tape and handcuff him until he was in the jeep. *He must have been too big to throw around,* I thought.

Almost immediately, the jeep veered off the highway to the right onto a very bumpy road. The pain in my hands was excruciating. I cried out, "*Por favor, mis manos!*"

Bruce yelled, "Shut up! Do you want to get us killed too?"

"But my hands are killing me!" A rifle barrel jammed into my back, and I bit my lip to control the urge to scream.

5
Five Hours Is Forever

WHEN THE VAN driven by Bruce Chapman was leaving the APLAR parking lot, Maria Alvarez pulled out behind it in her sedan. She was a quality control inspector at APLAR, and she was glad the week was over. Señor Bucheli was helping the staff to increase productivity, yet she couldn't help but worry about the future. What was Hartell going to do? Was the plant going to stay open? Would she be able to keep her job?

She hadn't been paying much attention to the traffic as she drove toward home. Suddenly a collision up ahead forced her to stop abruptly. She watched, uncomprehendingly at first, as fifteen armed young people poured out of a jeep and a truck and surrounded Chapman's van. One of the men opened fire with a submachine gun into the passenger side. More guns were firing. She couldn't see clearly, but it looked as though the gang was pulling men from the van. Yes, two men were led away and pushed into the jeep. Then the commandos sped away, and a few people began to emerge from stopped vehicles and cautiously approach the bullet-riddled van.

Maria, shaking from what she had just witnessed, managed to make a U-turn and drive back toward the plant. She spied a pay telephone booth and stopped. Her hands trembling, she found a number, inserted some *colones* in the slot, and dialed.

"Is this Mrs. Chapman?" she asked when a voice answered.

Linda Chapman, on the other end, tried to place the voice. "Yes, this is Mrs. Chapman."

"Can you tell me, *señora*, what kind of car Señor Chapman drove to work today?" asked Maria.

It sounded to Linda like one of the women from APLAR, but she couldn't be sure. "He drove the Dodge van, just as he always does," she replied. "Why do you ask?"

"Thank you, *señora*," replied Maria, without explaining. Then she hung up.

Linda heard the phone go dead. "Wait!" she called out in vain. Immediately pain grew in the pit of her stomach. About six months before, she and Bruce had flown to Miami for counterterrorist training. She had been living in dread ever since. There was no question in her mind why that voice wanted to know about Bruce's van. The only question now was, Is he alive or dead?

Maria fumbled through the directory until she found another number. She inserted more coins and dialed again. Raul, the No. 2 man at APLAR, had just walked in the door of his house when the phone rang.

"Hello!" he answered.

"Señor Raul, this is Maria Alvarez." Even her voice was quavering. "I just saw a gang of young people attack Señor Chapman's van on the Boulevard del Ejército Nacional! There was a lot of shooting and Señor Paz may be hurt or even dead! But I think Señor Chapman and Señor Bucheli are all right! The guerrillas took them away in a jeep." Maria was in tears.

"O.K., Maria!" said Raul. "Thank you for letting me know! I'll take care of things. You go on home now—and be careful!" They hung up.

Maria slumped to the floor of the phone booth and wept.

† † †

TIME IS hard to gauge under such circumstances. It may have been a half-hour that we bounced along that excuse for a road in silence. My hands were growing cold, my wrists were in agony.

Eventually, we stopped.

Our captors took us from the jeep and led us to the back of a bluish-green van. Four men were waiting there. They told us to lie down in the van. I crawled in and lay on my stomach, with my hands up under my chin. Bruce got in beside me, on my left. The men tossed cardboard boxes on top of us, and when we were fully camouflaged, the doors slammed shut.

"Bruce!" I rasped. "My hands!"

"Listen to me, Fausto!" he whispered. "We are the first Americans they have kidnapped. But don't worry! We'll get out of this before long. Just do whatever they tell you. They probably just want money. If they keep us together, let me do the talking. If not, just cooperate with them."

"What do you mean we are the first—"

"Shhh!" he ordered.

The driver's door opened, then the passenger's door, and two men got in. The doors slammed shut together. The engine revved to life, and we pulled away.

Again I lost track of time. My brain was in a fog. I was certainly in shock, just from witnessing the brutal slaying of Luis Paz—that scene kept replaying itself in my mind. And Bruce's words, instead of comforting me, distressed me even more. He seemed to know what was happening, who these people were. What did he know? How did he know? Why hadn't he told me more before this happened? How could he have let this happen?

After a drive of perhaps forty-five minutes, the van pulled into a garage. I had no idea where we were. We could have been close to the ocean, near the border of Honduras, or just outside San Salvador. I heard a garage door—one of the kind that rolls down on tracks from above—bang shut against the cement floor.

The back doors of the van opened, boxes were pulled off us, and I was helped out. There was a light on in the garage, but my captors did not realize that I could see. One man was wearing a white T-shirt and blue jeans; the other had on a white short-sleeved shirt and brown pants. They helped me to sit on the back of the van. I was so weak and shaky I didn't know if I could walk. They got on either side of me and held me up; the pressure sent shock waves of pain through my wrists.

We turned to the left and walked alongside the van. We went up a few steps, then went through a door that was too narrow for all of us. They pushed me on ahead of them, then continued to support me as we walked across a room to another door.

We entered a very small room that I could not yet fully survey. I was steered to a wooden chair and told to sit down. I was glad to do that.

"Just relax," said a voice, "and keep quiet. Nothing will happen to you if you do as you are told. Just be quiet and cooperate and you will be all right."

Cooperate? That's what Bruce had said. Where have you taken him? Sure, I'll cooperate. What could you want from me?

"Please, *señor*," I begged, "my hands are really bad. Can you remove these handcuffs? I can't feel my fingers any more. Please!"

"I'll be right back," said the voice.

Soon a third man entered the room with the first two. He took hold of my hands and lifted them up to look at them. I cried out. Tears were trapped by the adhesive tape, turning the lenses of my glasses wet. He dropped my hands back on my lap—more agony.

"Quiet!" he hissed. "Take them off!" he ordered one of the others.

"We can't find the key" came the reply. "It must have fallen out when we changed over to the van."

"Well, go get it!" said the boss. "Those things have to come off!"

† † †

"WHAT A crazy country this is to live in," thought Raul when he had hung up the phone after speaking with Maria. Several months ago, he and Bruce Chapman had reviewed the procedures he should follow if the unthinkable happened. But his notes were at the office. They included the names and phone numbers of people he would need to contact.

As he drove back to the plant, Raul stopped at the site of the ambush. The van was still there, along with a crowd of curious bystanders. Two policemen guarded the vehicle. Raul grimaced when he saw that the windows had been shot out. *It's a wonder that anyone got out alive!* he thought.

He identified himself to one of the policemen and asked what had happened, but the policeman knew nothing more than Maria had reported—except to confirm that Luis had been killed. As Raul looked at the front seat, he became nauseated. Overcoming the urge to vomit, he got back in his car and drove to the plant.

At his office, Raul located the Terrorism file. He reviewed his notes briefly, then placed the first call to Hartell Industries. He knew that everyone in the office complex would be gone for the weekend, so when the night-shift switchboard answered, he gave the prearranged code statement to indicate a bona-fide emergency. It took the operator several minutes to connect him with Carl Reynolds, the company vice-president for legal affairs.

Reynolds was in the middle of dinner at his home. "Hello," he said, a trace of irritation in his voice. He could hear the static of a long-distance connection.

"Mr. Reynolds, this is Raul in San Salvador. I'm sorry to disturb you tonight, but Bruce told me that I should call you if we ever had an emergency."

"What's the problem, Raul?" asked Reynolds, his interest quickening.

Raul took a deep breath. "It looks like a band of terrorists have kidnapped Señors Chapman and Bucheli! I am pretty sure that our men are alive, but the guerrillas killed the man who was Bruce's bodyguard!"

Reynolds gasped. "Oh, my! . . ." His voice trailed away. "How did it happen?"

Raul gave him the details he knew. Simultaneously Reynolds jotted notes and began developing a plan of action. When Raul finished, he said, "All right, Raul. You are going to be in charge of everything down there until we get this straightened out."

"Yes, sir!" Raul said.

"Does Mrs. Chapman know what has happened yet?" asked Reynolds.

"I don't know," replied Raul. "I called you first. I don't think Maria told her anything. But I also don't know whether the authorities have contacted her."

"Then the first thing you will need to do," Reynolds instructed, "is go out to Chapmans' and make sure that she and the children are all right."

Raul wasn't thrilled about that aspect of being in charge. "Yes, sir!" he complied.

"Then just sit tight until the kidnappers contact you. Set things up so that they only speak with you," he ordered. "Don't let Linda Chapman get involved. It would be too much for her to handle."

"Right!"

"When they contact you," Reynolds continued, "tell them that you are in touch with us, and take any information they are inclined to give. But make it clear that you don't have any authority to negotiate. We will send in special people for that."

"Good!" Raul said.

"Now I want you to write down another phone number where you can reach me as soon as the kidnappers contact you," concluded Reynolds. When the number was transmitted, both men hung up.

As Reynolds began placing a call to Russell Shannon, president of Hartell Industries, Raul had one more call of his own to make. He again contacted the overseas operator and this time gave her a number in Miami, Florida.

A woman's voice answered: "Rayne International."

"I need to speak with Mr. Fred Rayne," said Raul.

"Mr. Rayne is in New York tonight," said the voice "I am his fiancée. My name is Ginger Martin. May I take a message?"

"I'm not sure." Raul hesitated. "This is a highly confidential business matter. It is also an emergency."

"Where are you calling from?" Ginger asked.

"San Salvador."

"Does this have anything to do with Bruce and Linda Chapman?"

"Yes, it does," Raul said. "I guess you know them."

"Yes, I do. We became acquainted when they came up for Fred's seminar. Is anything wrong?"

"Yes, I'm afraid there is. Señor Chapman was kidnapped this evening. Also a Señor Bucheli from California who was sent down here by Hartell to do some special work."

"Oh no!" Ginger groaned. "Do you have any idea who is responsible? Fred will want to know that."

"No one has contacted us yet," replied Raul. "It could be any number of groups."

"Well, I'll call Fred right away," she promised, "and he will get in touch with you as soon as possible."

"Thank you, *señora*," said Raul. *"Adios!"*

"Good night!"

Ginger Martin hung up the phone and went into the study to find the information on where Rayne was speaking that night. Fred Rayne was the president of his own security consulting firm, and Hartell Industries was one of his clients. This particular evening he was the featured speaker at a banquet in New York City. His subject: "Developing Security Strategies Against Terrorism."

Just as she found the number of Fred's hotel, her phone rang again. She answered: "Rayne International."

It was Carl Reynolds of Hartell. Ginger told him of her conversation with Raul and said she was about to call Fred in New York.

Fred Rayne was in the middle of his main course when the headwaiter leaned over his shoulder and whispered, "Mr. Rayne, you have a long-distance call from Miami. It is your fiancée, and she says that it is an emergency."

Rayne placed his napkin beside the plate, rose from the table, and followed the waiter to a courtesy phone outside the banquet room. He picked up the red receiver. "Hello."

"I'm sorry to bother you, Fred," apologized Ginger, "but I just got two telephone calls—the first from a man named Raul in San Salvador, the second from Mr. Carl Reynolds of Hartell Industries."

"Damn!" To Fred, those calls could mean only one thing. He let Ginger continue.

"Apparently two Hartell men have been kidnapped by an unidentified gang of terrorists. One was Bruce Chapman. The other was a Mr. Bucheli who was there on a special assignment from Hartell."

"I told them to get an armored car!" Fred fumed. "Oh well, even that might not have been enough!"

"Probably not," Ginger agreed. "The kidnappers murdered Bruce's bodyguard!"

"They mean business!" he remarked, as much to himself as

to his fiancée. "I'll catch the next flight to Miami as soon as I've finished here. We'll set our negotiation plan into operation immediately. I think I have time to call Reynolds before I have to speak. He can begin setting the machinery into motion from that end."

"Is there anything else you want me to do?"

"Yes, there is. Call Juan Ortega and tell him to meet me in the office tomorrow morning. He's going to see some action."

"All right!" she said. "See you later!"

"You did the right thing, calling me, honey," he said. "Thanks! Good-by!"

† † †

TIME AND space ceased to have any meaning for me. There was only one dimension—pain. One does not normally think of the hands and wrists as centers of pain. But at that point, the tourniquet effect of the handcuffs was drowning out every other impulse in my brain, except one. The replay of the demise of Luis Paz haunted the movie screen of my mind. I could no more escape the continual reliving of those moments than I could extricate my hands from the fire that bound them. If hell is the perpetual experience of the worst moments of one's life, I was in hell. And I was too engulfed in physical and mental pain to ask why.

The only other stimulus in the environment was heat and humidity. I didn't know if I was alone or guarded by a silent watchman. By the time my captors returned, my clothes were drenched with sweat.

I was startled by the sound of the opening door. "You are lucky, *gringo!* We found the key!" I tensed, anticipating more pain in the process of release. It came as rough hands jostled the handcuffs trying to insert the key in the lock. Finally steel pulled away from flesh. I began moving my arms, rubbing my hands. There was little lessening of the pain right away.

But what happened next made me forget about my hands for a moment. Someone began ripping off the adhesive tape. I felt as if I were being scalped. Hair from my head and eyebrows was being ripped from the skin. I cried out and instinctively tried to grab the offender to stop him.

"Shut up!" commanded a voice in a whispered shout as another pair of hands immobilized my ineffective arms. "Hold still, or we'll put a bullet in your brain!"

I didn't doubt it and had no intention of resisting further. But the human organism responds to acute pain by reflex. "Please!" I begged. "Be careful! It hurts!"

The scalp torture ended when the last of the tape was removed, and I could see without restriction for the first time in several hours. In the dim light of the room I looked down at my hands: they were black and blue. The nails were black. *I'm going to lose my hands,* I thought.

Someone pulled off my glasses. It didn't affect my vision much, because my eyesight isn't very weak. I looked at my captors. They were wearing dingy, light-green pillowcases over their heads. Two of them bore two eye-holes. The third man, who also wore glasses, had a third opening, for his nose. *So he won't steam up his glasses,* I thought absently. All three wore old cotton coats over their gray-and-black clothes. And all three held submachine guns.

Señor "Glasses" pulled my pens, notepad, and passport from my shirt pocket and read the last.

I looked around the room. It was about six feet wide and ten feet long—too big for a closet, too small to be a living area. A storage room, maybe. It was all of cement—walls, ceiling, floor. Cracked cement, and dirty. Filthy. Dust and cobwebs.

The single source of light was a bare forty-watt bulb suspended from a nail in the center of the ceiling. The electric wire ran to the top of the door and disappeared outside. There were no real windows. On the wall opposite me, behind Señor Glasses, was an opening about one foot square. It was near the top of the wall, where one would expect a window to be in a cellar. It was boarded over with plywood.

Señor Glasses did the talking. "Born in Ecuador," he read. "Yes, I thought you were a Latino. But you are one of them! A *gringo!* A traitor!" He spat. He became abusive and vulgar in his language. "O.K., *gringo,* let's see what kind of man you are! Take off your clothes!"

I began to undress. Because my hands were swollen, It was a slow, painful process. At last I was down to my undershorts. I sat down again.

"Take off everything!" Señor Glasses commanded. "Your watch, your rings, your shorts!" I was appalled and didn't respond at first. But three submachine guns were trained on me. I pulled off my watch and glanced at the face just before it was snatched from my hands. It read 10:25.

My swollen fingers made removal of the rings almost impossible. The larger one finally came off, but the wedding band refused. One of my captors left the room and quickly returned with some soap scrapings. Still the ring would not slide over the knuckle. Finally they gave up on it.

"Now the shorts, traitor!" I removed them. It was for me the ultimate humiliation. I was brought up in a very proper family. Modesty was highly valued and privacy was strictly maintained. No one ever saw another member of the family naked. Having no covering reduced me to nothingness.

One terrorist collected my valuables; another gathered up my clothes. Señor Glasses said, "You are going to be here for a while. If you keep quiet and cooperate, you will be all right. If you resist, you are a dead man—just like your policeman friend!"

The three left and another took their place. He had a submachine gun in one hand and a stack of books in the other. "Lie down over there!" he ordered, using the gun to point to the corner behind me and to my right. I saw a row of boards laid out side by side, forming a wooden pallet. There were six or seven slats about three feet long and one foot wide. They covered over a quarter of the floor.

I eased myself onto the boards. They felt rough and splintery on my tender skin. I wished I could cover myself—I felt totally exposed.

The hooded guard turned the chair toward me and sat down, placing the books on the floor near my head. "These are for your entertainment," he mocked. I read the titles:

The Biography of Ché Guevara
The Socialist in Latin America
The Marxist
The History of Lenin
The Only Solution Is Communism
The Freedom of Cuba
Biography of Fidel Castro

When I turned back to the guard, I found I was looking up the barrel of the submachine gun. "I don't feel like reading right now," I said. He said nothing.

The door opened and another hooded figure entered with a five-gallon can, which he put in the far left corner. Then he left. "That is your toilet," announced the guard. It occurred to me that I might be here for a while.

I lay on the boards in silence. Pain and shame continued to plague me. I looked over at my jailer. He was wearing a three-hole pillowcase, a brown coat, and light-blue pants. No shirt, no shoes. His hands were rough and callous, like a farmer's. His toes would be uncomfortable in shoes. I thought, *He must really be hot under that jacket and hood.*

After a few minutes, I said, "Listen, *señor,* I'm not going to give you any trouble. Would you mind pointing that thing someplace else?" He didn't move or speak. I held up my hands. "Could I have some medicine for my hands? They really hurt!" No answer.

I tried again. "Please, *señor,* may I have a glass of water?" No answer. "*Señor,* what is your name? Won't you talk to me?"

He talked to me: "Shut up! You were told to be quiet! If you make any more noise, I will silence you for good!" He sighted down the barrel of the gun.

I tried to roll over onto my side, but the boards bumped against each other, pinching my skin. "Ouch!" I whispered.

"Shhh!" ordered the guard.

I remembered my watch: 10:25. Five hours to age five years—or five decades. How many more hours would this go on? How many more hours would I live?

Rita had been right. "Oh, my God, Rita!" What was she going through? What did she know? Who would take care of her and the kids? Would I ever see them again? If only I had listened to her! If only—oh, if only she had kissed me good-by! A knot welled up in my throat; tears spilled down my cheeks.

"Please, dear God, take care of Rita! Take care of my dear children!"

6
Blessed Are Those Who Mourn

Day 1 *(Friday, 21 September)*

DAVE SOLANO WAS beginning to get drowsy as he sat watching TV, relaxing after a busy week at his new job in Riverside. The nine o'clock program had just started and the plot was developing when the telephone rang. Dave hoisted himself out of his easy chair and grabbed the extension phone in the kitchen. "Solanos'," he answered.

"Dave," a woman said, "this is Wanda Chilcote."

"Wanda!" Dave was surprised. He had known her in Berne when she worked at C.T.S. Her husband had gotten a job in the Oakland area, and they had moved to California shortly before the Solanos had also migrated west. "How are you?"

"I'm fine," she said politely. "Have you heard the news tonight?"

"No, I haven't," Dave replied. "I've been watching TV, but the news hasn't been on yet down here. Why?"

"The channel we were watching had one of those on-the-hour updates," she explained. "I think I heard the newscaster say that Fausto Bucheli has been kidnapped by terrorists in some country in Central America."

Dave was incredulous. "No, that's not possible!"

"Well, how many Fausto Buchelis could there be?" she reasoned. "Do you know where he is?"

"Yes," said Dave. "He is in El Salvador. He is due back home tomorrow. Our family is going over there for a barbecue tomorrow night."

"I sure hope that I heard wrong, or that this is all some kind of mistake," said Wanda. "But I thought I should check with you anyway. Let me know if there's anything we can do—you know, if the report is true."

"Sure," Dave mumbled, his mind racing. "I'll look into it and get back to you. Thanks for calling. Bye!"

"Bye!" They hung up.

Dave's wife, Pauline, came into the kitchen. "Who was that?"

"Wanda Chilcote," he replied.

"Wanda Chilcote?" she said. "Aren't they in Oakland now?"

"Yes."

"Well, why did she call?" Pauline was perplexed by the dazed expression on Dave's face. His mind seemed to be someplace else.

"She said she heard on the news that Fausto has been kidnapped."

Pauline went to the kitchen table and sat down. After a few moments of silence, she said, "What do you make of it?"

"I'm not sure. I was just thinking about the last time we were over at Buchelis'. Do you remember? Fausto had just gotten back from El Salvador. He seemed preoccupied. I thought maybe he was worried about something; but he didn't appear to want to talk about it. I think maybe he was afraid something like this would happen."

"What do you think we should do?" questioned Pauline.

Dave picked up the phone directory. "First, I have to find out if it really happened."

"How are you going to do that?"

"All of those television and radio stations get their first information from the wire services. I'm going to call some local radio stations and see if one of them will confirm the report."

For several minutes, Dave called numbers that he located in the Yellow Pages. At that hour, all he got was recordings, busy signals, or no answers at all. Finally a man answered at a small local station. Dave told him why he was calling and waited while the engineer skimmed over the wire copy. The man returned to the phone with the report. There was nothing in the story about the killing of Luis Paz, but it confirmed the abduction of Fausto Bucheli and Bruce Chapman. Dave thanked the man and hung up.

"It's true!" Dave told Pauline. "There are no details at this point, but Fausto and some other man were kidnapped."

Pauline paled. "I wonder if Rita and the children know."

"I would expect so," replied Dave. "Don't they have to notify next of kin before they release that kind of news to the public?"

"If that's the case," she responded, "we should go over there and be with them. We're the closest friends they have in this area."

"We may be the only friends they have!" replied Dave. The Solanos and the Buchelis had been friendly acquaintances in Berne, where Dave had been born. But since both families had moved to the same general region of Southern California—the Solanos preceding the Buchelis by about a month—their friendship had deepened significantly.

"Still, I don't want to go rushing in on them if they haven't heard," said Dave. "On the other hand, if they don't know yet, maybe we should be the ones to tell them."

"Oh, that would be hard!" Pauline shuddered. "But you are right! The question is, How do we find out what they know in a tactful way?"

Dave had an idea. "The FBI—they know what the procedures are in these situations. I'll call them!"

The agent on duty assured Dave that the family would certainly have been informed by this time.

"Well, that settles that," sighed Dave. "I think I'd better call Rita and let her know we're coming over."

"We'll have to pick up Dana at the football game first so she can be here with Doug and Joey."

Dave agreed. "That won't take long. The game should be winding up right now." He dialed Bucheli's number.

Most of the Bucheli clan were watching television in the family room when the phone rang at 9:30 P.M. Fausto Jr. got up from the floor, went into the dining room, and answered the phone on the counter that runs along one side of the electric range. "Hello!" he said casually.

Dave Solano had expected that his call would intrude upon a family in upheaval. Immediately he sensed that the news had not descended on these people: Fausto's voice was much too normal. "Uh, hello, Fausto!" he said, shifting mental gears. "This is Dave Solano." He had not prepared what he would say in the event that he had to break the news. "How are you doing?"

"Fine!" Fausto replied. He figured Dave must be calling about the picnic scheduled for the next day.

"Have you heard anything—uh—about what's going on?" stammered Dave.

"I guess not," said Fausto. "Is something wrong?"

Dave took a deep breath. "Fausto, is anyone else on the phone right now?" There are phones all over the Bucheli residence. But the girls were all watching television. Rita, heading for the shower, came walking down the hall with a towel over her shoulder. Rita's mother, who had been living with the family for some time but spoke no English, was in her bedroom.

"No, Dave," Fausto reported, "it's just you and me!"

"I think," Dave began, "that there's a good chance that your father has been kidnapped."

"What?"

"It just came across the news. Apparently some anti-government terrorists have kidnapped your dad and one other man." Fausto was speechless. "I don't know whether the report is true, but Pauline and I are leaving right now to come over there, at least until we hear more."

Fausto didn't say anything more to Dave. Instead he called out to his mother, "Mom, wait!" Rita stopped at her bedroom door and walked back down the hallway to the dining room. She saw that the color had drained from Fausto's face. "It's Dave Solano!" he reported. "He said that daddy's been kidnapped!"

Rita laughed nervously. "Oh, that Dave, he's always kidding around!" Which was true enough. But Fausto didn't accept it.

"I don't think he would kid about something like that! He said he and Pauline are coming over here!"

Absently Fausto put down the receiver. He never said good-by.

"They are coming over here?" repeated Rita.

"Yes," Fausto said. "Would they come at this time of night if he wasn't serious?"

All four girls had entered the dining room and were listening intently. Fausto gave his report, and they believed it. They burst into tears. Their worst fears were being realized.

Rita held out longer. "If that is true," she reasoned, "then someone at Hartell must know about it!" She sat down at the table. "Call John Pike and see if he knows anything." John, Rita's car-pooling partner, had been Hartell's recruiter when Fausto was considering the move to California. He had also been instrumental in helping the Buchelis find a home and move their possessions from Indiana. His position in public relations and his acquaintance with the family made him the logical source of information. Fausto Jr. placed the call. Seventeen-year-old Barbara Pike answered.

"Good evening, Pikes."

"Hello, Barbara, this is Fausto Bucheli!"

Barbara gasped.

"May I speak with your father?"

"Uh, my dad and mom are on their way over to your place now," she answered. "They should be there any moment."

Fausto was astounded. "Do you know anything, Barbara?" he asked. "Do you know why they are coming here?"

Barbara was on the verge of tears. It was all she could do to talk. "No! They'll tell you everything when they get there! Good-by!" she said hurriedly and hung up.

As Fausto relayed the conversation to Rita, her mother emerged to investigate the commotion. Briefly Rita explained in Spanish what had transpired. Grandma almost fainted. Fausto caught her and helped her back to her room. She remained there the rest of the evening.

Shortly, John and Karen Pike arrived. John tried to be lighthearted. "Hi, Rita! How are you doing?" Even as he spoke, he saw the red, swollen eyes of the girls in the room. That scene wiped the smile off his face. He realized that they knew.

Rita said, "John, I only want to know one thing—is it true what we have heard about Fausto?"

He nodded. He and Karen sat down on one of the two, brown-plaid couches. "I'm sorry we didn't get word to you sooner, Rita! The company wanted to get confirmation whether or not Fausto is still alive. What have you heard?"

Rita related the substance of Dave's phone call. John shook his head. "It hit the news already!" he said in frustration. "That happened much quicker than we thought it would!"

"Do you know any more news?"

"What we've been able to piece together is that Fausto had left work with Bruce Chapman and Bruce's bodyguard, a man named Luis. They were driving into San Salvador when their van was stopped by two vehicles carrying the terrorists. The commandos shot up the van with submachine guns and killed the bodyguard."

This was new information to the family. John sensed the impact of the news of the killing. He added quickly, "But there were witnesses who saw both Fausto and Bruce walking away from the van. We are almost positive that they are all right!"

The girls broke down again. Fausto Jr. turned and walked away. Nine-year-old Tina, the youngest, fled to the backyard. Veronica, the eighth-grader, left through the front door. Not going anywhere in particular, she saw the next-door neighbors, the Verhoevens, pull into their driveway from an evening out. Their daughter, Denise, was a year older than she. Veronica ran to their car, tears streaming down her face. "My dad's been kidnapped!"

Gert Verhoeven put her arm around Veronica and took her into the house. The neighbors from across the street came over and listened as Veronica filled them in on what had happened. There was little they could say or do. After a while Gert took Veronica home.

By that time Dave and Pauline Solano had arrived. They were brought up to date by John. Rita sat by herself on a couch and pondered what she was going to do with five children and no husband.

Gert stayed just long enough to express regrets to Rita. The two neighbors had not yet spent much time together. Gert offered to help in any way she could, then went home.

Rita thought, "How sad it is that this has had to happen when we are so far away from our dearest friends." Then she said to Veronica, "Would you like to call someone in Berne?"

Veronica nodded. "I would really like to talk to Amy." In the kitchen she dialed the still-familiar number of the Habegger residence. Pretty soon the rest of the family could hear Veronica weeping over the phone. It helped all of them to know that a real friend was sharing the sorrow.

After a time Veronica called, "Mom, Amy would like to speak with you!" Rita took the phone. There was a long silence on the other end as Amy tried to talk. Nothing would come out—except sobs. It was Rita who spoke: "He's going to be all right, Amy! God will take care of him!"

Finally Amy was able to say, "I'll call Anita and Doris for you. They will want to know."

"Thank you, Amy!" replied Rita. "Good night!"

Fausto Jr. returned to the family room and said, "Mom, I think we should call dad's brother in Detroit."

Rita agreed. "I think that's a good idea. I've been thinking about calling our families in Ecuador, but it's two or three in the morning down there. Those calls will have to wait until tomorrow."

Fausto placed the call to Michigan.

"I think Reverend Crocker would like to know what has happened, Rita," suggested Dave, as Fausto completed his call. "Do you want me to call him?"

"No," Rita said, "I'll do that. I was just thinking the same thing. It's just that my mind has been a little numb."

The call to Don Crocker was the last one made that evening. He was so dumfounded by the news, he asked Rita three times to repeat it to make sure he understood her right.

Rita started probing Fausto Jr. with questions about the trip to the airport on Monday. She was feeling both sad and guilty about not having kissed her husband good-by that morning. If that turned out to be her last moment with him, the memory of her withdrawal from him would torment her the rest of her life.

As for Fausto Jr., her questions brought to his mind the parting admonitions his father had given him—and his promise to care for his mother and sisters in his father's absence. He didn't tell Rita about that conversation; it was his private heritage. It struck him that his father's words, which had made him feel somewhat uncomfortable at the time, were the sort of thing a man might say if he never expected to see his son again.

"Did he kiss you good-by?" That may have been the most important question for both Rita and her son.

"Yes, mommy, he did," choked Fausto. "And he said, 'I'll see you on Saturday.'" Fausto got up and went to his bedroom. No one saw him again, for all intents and purposes, for two days.

Don Crocker arrived with another man from the church, a psychologist. The pastor had seen the family only twice, both times at church. But it was clear that he felt responsibility toward them. John and Dave took the newcomers into the kitchen and told them what they knew. As they were talking, the eleven o'clock news came on. Everyone but Fausto Jr. and Grandma went into the family room to watch.

As anticipated there was a report about the kidnapping. The content was identical to what the family had already heard, with the exception that the newscaster couldn't pronounce Fausto's name correctly. It provided comic relief to some who watched; for others it was like pouring salt into a wound. There was a quote from Carl Reynolds expressing Hartell's concern for the men and the company's pledge to do everything possible to insure their safe return.

When the news broadcast moved on to other items, Don Crocker turned off the television. "I think it would be a good idea for us to pray together, don't you agree?" Everyone did. The room became very quiet, the silence punctuated only with periodic sniffs and the occasional blowing of a nose. Four girls, three women, and four men filled the family room, occupying both couches, the easy chair, and the carpet. It was a solemn moment.

"Dear God," began the pastor, "we understand neither what has happened nor why it has happened. You know the tremendous weight of grief that we feel tonight, and we come to You for comfort.

"We ask You to care for Fausto in Your great mercy. We have no idea what he has gone through, or what he is going through right now, but we ask You to protect him and the other man that we do not know. Give them strength to endure whatever ordeal they must face. Be with them, and guard them with Your grace.

"I pray as well, O God, for Rita, and the children. Help them to not be overwhelmed by what they do not know. And give them the strength to deal with what they do know. I pray that especially now they will cling to You in faith. May this experience, as difficult as it is, build them up rather than destroy them.

"Our Father, tonight we claim Your promise that 'all things work together for good to them who love God, to them who are called according to His purpose.' Prove that promise to be true to each of these dear children.

"And God, I ask that You would provide Your peace in the middle of all this anxiety. Help us to get some rest tonight so that tomorrow can be faced in Your strength. I pray these things in Jesus' name, Amen."

When he finished, the phone rang. It was the first of several calls Rita would receive from Berne, even though it was well past midnight there. That night Rita had comforting, bittersweet conversations with Doris Liechty and Anita Wenger, two "best friends" who had been alerted to the situation by the Habeggers.

It was after midnight when Don Crocker and his companion went home. No one else felt like leaving or going to bed. Over the next couple of hours, the adults sat together, talking about things that no one can remember, or just letting silence bathe the room. The girls began to drift to sleep in various positions on the floor.

At three in the morning John and Karen Pike reluctantly went home, promising to check back with Rita later in the new day.

With the Pikes' departure, Rita decided to put the girls in bed. The two who were awake couldn't bring themselves to pray, as was their bedtime custom. Rita tucked them in and kissed them good night.

As she returned to the family room and saw Dave and Pauline Solano sitting together, husband and wife, she was overwhelmed with a sense of loneliness. She had cried off and on through the evening. But the grief had been banked behind a wall of reserve in the presence of her children and people she did not know well. Even when friends had called on the phone, Rita retained a measure of composure because it was the caller who invariably broke down.

But now the stored-up emotion came pouring out in racking sobs. Dave and Pauline were momentarily startled by the intensity of her grief. Neither said a word, but Dave came to Rita, put his arms around her, and held her until her broken heart was spent. She cried hard for fifteen minutes. The tension of pent up grief was replaced by the sweet relief of sorrow expressed. God's peace became a reality. Rita excused herself, retired to her bedroom, lay across the bed, and let sleep overtake her. Her last conscious thought was, *At least he speaks Spanish. He will be able to talk to those people.*

Dave went around the house turning out lights. He found a couple of blankets, and he and Pauline completed their vigil in the Bucheli family room, each finding welcome slumber on a couch.

† † †

SLEEP, THE one refuge that offered escape from my misery, eluded me. Two factors conspired to prevent my rest. One was physical. The room was oppressively hot and humid. I lacked the cover to which I was accustomed. Abrasions and bruises multiplied over my body as I shifted about on my "bed." I had no pillow. My hands continued to throb.

Thirst was beginning to become a major affliction. The light remained on all night. The guard and the gun kept me in their sights. My entire system had endured the greatest physical trauma of my forty-one-plus years.

Even more disruptive was my mental-emotional state. My whole body literally shook with fear. Luis Paz had not just been shot before my eyes—he had been mutilated by submachine gun fire not two feet from me. And one of those same guns remained trained on me, threatening me with that same hideous extinction. I was terrified.

In those moments when my mind made an effort at rational thought, the magnitude of what had happened, and was happening to me, began to dawn. The first stirrings of anger—at these animals who held me, at Bruce, at Hartell, at myself, at fate—began to well up within me. *Why me?* I wanted to scream at someone. *Why me? What have I done to deserve this?* I hadn't been so bad, so wicked. Indeed, I was trying to help these people, to be loyal to my employers, to provide for my family. This was more than unfair—it was obscene.

From another part of my mind came a different line of thinking: *You're lucky even to be alive. You could have been killed with Luis. You could have been shot any number of times. These men have said you will be all right. Maybe you will survive through all this.* But that theme would invariably surrender to the voices predicting destruction.

An accompanying emotion was grief. Ironically I shed no tears during those hours, either for Luis, whom I had not really known, or for myself. I wept, like a man attending his own funeral, for my family. Already I was realizing how ill-prepared they were for my absence. I handled everything even remotely related to finances, business, and insurance. Rita wouldn't have a clue even how to begin to do any of this. Would Hartell provide for my family? Could I have any faith in this company after what they had allowed to happen to me?

I thought, sadly, about my parents in Ecuador. My mother was not in good health. What would this news do to her? Did they know? What would they do?

Such were the thoughts, emotions, and conditions that tormented me through the remainder of that night.

7
For They
Will Be Comforted

SEPTEMBER 22, 1979, was a good day for telephone companies all over the western hemisphere. It was a tough day for most of the relatives and friends of Fausto Bucheli. For virtually every one of them, the telephone was a bell that tolled bad news. And it rang everywhere.

Probably the earliest calls were those that woke Antonio and Maria Bucheli from their slumber in Quito. An official message was sent personally by the Ecuadorian ambassador in San Salvador. He assumed the responsibility for communicating to the senior Buchelis that their son had been kidnapped.

Shortly thereafter, another call got through from Detroit. Mama and Papa Bucheli learned about the situation of the family in America from a concerned son, Fausto's brother, who had decided not to interrupt his parents' night's sleep.

The news hit hard. Even though Fausto had fallen out of favor with his parents because of his marriage to Rita and had been out of the country for more than fifteen years, he was still their son.

The news of Fausto's abduction received front-page attention in the Ecuadorian press. Before noon, a crew from the major television station in Quito arrived in the front yard of the Bucheli residence. The interview gave Antonio his first opportunity to appeal to the terrorists in El Salvador to release his son—a fellow Latino.

In Miami, the telephone served summons to three former FBI agents who were recruited by Fred Rayne to serve on his negotiations team. Along with Juan Ortega, a security specialist, they met at the offices of Rayne International to review both strategy and tactics for the anticipated assignment.

In Berne, Indiana, the grapevine came alive a little earlier in the day than usual. By noon those who had not heard of the kidnapping by word of mouth were learning of it from local radio stations WADM and WBCL. Immediately prayer chains were formed in several of the churches. A prayer vigil was maintained in that community every day of the ordeal.

It was the telephone that signaled the start of a new day in the Bucheli household in Chino. It started ringing early in the morning and didn't stop until one o'clock the next morning. Someone was manning the phone almost constantly.

More calls came in from friends in Berne, all bearing the same message: expressions of sympathy, assurances of prayer, offers of help—financial and otherwise. "Call us, collect, any time you just want to talk" was a frequent exhortation.

John and Karen Pike returned and brought some food with them. John took all calls from the local media: "The Buchelis are not giving interviews at this time."

Rita and Dave Solano did talk with correspondents who called from Berne and Decatur, a small city nearer to Fort Wayne. Sharon Little filed the first newspaper story that day in the *News-Sentinel,* citing several statements by Rita.

By midmorning the telephone operator placed a call to Rita herself. "There are so many long-distance calls coming through, people are waiting in line," she reported. "Do you want to take all of these calls?" She was concerned that the volume might unintentionally be harassing the family.

"Let them come on through," said Rita. "They are all from friends who want to help us through a family crisis." Then she added, "I appreciate your concern. I'm glad the phone system isn't completely automated."

One local call that got through was from Tom Elliott, the engineer who had accompanied Fausto on his final trip to APLAR. He was mortified by what had happened. "Rita, I'm so sorry about what happened to Fausto! If he hadn't sent me home early, I might have been in that car with him!"

"You were very lucky," observed Rita.

"Yes, I was," Tom agreed. "I promised Fausto that I would call you when I got home. I should have done that right away, but I decided that it could wait until this morning. I feel really bad about not calling sooner."

"That's all right, Mr. Elliott. I understand. Was there any special message that he wanted you to give me?"

"Yes, there was," he replied. "He wanted me to tell you that he was all right"—he hesitated, trying to suppress the lump swelling in his throat—"and that he loves you!"

Even though it was coming through a stranger, this was a message Rita was glad to receive—especially in view of the way she and Fausto had argued just before he left. She now had a new "last memory" to cling to.

"I thought," continued Tom, clearing his throat, "that perhaps tomorrow you might like to go for a ride with my wife and me. It will probably be a madhouse around your place today. But if you want to get away for a while tomorrow, you could ask me any questions you have about Fausto and what we did during the past week."

"I would like to do that very much," agreed Rita. "That is very thoughtful of you. I will be going to church in the morning, but tomorrow afternoon would be a good time."

"Then we will pick you up at one o'clock," Tom said.

"Fine! Thank you for calling. Good-by!"

There were also some out-going calls to be made. After several attempts Rita succeeded in getting through to Fausto's family in Ecuador. By then, of course, the news was all over the country. But it was good to establish contact and let them know how the family in Chino was doing.

Dave Solano had a call of his own to make. The more he thought about what had happened and the way things were handled, the angrier he became. The thought that kept running through his mind was, *What if Wanda hadn't called me when she did? What if Rita and the children had heard about the kidnapping from the evening news report?*

During a lull in the incoming barrage, he placed a call to the State Department. When the phone at the L.A. office was answered, he asked to speak to the person who was in charge for the day. An unidentified official came on the line.

Dave laid out the whole scenario from the night before. Then he asked, "Isn't there some control over the release of news? I contacted the FBI last night, and they assured me that the family would certainly be notified in such a situation before the identities of the victims would be made public."

The man responded: "Normally, sir, that is the case with tragedies that occur within the United States. Law enforcement agencies have a measure of control over news reports of domestic situations. But no one exercises restraint over news stories that originate outside of the country."

"But shouldn't a television station check to make sure that the immediate family knows before they broadcast a story like that?" questioned Dave.

"It would be nice of them to do something like that," the official agreed. "But in reality, they are no more eager to break the news to loved ones than anyone else. And there is some doubt as to whether such an inquiry is any more gentle for the family than learning about the event on television. For the most part, I suspect that the media people are of the opinion that the task of notifying the family belongs to somebody else."

"Well, it shouldn't be that way!" fumed Dave.

"I sympathize with you," the man said. "But that is how things are. And I don't see any way to change it."

Dave knew it wasn't that man's fault, but he was still upset. He simply hung up the phone in frustration over a system that was too big and too complex to change.[1]

John Pike made a few contacts with the command post at Hartell. There was no more news. Everyone was just waiting—waiting for someone to take credit for the abduction, waiting for a ransom demand, waiting for some kind of communication.

The extent to which the news of the kidnapping had spread became evident later in the day. A telegram in Spanish arrived from Esmeraldas, Ecuador. Translated, it said: TO RITA BUCHELI AND FAMILY, WE ARE WITH YOU IN OUR PRAYERS. WE ARE SURE THAT GOD WILL BE WITH YOU ALL THE TIME. WITH LOVE, THE ERDEL FAMILY.

[1]What finally calmed Dave was the realization that in fact Wanda *had* called him and *he* was the one who told the family. The "uncontrollable system" had been overruled. God, he had reason to believe, was still in business.

For Rita, this telegram, as much as anything else, summarized the experience of the entire day.

On Saturday morning, September 22, the following article (translated from Spanish) appeared on the front page of *La Prensa Grafica* (The Graphic Press), the largest newspaper in San Salvador:

MANAGER OF FIRM KIDNAPPED
AND EMPLOYEE KILLED

Kidnapped yesterday in the free zone of San Bartolo, was Mr. [Bruce Chapman], 48, the general manager of the APLAR factory.

In the act of the kidnapping, the kidnappers shot to death the bodyguard José Luis Paz Viera, a retired sergeant of the National Guard, who had for some time given his services to the captive, Mr. [Chapman].

According to the official version, the perpetrators of the kidnapping used two vehicles in order to fake a collision on the Boulevard del Ejército, in the vicinity of the Matazano detour.

After killing the bodyguard and taking Mr. [Chapman] away, the kidnappers fled in the pickup used to crash into the back of the panel [truck] in which Mr. [Chapman], his chauffeur and bodyguard were riding.

About two hundred meters away from the site of the kidnapping, they abandoned said pickup, stopped a light truck that was driven by Mr. Armando Antonio Garay, and left him on foot. When Mr. Garay informed the authorities, he indicated that the vehicle belongs to a window manufacturing firm.

As of last night, [the authorities] had not yet identified any extremist group as being responsible for the kidnapping of Mr. [Bruce Chapman], according to information received from police authorities.

† † †

I DID NOT know whether it was morning when the door opened. The square "window" was completely sealed off. Not even cracks of light squeaked through at the edges. Nevertheless, the same person who had brought in the "toilet" some hours before now brought me "breakfast." It consisted of fried bananas and a liter of water. The water was in a brown plastic container about the size and shape of an oatmeal box. I was so dehydrated, I began to gulp the water down.

"Not so fast," warned the guard, breaking his silence. "That is all the water you will get today." Having drunk a little, I had no will power to conserve. I swallowed every drop.

When I turned my attention to the bananas, I realized for the first time that, if this was indeed morning, I had not eaten anything substantive for twenty-four hours. I was en route to supper when captured. I had worked right through lunch. My last meal had been coffee and a roll with Tom Elliott at the hotel. Within a single day I had been reduced to the status of those poor Salvadorans I had pitied two weeks before. My empty stomach notwithstanding, I let the bananas pass.

After a few minutes I traded my tray and pitcher for a morning newspaper. It had been liberally edited with a pair of scissors. There was no reference whatsoever to the abduction. The only articles that survived dealt with acts of violence either by government forces or by right-wing terrorists.

I doubt that the paper made the impression my captors had hoped for. I was politically naïve. In Berne we paid attention to what was happening in Decatur, Fort Wayne, and maybe Chicago and New York—but El Salvador could have been on the moon. I could tell from my recently acquired library that my adversaries were Communists, but even that didn't mean a lot to me.

I put the newspaper to good use. I rolled up pieces into long tubes and placed them between the boards of my pallet. They served as shock absorbers and greatly reduced the noise of the slats knocking against each other every time I moved. The remainder of the paper I placed next to the five-gallon can for future reference.

With breakfast and the morning paper came a changing of the guard. The submachine gun and the "uniform" were the same. So was the sinister silence.

Abruptly the three hooded kidnappers who had stripped me hours before strode into my cell. They were angry. "You capitalist, imperialist pig!'' snarled Señor Glasses with a string of curses. ''We told you not to try anything! We ought to shoot you right now and ship your traitor's carcass back to your blood-sucking company in a bag!''

I was looking up the barrels of four guns. I didn't know why, but it was obvious that the men holding these weapons needed only the slightest excuse to empty them into my body. ''Please, *señor*,'' I pled, ''I have done nothing!''

''Nothing?'' he roared. ''You call this nothing?'' There were broken, twisted fragments of gold metal in his left hand. He shoved them under my nose, and it took a few seconds for me to get them in focus. I was looking at the remains of my digital watch.

''That's my watch!'' I said in amazement. ''Why did you smash my watch?'' I must have sounded like a child. ''That was a good watch,'' I babbled on, ''a Seiko!''

Señor Glasses hurled the pieces into the can. ''You had a transmitter in that watch!'' he accused. ''You were sending out a signal so that someone could come here and find you. That's why we smashed it! We ought to smash you!''

I was dumbfounded. ''A transmitter? That's crazy. What made you think—''

''Crazy?'' The second man raised his fist to strike me. I cowered in the corner.

''No, wait!'' I cried, trying to think. Then a thought struck me. ''Did you hear a 'beep'? Is that the signal you are talking about?''

The second man turned to Señor Glasses. ''I knew he would confess!'' Señor Glasses held up his hand to silence his comrade.

''That was an alarm,'' I tried to explain. *Alarm* wasn't a very good word to use at that point. I tried again. ''What I mean is, that 'beep' you heard was not a transmitter. It was a sound that was supposed to wake me up this morning. It was set for six o'clock. Really! I wasn't signaling for help! I won't cause you any trouble!''

The situation would have been funny, hilariously funny, if it hadn't almost cost me my life. Señor Glasses, as it turned out, was a fairly sophisticated man. he could tell that my reactions were spontaneous. I had convinced him that they had hammered a perfectly harmless watch to bits.

"We'll let you live this time, traitor," he spat, "if you cooperate with us from now on."

I swallowed hard and nodded. My heart was racing and I was sweating profusely. I wondered how much more of this I could take.

"We are members of the Partido Revolucionario de los Trabajodores Centroamericanos, the Revolutionary Party of Central American Workers," announced Señor Glasses. "Your kidnapping was the result of a brilliantly executed operation!" He thrust his fist into the air. "Glory to our fighters fallen in battle: David, Jaime, and Raul Antim! Viva Nicaragua Sandinista!" He looked down at me. "We have some questions for you. If you give us the answers we need, you will live."

"May I please sit up?" I requested.

"No!" he snapped. "Stay where you are!" Then he turned to the third man and said, "Get him a pillow." The man left.

While he was gone, I studied the two men who stood over me. Señor Glasses was of average build. Beneath the gray-and-black topcoat he wore a fairly nice sport shirt and neatly pressed brown slacks. Of the three, he was the only one who wore shoes. I thought he might be a teacher. He was clearly in charge.

The second man was big, about six-feet-two and easily over two hundred pounds. His coat was too small for him. He wore a white T-shirt and blue jeans. When he raised his hand to strike me, the hood rode up on his face and I could see that he had a mustache. Since his pillowcase had only two holes, the mustache wasn't ordinarily visible. Señor Mustache seemed to want to hurt me. I was always more afraid of him than the others.

The third man returned with a small pillow, which really helped a lot. He was smaller than the others, sort of skinny. He wore blue jeans and no shirt at all beneath the open coat. He had not spoken. I surmised that he was more sympathetic to me than the others.

With my head slightly propped up by the pillow, Señor Mustache began the interrogation: "We have just talked with Chapman. He already gave us some information. He was very helpful. If you cooperate like he did and answer our questions, everything will be O.K."

"If I know the answers, I will tell you," I promised. I didn't think I had any knowledge that could be damaging to Hartell.

"So, how much money do you think you are worth?" Señor Mustache got down to business.

"I've never thought about that before," I said. "My wife and I are preparing to buy a house, and I have some money in the bank from the sale of—"

"No, no no!" he interrupted. "I'm talking about your company! How much are you worth to Hartell?"

I shrugged. "I don't know! I've only been working there for seven weeks, and I've been in El Salvador for three of those weeks." My brain felt sluggish. How does one answer such a question? I looked up at Señor Mustache. "I will be very honest with you. They haven't ever told me how much money I am worth to them. I only know what they pay me. If I say a very high amount, they may refuse to pay it because it is too much, and you will kill me. If I say a very low amount and you think I am trying to cheat you, you will be angry with me, and perhaps you will kill me. I am afraid to say anything. I just don't know."

"Chapman said we should ask for something between one and twenty million dollars," said Señor Mustache.

"If that's what Señor Chapman said, I will say that too," I replied. "But I really don't know."

Señor Glasses took over. "Who else travels overseas for Hartell?"

"I don't know!" I said. "I told you, I am new with the company."

"You are a liar!" charged Señor Glasses. "There was another North American with you this week!"

"I am not lying!" I insisted. "That man is an engineer at our Fullerton plant. He made one trip down here. He doesn't normally travel to other countries, and he isn't coming back down here." That was a safe statement.

"What about other countries—like Italy? Who goes to Europe?" he pressed.

"I really do not know." They did not like this answer.

Señor Mustache must have been the money man. "What was Hartell's total sales last year?" he asked.

"I don't know—" I caught myself. "I'm not sure. It may

have been something like 400 million dollars. You can find out by reading the stock reports in the *New York Times*."

"But we want to hear it from you!" he insisted.

"Well, that's the best I can do! My guess is 400 million, but it may be wrong."

"Do you have a name of someone in the company that we should contact to negotiate for your life?" Señor Mustache asked.

Several names crossed my mind, but I didn't know if saying them would put the people in danger. "I don't have a specific name," I replied. "Perhaps if you just contact the company, they will put you in touch with the right person." That sounded reasonable to me.

But they didn't like it—I was flunking their test. "Chapman gave us a name!" growled Señor Mustache.

"He did?"

"That's right! It was written on a card in his pocket." I was stunned. *Can I believe that? What name did he give them? Where is he?*

"All that we found in your pocket was this passport, *gringo!*" Señor Glasses was getting worked up. "It says you are a traitor! You should be on our side, but they brainwashed you! You are a *gringo!* They sent you over here to steal money from us! For every dollar they bring in, they take out two or three!"

"That is not true!" I protested. "My company sent me down here because they *lost* two million dollars last year!"

"How can you say that?" he objected. "How can you hate the Salvadoran people so much?"

"I'm not saying anything against the Salvadoran people!" I said. "I'm just telling you that the reason I was sent down here was because APLAR lost money the last two years. I came down to help your people, to train them to do good work, to give them jobs."

"To steal our money!" interrupted Señor Glasses.

I should have kept my mouth shut, but I didn't. "You can say what you want about America," I argued, "but when I went there, I didn't have anything. I had many opportunities to learn, to improve myself, to advance, to get a better job. They gave me opportunity, and I became one of them. I'm not better than anybody and I'm not less than anybody."

I wanted to say that I was trying to share what I had learned with my fellow Latinos. But I never got that far. Señor Mustache ended my little speech with his fist. I ducked, but there was no place to go. His knuckles smashed into my left jaw.

"Traitor!" he screamed. "You are a filthy *gringo!*" The vilest curses poured out of his mouth. I spat blood to the floor: he had broken a bridge on the upper side of my mouth. My gums and lip began to swell.

Señor Glasses grabbed Mustache by the arm and began to withdraw from the room. "Next time you talk like that, *gringo,* we'll put a bullet in your brain!"

"Yeah!" taunted Señor Mustache. "Like your friend Luis Paz—that murderer! He used to be in the National Guard. He was number one on our list, and we got him! You should choose your friends more carefully!"

"He wasn't my—" The door slammed shut. I was alone with a new guard and a new misery. My mouth was afire with pain.

I just lay there for a long time, looking at the cobweb-patterned ceiling, but seeing nothing. I was exhausted from the ordeal of the inquisition I had just survived.

I *had* survived. Again.

My pulse slowly returned to normal as the adrenalin was absorbed into my beleaguered system. With my tongue I explored the battered interior of my mouth. The bridgework on the upper jaw had been demolished; any pressure there sent shock waves of pain through the region. If I was ever to be given solid food, it would have to be processed through the right side. I was paying dearly for my outburst of patriotism.

But more damage had been done to my spirit than to my mouth. It crushes a man to be subjected to such mental abuse. It was utterly frustrating to be unable to make an acceptable response to these barbarians. Attempts at reasoning fell on deaf ears. Sincerity was met with more malice. My impotence had been dramatically reinforced. I was completely at the mercy of men who didn't care one whit whether I lived or died.

My feelings of helplessness were compounded by the senselessness of it all. I could not comprehend why I was being treated in such a way. These people acted toward me as though they hated me—yet they didn't know me. I had never been the object of hatred before. What they had done to Luis with bullets, they were doing to me with words and actions. Perhaps Luis was the lucky one.

Feebly the track in my mind that searched the darkness for any glimmers of hope registered its findings. Things had changed, and not all for the worse. I now had a pillow! And the newsprint shock absorbers were functioning admirably: I could turn over without causing the guard to jump. Acute thirst was no longer a source of agony, at least temporarily.

And I knew more than I had known. I learned that my captors had some connection with the Nicaraguan revolution that Rita had told me about. I now had reason to believe that I was of more value to them as a live hostage than as a dead "traitor's carcass." Regarding time, there were several clues to the effect that it was morning—Saturday morning, September 22, the day I was to have flown back to California for good.

The realization that I was not on my way home—and would not be going home—canceled out whatever ray of encouragement these new factors might have brought. I was plunged into depression. I rolled over on my side and stared at the wall like a catatonic patient in some padded cell. Would that this one were padded! My last conscious thought, maybe for several hours, was that Pan Am was probably angry at me for not canceling my reservation.

8
Rayne, of Terror

Day 3 *(Sunday, 23 September)*

THE ONE MAN who, more than any other, would determine the fate of Fausto Bucheli and Bruce Chapman spent the better part of Sunday flying from Miami to Los Angeles. Had the two hostages known of all the available resources in the country and of all the experts in the field of counterterrorist negotiations, it is very likely that they would have selected this man themselves to direct the efforts to secure their release. At age fifty-eight, Fred Rayne was at least one of the best in the business—possibly the best.

By temperament and experience, the president of Rayne International was ideally suited for his highly specialized vocation. By no choice of his own Rayne experienced terrorist activity at an early age. Born in Germany to an Aryan father and a Jewish mother, he was one of a group of teen-agers rounded up by Nazi agents in 1937. The young people were herded into a horse barn, which was set afire. The horses were going crazy with fear. Seventeen-year-old Fred shinnied up a pole to avoid the horses and the flames. When the barn doors finally burned down, he raced through the opening to safety.

He never looked back until he arrived safely on the shores of England. He enlisted in the British army and fought as a private in France. In 1942 he was given a position in British

Intelligence, initially interrogating German POWs. His code name was "Montague Rayne"—an alias transferred to him from an officer who had been killed in battle. In the course of the war he advanced to the rank of major. And when the fighting ended, he transferred to the German section of the British Foreign Office.

In all he served nine years with British Intelligence, developing the skills he would later use in various clandestine operations. He also legally adopted the English name, retaining "Fred" (his middle name) as the only vestige of his childhood identity as Manfred Reinefeld.

Though he stayed with his next vocation for over a decade, he eventually decided that circling the globe as a salesman of women's underwear and swimsuits was too tame. In the late fifties he entered the security business, which became the springboard for establishing his own company. Rayne International, one of the first firms to specialize in counterterrorist security for multinational corporations, was started in 1975. By the time the president was making this particular transcontinental flight four years later, the company was employing a staff of sixty-five agents working full- or part-time in the U.S., Europe, and Latin America and had a gross annual income of a million dollars.

Rayne had made trips such as this before. But the negotiations aspect of dealing with terrorists was not where he placed his emphasis. He invested most of his energies and creativity in prevention. He specialized in setting up counterterrorist security systems and training American executives living abroad in the fine art of avoiding abduction or worse. The techniques employed by Bruce Chapman during Fausto's third visit had been taught to him by Fred Rayne.

Only when the prevention methods did not work—an inevitable fact of life—did Rayne have to don the negotiator's hat. That he did marked him as unique in the security field. When a kidnapping did occur, Rayne offered personal "postevent assistance." He insisted on being a member of the "crisis-management team." And he assumed full responsibility for the sensitive roles of "courier" and "negotiator." Among security agency heads, only Fred Rayne took it upon himself to secure the release of hostages employed by client companies.

During the week ahead Rayne would meet with the other members of the "crisis-management team" of Hartell Industries in Fullerton. He would delineate their options and help formulate strategy. He would determine the extent of the company's kidnapping insurance and ascertain whether the company would be willing to pay even more than the amount of their coverage if necessary. He would obtain written authorization to represent the company in the negotiations and compile a list of names and phone numbers of Hartell executives who could authorize him to act or give him instructions on a moment's notice. He would set up procedures for securing large amounts of cash on any day of the week, any hour of the day. He would visit with the victims' wives to secure information that would enable him to confirm unmistakably the identities of the hostages.

And he would wait for the kidnappers to make their first move.

What he would not do is negotiate his own salary. That had already been established at $500 a day plus expenses: combat pay.

Traveling with Rayne were two other members of what would become the negotiating team. They were former FBI agents who would serve as his bodyguards and undertake any particular missions he might assign. They were, in short, sophisticated, highly trained errand boys who risked their lives on every assignment.

Two other team members remained behind in Miami, ready to fly to San Salvador on a moment's notice. When that moment arrived would depend on the terrorists.

† † †

WHATEVER I did as I lay on my pallet of boards could not be rightly termed sleeping. I tried to sleep—I was so tired. But no rest came.

By the third day, a recognizable pattern, a sort of daily routine, began to emerge. Some of the details didn't fall into place in my disturbed mind at first. But the elements were all in place by Sunday.

In the absence of any sunlight, there were three indicators that enabled me to remain oriented to time. First, there was the changing of the guard. Four men did sentry duty in sequence. They wore identical disguises, but I learned to tell them apart by their hands and feet. One of them wore a watch.

The second clue was provided by a boy—I guessed he was about age fifteen—who was my personal "valet." I later learned that his name was Ocho, a sadly uncreative name to denote one's eighth child. He also wore a hood, but his sparse peasant's attire revealed the frame of a teen-ager. Ocho brought my daily ration of six bananas and one liter of water. He also had the task of emptying the can when necessary. Ocho was the only one who ever communicated with me as a person. It was many days before he broke his silence, but his eyes told me he was not like the others.

Ocho's visits coincided with the changing of the guard. Three times he would bring the bananas—sometimes fried, occasionally raw. Then the guard would change without him. Then he would come with bananas and water, and check the toilet. Water, I finally determined, meant morning. And the guards were sweating six-hour shifts.

The third indicator was a daily ritual that occurred outside my cell. A rooster would crow and an irate dog would chase it. The rooster was apparently faster, for it never retired from being the canine's alarm clock—or mine.

On Sunday, when Ocho made his breakfast call, I was relieved to see no sign of the three hoods. I was also glad to see the canister of water. This time, though my thirst was great, I managed to discipline myself to drink only half the liter. I also tried a few pieces of banana, but gave up when the throbbing in my gums became too intense.

Not knowing the house rules yet, I asked Ocho, when he returned for my tray of bananas, if I could perhaps have a cup of coffee. He gave no indication one way or the other. But when he returned in a few minutes carrying a blue plastic cup, I could scarcely believe my good fortune. There in the stench of that unvented cell, I imagined I could smell the incomparable aroma of Salvadoran coffee.

It was only imagination. The cup held coffee all right. But it was tepid. And on the surface floated a big black roach, presumably dead. I poured the coffee into the can and gave the cup back to Ocho. The cruelty of such a hoax flogged my already exhausted emotions. I lay down on the pallet and cried.

† † †

AS THE wide-bodied jet transporting Fred Rayne and company flew over the plains of mid-America, the citizens of Berne, Indiana, were making plans of their own. Special times for prayer were inserted into the schedules of virtually every church service and most of the Sunday school classes in town. There had been a run on sympathy/encouragement cards the day before, and many of those made the rounds of the various study groups before being dropped in the mail. The Freshman Girls' Sunday School Class of First Mennonite Church drafted and signed their very own letter to the Bucheli family.

On the other hand, informal discussions as to what the community should do in the event that Fausto was killed led to the selection of a dozen representatives who volunteered to fly to California for the funeral. A local travel agent began monitoring the computer listings of reservations in order to secure space on a single flight, if possible, at the earliest possible time. The prearranged travel plans would be activated by the announcement of Fausto's death. Rita's friends would not allow her to go through that experience alone.

Out in California, Rita took her first venture out of the house: she and the girls went to church. It was a strange experience. The first two times they had attended Faith Missionary Church, they had been "those people with the Spanish accent who just moved here from Indiana." This time they were the family whose father was kidnapped in Central America. It was difficult for people who were not well-acquainted to know what to say or do. Several individuals and couples expressed their sympathy to Rita and the girls, and there were offers of assistance and food. Even though they were still strangers among the Californians, it felt good to Rita to be among fellow Christians and to know that this concern was genuine.

It felt even better to be in a worship service. The singing of hymns, the pastor's prayer, the message from the Bible all contributed to bolster Rita's confidence in God. There was something about worshiping with others of like faith that put the present circumstances in a broader perspective. She knew that hundreds of people all over the country were praying for Fausto and for her and the children. But somehow it helped to hear some of those prayers with her own ears. She was reminded of Fausto's promise, made to Pastor Crocker the week before, that he wanted to discuss church membership when he returned from El Salvador. She wondered if she would ever see him fulfill that promise.

That same day, an American real estate agent, William W. Hom of San Francisco, and two Salvadoran friends were shot to death during a leftist guerrilla attack on the presidential palace in San Salvador.

Approximately fifty armed men mounted a twenty-five-minute assault on the Armed Forces Communications Training School. Hom, who was vacationing in El Salvador and who had apparently been returning from a trip to the beach, got caught in a cross fire. The leftists retreated when the fifty soldiers stationed at the school were reinforced by other troops located nearby.

In another part of the city, national police attempted to force some four hundred demonstrators out of the Labor Ministry headquarters, which they had seized on Friday. After cordoning off the usually crowded section of the city, Police lobbed between twenty-five and thirty tear gas shells into the building. They failed to dislodge the protesters.

The government facility had been occupied by leftist members of the "28th of February Popular League," which took its name from the date of a violent antigovernment protest in 1977. Spokesmen for the demonstrators maintained that three of their members had been arrested by police in April and had not been heard of since. The seizure of the Labor Ministry building was intended to secure the release of the three prisoners.

In still another section of the capital, police located the getaway car used by the gunmen who kidnapped Fausto Bucheli and Bruce Chapman. As of that date, no group had claimed responsibility for the abduction, and the condition and whereabouts of the two American businessmen remained unknown.

† † †

"LUNCH" WAS the occasion that reactivated the thinking process. When Ocho delivered the tray of bananas, he looked at me—and there was sadness in his eyes. He used hand signals to try to encourage me to eat something. When I set aside my self-pity enough to pay attention to him, I realized that this boy was sending me a message: "The roach wasn't my idea. I'm sorry you hurt so bad."

Gingerly I put some banana into my mouth and, with great effort, managed to chew then swallow it. Ocho nodded his support. It was like a standing ovation. I took a sip of water and tried to smile. Ocho glanced at the guard and abruptly left the room.

A gesture, a nod were the first "encouraging words" I had received in these recent days. I was deeply grateful. I had just had communication with someone who did not find me detestable. In my confinement I was not completely without a friend.

Ocho's expression of sympathy freed me momentarily from the overwhelming gloom of despondency. Every previous attempt to evaluate my situation had generated such acute pain that I sought to escape in sleep. Thoughts of my family and what they might be experiencing had been too much for my mind to contemplate. But now I thought of them, and the pain was accompanied by comfort.

The comfort stemmed from the realization that, when allowances were made for time-zone differences, it was very likely that Rita and the children were in church. I could visualize them surrounded by caring people. I could see Pastor Crocker leading the congregation in prayer for my safety and my family's strength. We were not alone.

By now our friends in Berne would have heard the news. There would be phone calls and cards and letters. The people in the churches would be praying for me. Rita and the children would have help and support.

I recalled my brief conversation with Pastor Crocker the Sunday before: it seemed like years ago. He had impressed me as a compassionate man; I hoped that he would be able to comfort my family. I also hoped that the prayers would accomplish some good. I didn't know much about that. My thoughts

about God over the past thirty-six hours had been pretty negative. It didn't occur to me until much later that the presence of
any comforting thoughts at all might be part of His answer to
those petitions.

What did occur to me is that more was at issue in my
situation than physical survival alone. A major offensive had
been launched against my sanity. I might not have any say,
ultimately, as to my physical survival. But I could resist the
onslaught directed against my mind. If I didn't do something to
fight back, it was conceivable that this creature might somehow
be released from the captivity of that cell no longer existing as
Fausto Bucheli.

What made me aware of this danger was the experience of
having my few positive thoughts turn on me. Thinking of the
friends who must be surrounding Rita accentuated my own
sense of loneliness. Visualizing the concern of the citizens of
Berne evoked anger with myself for having moved from there.
Images of people praying raised the whole issue of the nature of
God. Ironically I entertained little doubt about His existence.
But what sort of God He was became a topic of serious debate in
my mind. His performance, or lack thereof, during the past two
days significantly undermined the validity of any claims to justice, wisdom, power, or love. Apart from its value as a gesture
of solidarity, I wondered if prayer had any genuine worth or
meaning.

While those were issues that I would have to come to grips
with, I knew that I could not handle them at this point. The
mental spiral was always downward. I had to do something to
engage my brain in a positive direction.

I considered reading. There was a stack of books to choose
from, if barely enough light to read by. I took the top volume
and thumbed through it. No, this would not work. My ability to
think straight was already seriously impaired. Further poison-
ing my mind with propaganda could send me over the brink.

So I turned pages and pretended to read.

The mental exercise I finally chose for preserving my ra-
tionality was reminiscence. I decided to try to remember the
happy memories from my past, to see how far back I could go,
to discover how much of what was recorded in my brain could
be recalled. It proved to be a healthful activity. In fact, my

ability to recount the details of my life, no less this story, is probably due to the reinforcement of memories resurrected and relived during the days of my captivity.

Of course, the extremity of my condition did not permit the detached kind of reflection in which one drifts back into the past and re-experiences events in the imagination. The present kept intruding into the recollections and I unintentionally, but continually, reminded myself of the contrast between past privileges and my present deprivation.

The first thing that struck me, as I reflected on my early childhood, was how protected I was by my parents. My earliest memories were of my father carrying me to bed and tucking me in. That image seemed to represent the strength and security he communicated to me.

From my youngest years I wanted to know what made things work. My engineer's mentality was apparent as early as age four. My father had a beautiful old clock that had been handed down from his father's father, a real heirloom. It fascinated me. The "tick-tock, tick-tock" was loud, and I was always curious as to who was making those noises. I asked my parents who was inside that clock: they thought that was cute. They told me that a little man lived in the clock and made it keep time. I wanted to see this little man. So one day, when no one else was around, I opened up the clock with my father's hammer—broke it into hundreds of pieces. A spring shot out of the mechanism and struck my bare leg. It made such a hole in the flesh that I still have the scar.

With blood streaming down my leg, I went crying to my mother to report that the little man had attacked me! That was only the beginning of my troubles. My father was so upset he stalked out of the house. I think he was afraid of what he would do to me if he disciplined me. My mother did not have such qualms about her self-control, and soon the pain in my leg was forgotten in deference to the sting of my backside. It might have been worse, but I suspect my parents accepted part of the blame for telling me about that "little man" in the first place.

I couldn't help but make the connection between my episode with the clock and the more recent smashing of my Seiko. Though the reasons for the demolitions were different, it certainly made the actions of my captors look childish.

As the oldest son, I held a special place in my father's heart. On the one hand, I was overprotected and spoiled. It seems that I was given virtually anything I really wanted. On the other hand, I seem to have gotten more spankings than any of my seven siblings. My mother explained, many years later, that parents want the older children to be a model for the younger ones. So I received more discipline.

When I turned twelve, my father gave me two very important things: My first pair of long trousers—the symbol in Ecuador that a boy has become a man; and a dog, a German shepherd that I named Pituco—"Handsome."

My father would tell me, "Fausto, you are my oldest son. You will carry on the family name. Always carry that name with honor. As a Bucheli, you will be an ambassador of your family, your country, your heritage. Don't ever do anything that will bring shame to our name."

My father was my idol, my role model. He was authoritarian in his home, eminently successful in his business, highly respected in Ecuadorian society. He earned everything he had by aggressiveness and hard work. I wanted to be just like him.

Though I was very shy and socially insecure as a child, I could be relentless in the pursuit of a goal. With characteristic tenacity, I trained Pituco to do remarkable things. We used to put money and a shopping list in a basket. He would carry the basket in his teeth to the little market a block away. A clerk would put the requested items in the basket, and Pituco would bring them home. He never touched a thing—not even meat.

All my life I tried to live up to the expectations of my father. And I felt that I had done well. Though it took awhile to gain acceptance, I eventually became a community leader in Berne. I started my own company and built it into a flourishing business through hard work and creative initiative. I wore the Bucheli name with pride, and I always felt that I brought honor to my family.

Until I was made a hostage. In a matter of hours, these ragtag guerrillas had taken a man with a strong sense of accomplishment and self-respect and had broken him. As I contemplated my naked, sweating body, I was filled once again with self-pity and despair. I realized that if Fausto Bucheli, the man of prominence I once was, were to walk into that cell and behold the shell of a man cringing helplessly in the corner, he would gag and turn away in disgust. Thoughts of my father produced an overwhelming sense of failure within me. It was almost more than I could stand.

In all the world, I thought, there was only one creature that could possibly regard me without revulsion—my beloved Pituco. Would to God that the dog outside were Pituco! I would have given anything to be able to put my arms around his beautiful brown neck, to feel his tongue licking the tears from my cheeks!

This was no world for children.

† † †

TRUE TO his word, Tom Elliott arrived at the Bucheli home at one o'clock in the afternoon.

Tom drove about the area as he and his wife and Rita became acquainted. Chino and the neighboring communities were still unfamiliar to Rita, so she paid little attention to where they were going. Mostly she asked questions and listened.

Tom had read most of Fausto's notes for the report he was planning to make to Hartell upon his return. He told Rita of her husband's dismay over the political conditions in the region, and the company's seeming lack of awareness and regard of the dangers to American personnel. He related what details he could remember of conversations and experiences, including the anxiety-filled experience of riding to and from the airport with Bruce Chapman.

The visit had a salutary effect on Rita. Though much of Tom's information confirmed her conclusion that Hartell had failed to take the danger signals seriously, her knowledge of Fausto's activities and thoughts during the past week helped her to feel closer to him. And that, in turn, helped to ease the pain associated with her memory of their parting.

While Rita was gone with the Elliotts, Fausto Jr. emerged from the long retreat in his room. Dave Solano who was watching over the household in Rita's absence, observed a look of resolve on the sixteen-year-old's face. *Something happened in there,* Dave mused. *I think that boy has become a man.*

9
The Way We Were

Day 4 *(Monday, 24 September)*

Monday DAWNED (I presumed) with the not-yet-familiar sounds of a crowing rooster and barking dog. Though restorative sleep continued to elude me, I must have drifted in and out of a dream world. The sound of the dog became the sensory transition between some fantasy about Pituco and consciousness.

Ocho was there with my fried bananas and water. The water presented me with a new dilemma. During the night I was rudely reminded of the catch phrase for North American tourists: "Don't drink the water." Dysentery, jokingly referred to in Central American countries as "Montezuma's Revenge," is no laughing matter under the best of circumstances. To put it bluntly, I had to choose between dehydration and diarrhea. At the moment, thirst was the deciding factor. I drank the water.

Even though I was not fond of my menu of bananas, I now knew better than to request any variation in food. I did ask Ocho, when he returned, if he would mind cleaning out the spider webs and whatever had been trapped in them. With great filth surrounding me, I was concerned about what small creatures might be lurking. To my surprise and relief, Ocho agreed to a spring cleaning.

Within minutes he returned with a mop. He swept the cobwebs from the corners of the room. Then he left to rinse out the mop, saturated it in a detergent solution, returned, and washed the walls and ceiling. He even took a swipe at the floor, but when that proved to be an exercise in futility, he gave up. The detergent bore a pungent aroma that had a deodorizing effect on the cell for the next few hours.

When this diversion was past, I faced once again the task of preserving my sanity. How was I going to occupy my mind constructively? The efforts of the previous day had been fruitful for a time. But if reminiscence was going to be a helpful pastime, I was going to have to exercise discipline in the directions I allowed my mind to go. I would have to let happy memories be just that—happy memories. I must not permit them to sit in editorial judgment on my present situation. I had enough tormentors without manufacturing more of my own.

My thoughts turned naturally enough to Rita. Resisting the urge to nurse the ache in my heart, I engaged my imagination to transport me backward in time over two decades.

My courtship of Rita was preceded by a two-year transition period during which I left my paternal home to go out on my own. I had been obedient to my father's wishes and my own aptitude in securing a degree in engineering from the University of Quito. But when it came time to get a job, engineering did not appeal to me. Flying did. So I obtained a job with F.A.S.A., an American crop-dusting firm in Esmeraldas. The city of Esmeraldas lies on the Pacific coast just south of the Colombian border. When I moved there, it was the first time I had lived any place besides Quito. And it was the first time I had lived by myself. It was a daring step for a boy who had been so dependent on his family.

I got a real education from the Americans. From them I learned how to build and repair biplanes; how to fly biplanes; and how to waste money on parties, drinking, and women. When I lived at home, my older sister had always taken care of me, right up to the time that she got married. She ironed and folded my clothes, told me what to wear, and made sure I was well groomed whenever I went out. But without Mary I didn't take good care of my belongings. After a while my appearance became shabby because I was throwing my money away in bars.

One day the lady from whom I was renting my house asked, "Fausto, did you just recently leave home?"

I said, "Yes, I just moved here from Quito."

"I thought so," she said. "You really aren't taking very good care of yourself." I knew that. "Would you mind if I helped you a little bit?" she asked.

"No, not at all," I agreed.

I began giving her part of my paycheck, and she helped me buy shoes and clothes and other things I needed. She helped me to learn how to function as a responsible adult.

After I had been with F.A.S.A. for two years, I had the opportunity to go to work for a larger company, with better pay, in the city of Guayaquil. I gave my two week's notice.

Three days before I was to quit working for F.A.S.A., I was celebrating my good fortune with a friend in a bar beside the ocean. My next-door neighbor came in and said, "Hey Fausto, today is my birthday! Why don't you fellows come over to my party? We're having ice cream and beer, if you want it!"

When we entered the house, I recognized several friends, including Yvonne and Jeanette, two sisters who were also neighbors. But there was another girl with them whom I had never seen before. And she was beautiful! I had never been so dazzled by a woman.

I asked Yvonne secretively about her.

"Oh, Fausto!" she laughed. "She is not your type! She is an Evangelista."

"*Evangelista?*" I replied. "What is that?"

Yvonne laughed again. "She is Christian."

"Christian? Is that her first name?"

"No, no no!" she explained. "Evangelicals are religious people who are not Catholic. They don't believe in doing any of the things that you like to do. They don't drink, they don't smoke, they don't dance, they don't do anything!"

As ominous as that sounded, I was undeterred. "Well, I'm going to go meet her!" I announced and began to walk away.

Yvonne grabbed me by the arm. "Wait, Fausto!" she hissed. "Take a look at yourself! You are almost drunk! You won't even get close to her!" She was right, and I was sober enough to realize it. I went into the bathroom, splashed water on my face, combed my hair, and began chewing a piece of gum. Then I returned and initiated the most important conversation of my life.

"Hello, my name is Fausto Bucheli. Would you like to dance?"

"I don't dance," she replied.

I wasn't going to be so quickly dismissed. "Then what are you doing here if you don't dance?" I pursued, smiling.

She appeared to waver for a moment. Then she got up and said, "All right! Just this once!"

And so we began dancing—I think it was a waltz. I talked as we danced. "You know, I've lived here for two years, but I don't think I've ever seen you before."

She didn't say anything.

I tried again. "You have probably been told that you have beautiful eyes." She smiled shyly. I took a deep breath. "I don't even know your name yet"—I paused, no reply—"but I will tell you this: you are going to be my wife."

Abruptly we stopped dancing. She stared at me. I thought she was trying to decide whether to slap me. Without saying a word, she turned on her heel and walked out of the house. I still didn't know her name.

I went to Yvonne. "Well, I told you she wasn't your type!" she chided. "What happened?"

I was still staring at the front door with a grin on my face. "I told her I was going to marry her!"

"You what?" Yvonne erupted. "You can't do that! You don't even know the girl! Her father is one of the leaders of Esmeraldas. He used to be captain of the police and a governor of the province. She is from a very important family!"

"Well, so am I!" I replied. "We will make a very good pair. By the way, what is her name?

"Rita."

I looked at Yvonne earnestly. "I have to talk to her again, Yvonne! Please help me!"

"I think you are hoping for a miracle," she replied.

"Well, I don't know about a miracle," I said, "but she is the closest thing to an angel I have ever seen."

Even in the gloom of my cell I think I smiled as that scene became frozen in my mind. The guard would have thought I was hallucinating had he noticed. Somehow it seemed as if I were observing someone else in my mind's eye—a young, moonstruck Casanova saying ridiculous things and doing even crazier things. Little had I known how true Yvonne's words were.

No, I hadn't known how improbable were the prospects of my marrying Rita. But even if I had, I doubt whether it would have made a difference. I now had a consuming goal in life. One of my most prominent personality traits—tenacity—took over my conduct. If a miracle was called for, I would bring it about.

The next morning, as I was leaving my home for a strategy-planning walk on the beach, my concentration was shattered by a honking horn. A chauffeur-driven Jeep pulled into my driveway bearing Yvonne, Jeanette, and incredibly, Rita. I walked over and said, "Good morning!"

Yvonne was the first to respond. "We brought Rita by so you could apologize to her and prove that you are a nice guy like we've been telling her!"

Everyone laughed. Rita looked embarrassed. I said, "I appreciate that, Yvonne, but I am not going to apologize."

Yvonne was shocked. "Now listen here Fausto!" she scolded. "You told me that—"

"I'm not going to apologize," I interrupted, "because I simply am not sorry. What I said was the truth. I like Rita very much. I think I may be in love with her. I've never met a girl like her before."

The expression on Rita's face made it clear that she had never met anyone like me before either. Yvonne was stunned into silence.

I addressed the sisters. "If it is all right with you, and if the young lady will permit me, I would like some words with her alone."

For some reason Rita agreed to walk on the beach with me. We began to get acquainted, and we were able to relax a bit. After a while I asked her, "What is this *'evangelista'* business? Yvonne told me that you are an Evangelical."

"Yes, I am."

"What does that mean?"

"When I was a small girl," she explained, "I asked Jesus to come into my heart and take away my sins. Ever since then, He has been my Lord and Savior—the most important person in my life."

"You are not like my mother, are you?" I queried, half-jokingly. "She is very religious. She made me go to parochial school and Mass and all of those things."

"Well, I don't know if I am like your mother," Rita replied. "I just know that I am like myself, and my relationship to Jesus and His church is very important to me. More important than anything else."

I had never heard anyone talk like this. It was hard to understand how such an attractive, intelligent woman could be so absorbed in religion. All the young adults I knew were interested in making a lot of money and having a good time.

"Our church is having a district convention, a special meeting tonight," she said, kicking a shell with her toe. "Would you like to come with me? It would be a good way for you to see and hear for yourself what Evangelicals believe, and what they are like."

"Oh, I don't know!" I said. "I've never been to a church like that before. I wouldn't know what to do, what to say, how to act."

"You don't have to worry about that. You will be with me and you won't have to do or say anything that will embarrass you."

"I don't know what to wear." A lame excuse.

"What you are wearing now will be fine," she assured me. "I will wait for you at the front door."

I never really said yes, nor did I say no. But that was the end of the conversation, because she took off running back to the Jeep. She jumped in, and as the Jeep pulled away, she smiled and waved. At that moment, if she had invited me to a meeting of witchdoctors, I think I probably would have gone.

But I wouldn't have been any more uncomfortable than I was that night in Las Palmas Missionary Church. As it turned out, the church was only two blocks from my house, but I had never noticed it before. I never had any reason to. The people there were not "my people." For the most part, they were of the lower classes. There were also a few Negros. Rita was the only high-class person in the entire church. I felt very strange, uneasy among people with whom I would never mix socially.

Three or four Americans were present also. I gestured toward them and whispered to Rita, "Who are they?"

"Missionaries," she whispered back.

"What are they doing here?"

"They are the ones who brought the gospel to us."

I had never met missionaries before, but I had heard of some while I was growing up. Our home, constructed during my childhood on the outskirts of Quito, was located not far from radio station HCJB, which was built and operated by American missionaries. Because they isolated themselves from the Ecuadorian people and lived in their own little community, they seemed aloof. They seemed to regard themselves as superior to us. So I carried a resentment toward missionaries in general for their attitude of superiority in the same way I harbored disdain for those I thought were beneath me. At the time I didn't see the inconsistency in my attitudes.

All that I noticed was that I was out of my element. I didn't hear anything said during the service. I could think only of getting out of there as soon as possible, which I did the minute the meeting was over. After politely greeting some of her friends, Rita joined me outside.

I took her out for a cola and we talked some more. My discomfort in her church had been obvious. "Those just aren't my kind of people," I tried to explain.

"I have learned that people are people," she replied. "Upper-class people can hurt you, and lower-class people can be the dearest of friends."

I couldn't imagine becoming friends with any of those people. My friends came from families and backgrounds like my own.

Rita continued, "When you are before the Lord, He doesn't pay any attention to whether you have light skin or dark skin, whether you are rich or poor, whether you are from the upper class or a lower class. In His eyes, all are equal. That's how I have learned to see people."

"Maybe that's how you see them," I replied, "but I don't! I am better than a lot of people."

The next day—Monday—I went back to F.A.S.A to talk with the general manager. "I came to see if I could have my job back. I want to stay in Esmeraldas."

"Well, I don't know," he toyed. "Why do you want to stay? I thought that job in Guayaquil offered more money."

"I don't care about that any more," I replied. He waited for an explanation. "I met a girl this weekend, and I am in love with her."

He laughed. "So now you are not so interested in money!" he kidded me. "O.K., you may continue working here. But you'd better not lose all interest in money—courting is expensive."

"I guess that's true!" I laughed. "Thanks for letting me stay on."

"By the way," he said, "I have to compliment you on your taste in women. That Rita is a very attractive girl. But I'm not sure she is . . . uh . . . well-suited to you. She is an Evangelical."

"You know her?"

"I know of her. Her family is very prominent in Esmeraldas. She is a school teacher—a very good one from what I hear."

This was new information, mixed in with another warning concerning Rita's unsuitability for a person like me or vice versa. Well, we would see about that. "I'd better get to work," I said, bringing the discussion about Rita to an end. "I don't want to get fired for goofing off! I need the money!"

After work I went looking for Rita. I learned that she taught first grade at Light and Liberty Christian School. I met her there when classes dismissed and invited her to go out for some ice cream. Glad to have something to talk about besides religion, I asked her about teaching school.

"That's an interesting story," she said. "I had many struggles in getting my teaching degree, mostly because of poor health. I asked the Lord to give me the strength to complete the program, because I really wanted to be a teacher. I told Him that if I got my credential, I would take whatever opportunity He might give me to use it in Christian education.

"When I graduated, I worked in a government school for a while. But when Paul Erdel, one of the missionary leaders here, wanted to open a Christian school, I left that post to help him start Light and Liberty. I had to take a 50 percent cut in salary, but the joy I experience instructing children in the Bible, as well as the other subjects, more than makes up for the money."

I could hardly believe that a conversation about teaching

ended up on the subject of religion again. Rita's life really did revolve around her Christianity. On the one hand, her preoccupation with her Evangelical faith was disturbing. I didn't understand it, and I couldn't see myself getting involved in something so foreign to my background and lifestyle. On the other hand, Rita was not obnoxious or preachy when she spoke of her faith. It was a natural part of her. I think she was the first young person I had ever met who was committed to something other than one's personal advancement or pleasure. This made her all the more attractive.

"I find that most admirable," I responded. "I can relate to sacrificing a better-paying job for something more important."

"Really?" she expressed surprise.

"That's right!" I replied. "Just this weekend I turned down a higher salary in Guayaquil because I wanted to stay in Esmeraldas." It was the perfect setup. All she had to say was . . .

"Why?"

She did it! "Because on Saturday night I met you!" Rita blushed. "And you are more important to me than more money. I fully intend to court you, and win you, and marry you!"

Rita laughed. "You certainly have a one-track mind. I am very flattered."

"Well, I'm serious!" I replied. "I'll do whatever it takes!"

"Including becoming a Christian?" she asked straightforwardly.

I hedged. "I am a Christian already. I am a good person. My only vice is a little bit of drinking now and then. And I like to go out with . . . uh . . . I used to go out with girls, but that's all over now. I'm not a sinner!"

Rita laughed again. But she was serious when she said, "Fausto, you *are* a sinner! We are all sinners! We are all in need of God's forgiveness. And that forgiveness is given to those who repent of their sins and put their trust in Jesus as their Savior."

"I don't understand what all that means," I replied. "I think it is fine for you to believe all those things, but I don't see what it has to do with my marrying you."

"As a Christian," she explained, "I am not permitted to marry outside of my faith."

"Who doesn't permit that?" I insisted, becoming a little angry. "The Church?"

"Well, yes," she replied. "But really it's my own conviction. The Bible says that we should not become 'unequally yoked' with unbelievers. And I am committed to obeying the Bible as much as I am able. . . . I like you very much, Fausto. And your decision about becoming a Christian is strictly between you and the Lord. But I cannot even consider marriage to someone who has not also made that commitment."

"I really do want to marry you, Rita," I declared. "But this religion stuff is all very foreign to me."

"I can appreciate that. I have a friend who is very good at explaining these things. His name is Doug Hodges—he is one of the missionaries."

"I don't think I want to talk to any missionaries," I objected. I told her of the ones I had heard about as a child.

"Doug Hodges is not like that," she assured me. "Just talk with him once. I know you will like him."

At last I agreed. The next afternoon Rita took me to meet the Hodges. Despite my apprehension, I found that Rita was right: I did like Doug. He was friendly, patient—not pushy. He showed me in the Bible some of the things Rita had said to me.

Doug said there was one verse in the Gospel of John that summed up the message of the Bible:

> For God so loved the world that He gave His one and only Son, that whoever believes in Him shall not perish but have everlasting life.

Doug explained that this "one and only Son" was Jesus and that God sent Him from heaven to earth to be the Savior of the world. "The reason we need a Savior," he explained, "is that we are all sinners." That's what Rita had said. "When Jesus died on the cross, God's judgment for our sin was poured out on His Son. He experienced the judgment that we all deserve. God then raised His Son from the dead to prove the sufficiency of His sacrifice for us. Those who confess their sins and trust in Jesus as their Savior 'shall not perish but have everlasting life.'"

When I suggested, once again, that I didn't think that I was all that bad a "sinner," Doug replied, "If we didn't need a Savior, do you think God would have sent Jesus to die on the cross?" Then he added, "That's also the reason we have come here—to tell the people of Esmeraldas this wonderful news: Everyone can know God, and live with Him, through faith in Jesus, His Son."

Frankly, I was not really interested in religion or Jesus or the church. What I was interested in was Rita. So I listened very carefully to learn what I had to do to marry her. And I told Doug I would think over everything he had said and become a Christian.

Despite my initial discomfort I faithfully attended church with Rita. I sang the hymns, listened to the sermons, attended the various church activities. I even acknowledged, when asked, that I had become a Christian.

But when I was not with Rita, I went out with my other friends. I still frequented the bars for a few drinks after work.

I was never baptized, but I did everything else Rita wanted me to do. As far as she knew, I had met her qualifications for a husband.

I courted Rita for five months. At that time couples did not date without chaperones in Ecuador. So when she finally agreed to marry me, I had not even kissed her. That abstinence remained in force right up to the day of our wedding.

When we were making the arrangements for the wedding, we encountered the first of several difficulties. The Ecuadorian pastor of Rita's church would not perform the ceremony, because he didn't think that I had been converted. We asked Doug Hodges if he would officiate. I said, "Señor Hodges, you are the first person I met in Rita's church. You are the first one who told me about God. I would like for you to perform our wedding ceremony.

He said, "It will be a privilege." So that was set.

The next problem concerned our families. My father would not attend a Christian wedding at all. My mother, being Roman Catholic, would not come to a ceremony in an Evangelical church. Rita would not be married in a Catholic church.

The manager of F.A.S.A., whom I had asked to be my best man, found a solution. When people are married in Ecuador, they go through two ceremonies. There is the civil wedding, officiated by an officer of the government. Then the bride and groom take their legal papers to the church and observe the religious rites. My friend suggested that we invite my family to attend the civil ceremony. Then, after the church wedding, there could be two receptions—one for my family and friends (complete with champagne), and one for Rita's family and church friends. (In spite of our efforts, my father refused to attend.)

Rita and I were married on November 19, 1960, in a beautiful wedding attended by some four hundred guests. The miracle had happened: I had won my angel. I was incredibly happy.

It was predictable that our marriage would have to weather some heavy seas. In our immaturity I'm sure we were persuaded that love would overcome any differences in our goals and values. But reality painted a different picture. And as I lay in the confines of my cell, I had to admit that if I lived to see our nineteenth anniversary (less than two months away), most of the credit for our marriage's survival would belong to Rita. I had certainly provided many reasons over the years for her to think she had made a mistake in marrying me.

In fact, she must even have felt this way on our wedding night. Recounting this incident gives me no pleasure, and remembering it during my captivity did nothing to help my state of mind. What occurred so epitomized what we were bringing to our marriage that I was forced to recall it then, just as I must retell it now.

After the wedding we went back and forth between the two receptions and received the congratulations of our friends and family members. As the time approached midnight, I prepared to take Rita away, as custom dictated. I told her, "My mother has an extra room at the hotel in town. We can go there to be alone."

But she said, "I don't think that is a good idea, Fausto." I was startled, but she explained, "You know we have to catch the bus to go on our honeymoon at 4:00 A.M. I am so tired now, I think it would be wise to get some rest so we can enjoy being together."

As anxious as I was to take her with me, I agreed that she was probably right. "Why don't you go to your mother's hotel," she continued, "and I will stay with the Hodges. They can take me to the bus station in the morning, and I will meet you there." Reluctantly I agreed.

But as I was preparing to leave the reception, some of my friends from work—pilots and mechanics—intercepted me. "Fausto," they said, "the night is young! You have your whole life ahead of you! Come with us and celebrate!"

I said, "O.K. But I have to be at the bus depot by four o'clock!"

"Don't worry!" they promised. "You'll be there!"

So we went to a favorite tavern, and I got thoroughly drunk. At 3:45, someone said, "Hey, we have to get him out of here!" They called a taxi.

When I got in the car, I absent-mindedly gave him my old address. But the taxi driver knew better. "Señor, you just got married last night, and your wife is waiting for you at the bus station. I will take you there."

When we arrived, everyone was waiting for me. They had even held the bus back from leaving on time. It was the first time Rita or the Hodges had seen me in a drunken condition. It was not a happy moment. They put me on the bus, and I passed out.

When I came to, we were almost to Quito. I felt miserable, physically and mentally. I could see the hurt in Rita's eyes. It did not go away for a long time.

Ironically, as I replayed that disaster in my memory in the cell, it did not have the same crushing effect as my previous recollections had. Instead it served to underscore the depth of Rita's commitment to me and to our marriage. Though she had threatened to leave me more than once, divorce was not in her vocabulary. And the threats to leave, though genuine, were mainly designed to get my attention. What she wanted, what she held out for, was a full-time husband. She deserved that.

These bittersweet memories also served to awaken within me the abiding affection I had always had for Rita. I had made my share of mistakes over the years. It was not proud of the way I had behaved to win Rita's hand and my subsequent reversion to my "normal" lifestyle. But marrying her remained the wisest thing I had ever done. My love for her was the one constant of my life.

Amid my reminiscing, the physical pain produced by fatigue, dysentery, aching hands and wrists, and broken teeth raged unabated. I continued to shiver in fear beneath the threatening muzzle of the ever-present submachine gun. But somehow my reflections about Rita increased my resolve to endure. More than anything else I wanted to celebrate that nineteenth anniversary. What I began to hold out for was another—no, a genuine—miracle.

It occurred to me, as the fourth day elapsed, that enough time had passed for my captors to establish contact with the company. Perhaps something was happening. Maybe some progress was being made. Possibly the deal was being struck that would extricate me from this hole.

It had better be soon.

10
Intimate Strangers

No NEWS WAS BAD news as far as Antonio and Maria Bucheli were concerned. It was time to do something about Fausto's situation. They knew people in high places. Surely there must be some way to exert diplomatic pressure to secure their son's release.

After a few phone calls they worked their way up the bureaucratic ladder. In a single morning they were granted audiences with the ambassador of El Salvador, Ecuador's Secretary of State, and finally President Jaime Roldós Aguilera himself. Every official was sympathetic and cooperative. President Roldós gave special passes to the Buchelis that would grant them virtually instant access to his office at any time. He also offered round-trip airplane tickets to San Salvador at government expense. The Buchelis decided to wait for further information about their son before making such a demanding trip.

Antonio asked the President and the Secretary of State whether they could appeal to the Sandinista-led junta in Nicaragua to send some kind of communiqué to the leftists requesting Fausto's release. He hoped that Fausto's Latin American origins would encourage sympathetic treatment from his captors.

The highest officials in Ecuador assured the Buchelis that

they would pursue every diplomatic avenue to secure their son's freedom. They followed through on that promise. The embassies of El Salvador, Ecuador, and the United States were in contact with the family virtually every day. By week's end the ambassador or Ecuador in San Salvador had succeeded in placing a full-page open letter to the kidnappers in the largest newspaper in the country. It appealed to them to release their fellow Latino for the sake of peace, for the sake of his family.

Antonio and Maria Bucheli returned home from their diplomatic mission exhausted. It was all Maria could handle. Already having a weak heart, she went into shock. Her doctor ordered her to bed, and she remained there, under the care of one of her daughter's, until Fausto's captivity ended. They had done what they could.

Rita had already decided Sunday night that on this particular Monday she would not go to work. Circumstances were too uncertain and emotions too frayed to go about life as usual. The children weren't capable of handling school; it was still foreign terrain for them. They had begun to make some acquaintances, but they had not had time to form strong friendships with classmates. They needed the refuge of their own home.

John Pike and Dave Solano both went back to work. But Pauline Solano was able to continue her vigil with the family. She had been there about a half-hour on Monday when Rita received a call from John Pike.

"Rita, the man our company has hired to negotiate with the kidnappers is here now. He would like to talk to you about Fausto. Can you come over to the plant?"

Rita looked at Pauline. "I think that Pauline could drive me over," she replied. Pauline nodded. "We'll be there in about a half-hour."

The receptionist at Hartell was expecting Rita. "You are to go to the executive conference room. Mr. Reynolds, one of our vice presidents, will meet you there." She gave Rita directions.

"Mrs. Bucheli," said a sober, silver-haired man, rising from his chair to greet her. "I am Carl Reynolds, company vice president for legal affairs. I am so sorry about what has happened to Fausto. We are going to do everything in our power to get him back home, safe and sound, as soon as possible." He turned to the man who had come beside him. "This is Fred Rayne, the man who will be negotiating Fausto's release."

Rayne extended his hand. *"Buenos dias, señora!"* Rita shook his hand and introduced Pauline.

Reynolds led Pauline to the waiting area outside his office.

Rayne took charge. "Would you prefer to converse in Spanish or English, Mrs. Bucheli?" He had done his homework, and Rita appreciated his thoughtfulness.

"I think I would prefer Spanish," she replied. They began speaking in that language, but Rita soon realized that Rayne wasn't fluent in her native tongue, and Reynolds was showing signs of uneasiness over not being privy to the discussion. "I think it would be fine to talk in English," suggested Rita.

"Thank you!" smiled Reynolds.

"Mrs. Bucheli," Rayne resumed. "When the kidnappers contact us and tell us that they have your husband, my first job will be to determine if they are telling the truth. You see, almost anyone could claim to have captured him." Rita hadn't thought of that. "So I have to make sure I am dealing with the right people.

"To do that, I need to know some things about him that no one else would know but you and him. Things like his favorite color, what his favorite foods are, events in his past life that a stranger would have no way of knowing. In particular, it would be helpful if you could tell me of any physical features that would identify his body—moles', birthmarks, or anything like that. Because frankly, Mrs. Bucheli, at this point we don't know for sure whether he is alive or dead. And if, God forbid, they have killed him, the physical identification will be crucial."

Rita thought a few moments. Then she replied, "You have his physical description from his file, don't you?" Rayne nodded. "O.K., the other detail that would identify him is a scar on his abdomen from an operation he had several years ago."

"Oh, that's very good," said Rayne.

"His favorite color is blue, and he cannot eat hot food because he has had to have extensive work done on his teeth, and his mouth is still tender where the dentist put in the bridgework." Rita went on to disclose a number of details from Fausto's past that Rayne could use if necessary.

Recalling features that made Fausto unique from all other men caused the grief to well up in her again and she broke down and wept. Fred Rayne put his arm around her. Reynolds found a box of tissues for her. As Rita wiped her eyes, she looked up at Rayne and discovered that he too was weeping. "It's hard to believe that we're having this conversation, isn't it?" he said at last.

Rita nodded.

"What you've told me will be very helpful," he assured her. "I don't have any more questions for now."

Carl Reynolds spoke. "Mrs. Bucheli, we'll do what we can to keep you posted on what we learn. And we want to help protect you and your family from the nuisance of always having to talk to reporters. So we're going to have John Pike stay with you and your family until this is over. He will make sure that you are cared for, and he can be there to handle the media."

That sounded all right to Rita. At least there would be someone there from the company who could tell her what was happening.

They left the conference room. Rita found Pauline, and they drove home.

Raul sat at his desk reviewing the new procedures the plant was trying to implement. He was pleased that work was continuing, even in Bruce's absence. Of course, Bruce had frequently been absent—most of the actual plant operation was already being directed by Pacho and Raul himself. But Bruce gave everyone a feeling of security. Nothing went wrong that he couldn't handle. Raul hoped that nothing would go wrong. He didn't want to have to send everyone home just because he couldn't figure out what to do.

His other great concern, of course, was what had happened to Bruce and Fausto. Where were they? Why had there been no word from the kidnappers? Should he be doing more to find out? The police couldn't give him any ideas.

The ringing of the phone startled him. "APLAR, this is Raul."

A man's voice commanded: "Don't talk! Just listen! I am a member of the Revolutionary Party of Central American Workers. We are responsible for the capture of your men, Chapman and Bucheli. They are both alive and well. If you want to keep them that way, you will get in touch with Señor Fred Rayne. Tell him to come to San Salvador immediately. We will talk only with him."

The line went dead.

Raul depressed the button and heard the dial tone. He called the overseas operator. The contest of wills had begun.

Rita sent Pauline home to take care of Dave and her own children. She just wanted to be alone for a while, she said. The emotional drain over the past few days had been considerable, and Rita was feeling the fatigue that comes with grief. She lay down across her king-sized bed and tried to turn off her mind for a few minutes of rest.

Rest wouldn't come. Rita was surrounded, literally, with reminders of Fausto. He had been gone so much during the past two months that he hadn't finished unpacking. Boxes lined the walls, making it difficult to navigate through a room that was already cramped because of the size of the bed. *Will he ever have the chance to finish the job?* Rita wondered. The thought brought more tears.

But the boxes prompted another kind of self-pity as well. They reminded Rita that she was alone in a foreign place. And this awareness generated another round of Why questions. *Why did this happen to such a man as Fausto? Why us? What have we done? Why did all of this have to occur when we moved so far away from our family and our dear friends? This wouldn't have happened in the first place if we had stayed in Berne where we were so comfortable. But now, not only has Fausto been kidnapped by violent men, but the family is left fatherless in a strange land.*

Fausto Jr. could hear the muffled sobs of his mother penetrating the walls into the hallway. He knew she wanted some time to herself. But instinctively he realized that without an audience, her sorrow would pull her down into dark despair. She needed someone to share her grief—someone who would be available, someone with whom she could be herself, someone to whom she could express her true feelings.

Assuming his new responsibility as protector of the family, Fausto came to a decision. He walked down the hall, through the dining room, into the backyard. He crossed the yard, jumped over the fence, and strode over to the backdoor of the tan stucco-and-brick house that occupied the adjacent lot. He knocked at the home of Gary and Gert Verhoeven.

"Oh, hello, Fausto!" Gert greeted him. "Come on in! Helen and Tina are already here!"

"Yes, I know!" he replied. The girls had already discovered this haven. "I was wondering if you might come over to our house for a few minutes," he said. "I think my mom needs someone to talk to."

Gert didn't even hesitate. "Sure, Fausto!" she responded. "Just a second!" She stuck her head into the living room and announced, "I'm going over to the Buchelis' for a few minutes! I'll be back in a little bit to get supper!"

This brief exchange between Fausto and Gert was one of those seemingly insignificant incidents that turns out, in retrospect, to be a crossroad. Life would never be the same for Gert Verhoeven. At age thirty-five, the tall, slender woman with the close-cropped red hair had lived most of her life within the clearly defined perimeters of the Dutch Reformed community. Her life revolved around her family, her bookkeeping job, the Christian school her children attended, and her church. As she entered the Bucheli home for only the second time, she stepped out of her own world. "Normal life" as she had known it would soon be placed on "hold" for the next two months. She would excuse herself from every responsibility except church choir; she would cancel a family vacation; she would keep house for two families.

Rita readily gave Gert permission to enter her private chamber. Within minutes she was giving tacit permission to enter the secret recesses of her mind and heart.

Not really knowing what else to say, Gert asked, "What are you thinking about, Rita?"

"I have been thinking about that stack of ironing over there in the corner," murmured Rita. "Those are Fausto's shirts. He only wears custom-made clothes, and he insists that his shirts be carefully pressed. I was going to iron them before he got back." She stopped talking as the tears welled up. "But now I don't know if there is any reason to do that!" she sobbed. "I don't know if he'll ever wear them again!" She buried her face in her pillow. Gert sat next to her and wept silently.

After a few minutes Gert spoke, quietly and firmly. "You are going to make it, Rita! Whatever happens, you are going to make it! The Lord will give you the strength to be what you must be, to do what you have to do."

Rita looked up, her face red and swollen, tear tracks streaking her cheeks. "I know He will," she whispered. "But sometimes it hurts so bad, and I just don't understand what is happening." She paused, trying to sort out her thoughts. "I know He is with me," she continued, "but I feel like I'm all alone."

"Well, you're not," Gert assured her. "Gary and I are here, and we will be with you. I will come over every day, if you want me to, until Fausto comes home.

"I appreciate that, Gert."

"I just want you to know," Gert continued, "that you can be yourself with me. I know that you want to be strong for the sake of the children. But there will be times, like now, when you don't feel strong at all. That's all right. When you want to talk—about anything at all—I'll be here."

Rita nodded and even managed a smile. Gert gave her a hug. "Tell you what!" she said. "I'll go fix supper for all of us tonight. You come on over in about an hour. That should give you enough time to get most of that ironing done."

Rita laughed, for the first time in four days, right out loud.

11
Mail Call

Day 5 *(Tuesday, 25 September)*

SHORTLY AFTER breakfast was served on what I reckoned to be Tuesday morning, Ocho returned with an unexpected luxury. He brought me two cans of water—not to drink, but to wash over my body. For cleanliness, it didn't accomplish much. In fact, the runoff turned the floor of the cell to mud. But in the ovenlike climate of that enclosure the water felt good.

Since this was evidence of generosity on someone's part, I decided to risk another request. I asked Ocho if he would ask the leaders to get me a Bible. Ocho stared at me, his eyes wide as if with fear. He said nothing, nor did he nod or shake his head. He simply took the two empty cans and left the room.

When he left, I began taking inventory of my rinsed-off body. My hands were still puffy, black-and-blue, and tender. All my fingernails were black. I knew I would lose them—and I did eventually. I realized one problem was that I was allowed absolutely no exercise, and this was restricting the circulation in my hands. I tried to rub them to promote blood flow, but the pain was too intense to continue.

The combination of enforced inactivity, chronic insomnia, and the diet of bananas and polluted water was beginning to take its toll. The first indications of a skin rash appeared on my legs. My physical condition—poor to start with—was deteriorating.

I had been telling myself that things couldn't get worse. The discovery that this was not the case was depressing. It led to the inevitable question of what else I might have to endure. Even worse was the related fear of how long this imprisonment might last. I spent most of this day futilely wishing that something, anything, would happen to get me out of there.

† † †

JOHN AND Karen Pike arrived at the Bucheli house around ten o'clock Tuesday morning. John opened his briefcase and proceeded to set up shop on the dining room table.

"You look like you're moving in!" said Rita, only half-jokingly. "Have you heard any news?"

"As a matter of fact, we have. We got a call from our Salvadoran plant manager. He was contacted by the kidnappers yesterday."

Rita's heart leaped. She sat down. "What did they say?" The children came running.

"Not much!" said John. "They assured him that both men are alive and physically all right."

"Thank God!" breathed Rita. "What do they want? When are they going to let them go?"

"They didn't make any demands at all. All they did was identify themselves as the Revolutionary Party of Central American Workers, or PRTC for short."

"Who is that?" asked Hilda Bucheli.

"Oh, it's some leftist militant group," answered John. "Nobody seems to have heard of them before. This is probably their first major operation."

"Didn't they say anything else?" questioned Veronica. "Weren't there any demands at all?"

"No," said John curtly. "I told you that they didn't say anything else. But we figure that they will get back in touch before very long."

"Well, at least we know that they are alive!" said Rita. "That's something to be thankful for!"

John reached into his briefcase. "I also brought you this,"

he said, handing Rita an envelope. "It's a letter from the president of Hartell."

It was dated September 25, this very day.

Dear Mrs. Bucheli,

All of us at Hartell were deeply shocked to learn of the abduction of your husband, Fausto, and Bruce Chapman in San Salvador. I want you to know that since the news first arrived here, the company management, with the aid of a professional security organization, has been doing everything in its power to keep abreast of events and to handle the situation in a way which we believe will best assure the safe return of Fausto to you and your children.

I have directed the appropriate management personnel within Hartell to continue to exert maximum effort in securing the release of Fausto and Bruce Chapman. If you have any questions which are not answered by those directly assigned to this task, please let me know.

Respectfully yours,

(Signed)

Russell T. Shannon
President

"It was very nice of him to write that letter to us," said Rita, handing it to Fausto Jr.

"You have the very best team working on this assignment," assured John. He cleared his throat. "While we're all here, there's something important that I need to talk to you about."

Fausto kept on reading.

"Fausto, that includes you!" John insisted. Fausto looked up. He didn't appreciate being addressed that way.

"I'm listening sir!" he said.

"Well, you'd better be, because this could affect whether or not we get your dad out of El Salvador in one piece."

He's being a little melodramatic, thought Hilda.

"It is very important that none of you ever give any information to reporters—from the newspaper, radio stations, or TV networks. In fact, the only way to really control the information is not to tell anyone anything about your father. If the wrong information leaked out, whether it was correct or incorrect, it could hurt our ability to bargain with the kidnappers. So anything that I tell you has to be kept top secret!"

The speech was over. "Do you mean," asked Rita, "that we are not to ever talk about Fausto to anyone?"

"That would be best. We must not do anything that would even remotely jeopardize the negotiations process."

"Well, you don't have to worry!" said Fausto Jr. "We care more about our dad than anyone else. We're not about to say anything to anyone that would put him in more danger."

"Good! From now on, I'll take all incoming phone calls. That way, if the media keep trying to get through, I can respond to them in the best way."

"May we be excused now?" Hilda asked with feigned politeness.

"Sure! If there's anything else, I'll let you know."

Rita rose from the table and went into the family room as her children scattered. She sat down in her chair, looked across at Karen Pike sitting on the couch reading a magazine, and smiled weakly.

"Dear Lord," Rita prayed silently, "I have one more reason for you to bring Fausto home. I don't think it is going to work to have these people in our house. They just don't belong here."

The telephone rang in the home of Linda Chapman. The maid picked up the receiver. "Hello!"

"I must speak to Mrs. Chapman!" a man's voice said.

"Mrs. Chapman is taking a shower right now. May I have her call you back?"

"No! Just tell her that the PRTC called. We are the ones who have her husband!" The maid gasped. "Tell her that we will call tomorrow at this time. If she wants to see her husband alive, she will be there to answer."

"Yes, sir!" stammered the maid into a dead phone.

At 3:00 P.M. the doorbell rang in the Bucheli home. John Pike opened the front door, but no one was there. "There are two front doors!" called Helen, hurrying to the entrance off the living room. "It must be the mailman!"

"I'll get it!" John ordered, but Helen was already taking a huge pile of mail from the carrier.

"There was too much to fit into the box," explained the mailman. "I thought you might want to collect it all at once."

"Thank you very much," John said.

Helen dumped the mail on the dining room table, and the rest of the family materialized with remarkable speed. "Wow, look at all those letters!" said Tina. Each member of the family had a handful. At first all they did was scan the familiar return addresses: the first shipment from Berne had arrived.

It took the rest of the afternoon for everyone to read all the cards and notes. There was a lot of sniffling and wiping of eyes as the expressions of sympathy made their impact. Everyone's "best friends" had sent some message of concern.

Typical among them was this handwritten letter:

Dear Tina, Helen, Veronica, Fausto, Hilda, Grandma, and Rita,

We are in Sunday School this morning and we are all thinking about you. We really can't imagine what you must be feeling and thinking right now. But we are continually remembering you all in our prayers.

We were studying Paul's letters (1 Thessalonians and Titus) this morning and we've seen how Paul encouraged the early Christians in times of trouble. He stressed that God is in control at all times. In thinking about Fausto in El Salvador it helped us to read Titus 2:14: "He (Christ) gave himself for us, to rescue us from all wickedness and to make us a pure people who belong to him alone and are eager to do good."

We trust that you can find strength in the Lord.

In Christ,

The Freshman Girls'
  Sunday School Class
Lisa Liechty
Anne Moser
Jackie Weaver
Tammy Van Gunten
Tammi Gilliom
Laura Lerdal
Julia Neuenschwander

There are almost as many telephone extensions in the Bucheli home as there are people, thanks to a father who specializes in electronic components. It was Veronica who placed the first of a series of calls. But each one was definitely a conference affair. It was hard to find any sense of order in the conversations, but the link between Chino and Berne was never stronger.

✝   ✝   ✝

AS THE day was wasting fruitlessly away toward late afternoon, the door opened. It startled me, because I wasn't expecting company for another couple of hours. My heart rate doubled when I saw that my uninvited visitors were none other than Señor Mustache and Señor Skinny, complete with hoods, coats, and submachine guns.

A host of possibilities flashed through my mind: Ocho had passed on my request for a Bible and they were coming to punish me; Hartell had rejected their demands and they were coming to kill me; Hartell had agreed to their terms and they were coming to set me free. The answer, as it turned out, was none of the above.

Señor Skinny brought with him a pad of paper and a pen. Señor Mustache did the talking: "Hey, *gringo*, today we are going to do you a favor! We are going to let you write a letter to your wife to tell her what a nice time you are having on your little vacation!" He punctuated his joke with a villainous laugh.

This is worse than a bad movie! I thought.

Señor Skinny handed me the pad and pen. I tried the ballpoint, but the room was so humid, it didn't work. Señor Skinny took it away, left the cell, and shortly returned with a pencil. I took it and began to write: "My dearest Rita . . ."

"Wait a minute, traitor!" snapped Señor Mustache, snatching the pad from my lap. He ripped the page from the tablet, wadded it, and threw the crumpled sheet into the toilet can. "You must write in Spanish," he ordered, "and write only what we tell you!"

It took painstaking effort to write at all. The pressure of the pencil on my damaged nails sent piercing pain through my fingers. But I managed to write as Señor Mustache dictated.

My mind was racing as my hands transcribed the message. One of my greatest concerns for Rita was that she was unfamiliar with our family business affairs. I doubted whether she even knew the names of our insurance companies. So when Señor Mustache finished his dictation, I took a chance: "Would it be all right if I tell her I love her and miss her and things like that?"

"Yeah, go ahead!" he agreed. "That will make the letter even better!"

So I wrote those statements. Then I added a sentence: "Say hello to Mr. Minnesota Mutual and Mr. Travelers and to Mr. Equitable Life, and tell them thank you. Greet John and Karen and kiss the kids for me."

I gave the page to Señor Mustache and held my breath. He proofread the contents with satisfaction until he came to my personal greetings. "Hey, what do you think you are trying to do, *gringo?*" he glared. "I didn't say you could say hello to anybody!" He destroyed that sheet as he had the first and deposited it angrily in the can. "Write it all again, and this time do as you are told!"

I sighed with disappointment and wrote their letter again. On the first draft I had pressed very hard on the paper with the pencil when I wrote the names of the insurance companies. I was hoping that the impressions would be engraved onto the next sheet and that some perceptive person on the other end would notice them. This was the first of two unsuccessful attempts to smuggle a secret message to the outside world.

What I don't remember, interestingly is the precise contents of that letter. This may be due to my preoccupation with the plot I was hatching as I was taking the dictation. Although Rita received the letter, it is the one piece of memorabilia that has been lost.

Satisfied at last, Señors Mustache and Skinny departed, leaving me to nurse my aching fingers and speculate on my fate. On the plus side, assuming that Rita ever received the letter, she would at least be assured I was alive. And someone might conceivably pick up my code. On the minus side, the time involved in getting the note to her virtually guaranteed that my "vacation" would last for some days rather than hours. Further, what effect would the receipt of that letter have on her and the children? It was bound to be more of an occasion of grief than of relief.

The whole situation sent me plummeting into fearful dejection. My body began to shake all over, and I found it very easy to cry.

12

A Fellow Inmate

Day 6 *(Wednesday, 26 September)*

IT WAS 9:00 A.M. when the telephone rang at the residence of Raul Hernandez. Raul was already at work, and his wife had left for the market, so the maid answered the phone.

"We are the PRTC!" a man said. "We must speak to Raul immediately!"

The maid had no idea what PRTC meant. "He is already at work," she replied.

"Then call him there!" the man ordered. "And tell him that for the sake of the two North Americans, he had better be at this number in thirty minutes! We have some instructions for him that are very important!" The man hung up.

The maid called APLAR. When Raul answered, she said, "Some man just called from a company called PRTC and left a message for you. I don't know why he didn't call you there at your office."

Raul felt the blood drain from his face. "Never mind that!" he almost shouted. "What was the message?"

"He said that he was going to call here in a half-hour with some information about some North Americans. He said you should be here."

Raul slammed down the phone, glanced at his watch, and ran out of the plant to his car. His home was on the other side of

127

San Salvador. His previous best factory-to-house time was twenty-three minutes. His car was no hot rod, but the tires screeched respectably as he wheeled out of the parking lot onto the highway.

Though an observer might have thought he was watching a madman roar down the boulevard, Raul was very much in control of himself and his vehicle. He could afford no mistakes. So even while he drove at the maximum speed possible, he studied the traffic carefully. At one point he eased up on the accelerator to avoid braking just before he down-shifted and stepped on the gas to go around a garbage truck.

Raul's mind was reviewing and evaluating the various routes open to him. He had to allow for the time of day, known detours where road construction would slow him down, and traffic signals. He chose a course that took him along less-traveled back streets. He knew they would be narrower than the main thoroughfares, but he was counting on fewer obstacles than he actually encountered. His main obstructions turned out to be living—canines and human beings who offered moving targets. Two or three times he borrowed portions of the sidewalk and sent pedestrians scattering for cover. But no damage was done, and he arrived home safely.

For the first time since he left the office, Raul looked at his watch. The second hand was sweeping toward the top of the face. Seventeen minutes. *I just wish I had that drive on film,* he thought. *It would have made a good movie scene.*

He jogged into the house, ordered a drink from the maid, and permitted himself a few moments to catch his breath.

He was half-way through his drink when the phone rang. Raul's stomach tightened as he picked up the receiver. "Hello," he said, "this is Raul!"

"I am glad to see that you know how to follow instructions!" said the man. "Because I have some more to give you!" Raul said nothing. He grabbed a pencil and prepared to take notes on a pad of paper.

"Go to the restaurant El Comal on Alameda Roosevelt," continued the voice. "Do you know where that is?"

"Yes!"

"As you enter the dining room, you will see some large open beams crossing over the tables. On top of the third beam there is a small package. You will be able to see part of it sticking out over the edge. Do not attract attention to yourself. But very casually take down that package and see to it that it is delivered to Fred Rayne. Is that understood?"

"Yes," said Raul.

"And Raul!" cautioned the voice. "Do not contact the authorities. You may rest assured that you will be under constant surveillance." The man hung up.

Raul took a deep breath, put down his pad and pencil, and took another swallow from his glass. Then he got up and returned to his car.

He drove carefully this time, making sure that he obeyed every traffic law. He could not afford to be stopped by a policeman for any reason. If he was being watched—and he could bet his life that he was—any conversation he might have with an officer for whatever reason would surely be mistrusted and misinterpreted.

Since it was only ten o'clock in the morning when he arrived at El Comal, there were few patrons in the place. In fact, as he surveyed the room while his eyes adjusted to the dim light, he was able to count six couples at the tables. It occurred to him that any of them—or all of them—might be PRTC. Trying to appear casual when he was sure that people could see his heart trying to pound through his rib cage was difficult. *This must be what robbers feel like just before they hit a bank!* he thought.

No one disturbed him as he wandered through the room. He pretended to be examining the décor and, after scrutinizing a few wall hangings, he surveyed the ceiling. He counted the beams—one, two, three. His eye followed the line across the center of the room. There it was: a white piece of paper protruding just enough to be seen. *Why did they have to put it in the middle of the room?* He didn't feel cut out for this cloak-and-dagger stuff.

There seemed to be only one way to reach the paper. He went to the table beneath the object, pulled out a chair, stood up on it, took an envelope off the beam, climbed down, and without looking at the envelope or the people in the restaurant, walked briskly out the door. It wasn't until he climbed behind the wheel of his car that he discovered he had stopped breathing. He put the envelope on the seat next to him and drove away.

† † †

THIS MORNING I did something that I had hoped would never become necessary. I began to make marks on the walls to count the days of my captivity.

It took great mental effort to compute what day it actually was. When one is in solitary confinement and denied access to the normal indicators of time, that dimension becomes distorted. It is frightening to become disoriented to how long something has been going on. An amazing amount of one's security is based on the simplest of reference points—most of which I was denied.

My hooded nemeses had left behind the paper and pencil. So I took the pencil in my hand, rolled onto my side with my back to the guard, and began the tortuous process of mentally chronicling my captivity. To that point, each day had had at least one distinguishing feature.

As each day came into focus in my memory, I made one mark with the pencil along the base of the wall, where no one else would see my record. I used the system I had learned in Ecuador as a child: the first four tallies established the sides of a square; Day 5 was documented by a diagonal line through the box. The sixth mark started a new square.

It was hard to believe that there were only six lines to show for all the time I had logged in that hell-hole. But at least I was oriented to time again. After this I made a mark with the arrival of every fourth guard.

This day saw my physical condition deteriorate further. The rash that had appeared on my legs the day before was spreading like crabgrass. Though I couldn't see it, a similar ailment was developing behind my ears. It required a lot of concentration not to scratch the affected areas. When I forgot, the pain in my fingers alerted me to my unconscious trespassing.

The final affliction to harass my system began this day—a case of the shakes. This could have been brought on by any number of things. A result of the dysentery. Or a physical response to the emotional stress of my captivity. I continued to feel terror from the submachine guns. One such weapon was always pointed at me—even when I crawled over to use the toilet. And every night I could hear the off-duty guards cleaning and loading their firearms in an adjacent room. The "click-click, click-click" of metal striking against metal curdled my blood. My whole body would begin to shake and I was powerless to stop it.

My captors were apparently becoming concerned about my obvious disintegration. One guard who came in with Ocho at "supper" gave me a pill and ordered me to take it. It was the first time I had heard that man say anything. I had no idea what the tablet was for, and I was afraid it might kill me. So I only pretended to swallow it. When the guard was not looking, I put it into one of the cracks in the cement floor and covered it with dirt.

The sum total of my agonies overwhelmed me. From childhood it had been ingrained in me that strong men do not cry. But with the rash and the tremors came this additional humiliation—an acute emotional sensitivity that triggered weeping spells. I recalled Rita's complaint, on the night that we watched "Holocaust" on television, that I was insensitive. Well, that problem was thoroughly solved.

RAUL WAS in place at the Chapman residence well before 3:00 P.M., the anticipated time of the phone call promised to Linda Chapman's maid. Linda had told Raul of the call the night before, and he had promised to be there to receive it. She had no quarrel with Hartell's desire to keep her out of the line of fire.

In the meantime Raul had addressed and mailed the envelope he had picked up in the restaurant. He had called Carl Reynolds at Hartell to inform him of what had happened to that point, especially regarding the envelope.

Raul was feeling more confident about his ability to fulfill his role in this bizarre affair. At the prescribed time, the telephone ran. Raul answered it.

"Mrs. Chapman is supposed to be on this line!" an irate man protested.

"I am sorry, *señor*," replied Raul, "but Mrs. Chapman is in no condition to be receiving any messages. I am Raul. If you have any information to pass along, or anything else, you must talk to me. I am the only one who can do anything."

The man cursed. There was brief silence on the other end. Raul could tell that the speaker had put his hand over the mouthpiece of the telephone. Then the man returned. "All right!" he said. "You followed your instructions well enough this morning. We will talk to you for now. But the man we need to speak to is Fred Rayne. Have you contacted him?

"Yes, I have," said Raul.

"Then why isn't he here yet?" demanded the man.

"These things take time!" explained Raul. "He will be here as soon as he can!"

"Well, he better get here soon or there won't be any reason for him to come! Do you understand what I mean?"

"Yes, I understand!" said Raul. He was beginning to grow weary of the braggadocio.

"We will call tomorrow," the man said. "We won't call your office any more—that line is probably already tapped. We'll call back here. And remember, no police!"

"What time—" began Raul, but the line was dead. *Oh well,* he thought, *I guess I can just move my office out here.*

Old family routines in the Bucheli household were being replaced with new ones.

One of the first traditions dropped was the mealtime prayer. At dinner it had been customary for one of the children to lead in a prayer of thanksgiving for the food and anything else that came to mind. The first time the whole family assembled for a "normal" meal after Fausto's abduction, it was Tina's turn to lead in prayer. She began,

Dear God, please be with daddy, and . . .

and that was as far as she got. Her throat swelled shut with emotion. When she couldn't speak further, the others at the table broke down in tears. Most got up from the table and never touched their food. Thereafter, for the sake of nutrition, the preliminary prayer of thanksgiving was abandoned.

The new routines included the daily arrival of John and

Karen Pike—with no new information from Hartell—and the evening vigil conducted by Gert Verhoeven.

The other individual who did more than anyone else to provide comfort and stability for this distressed family was the pastor of Faith Missionary Church, Don Crocker. Ironically it was once again a virtual stranger who came to occupy the place of highest regard in the esteem of the family Bucheli.

Don Crocker was a soft-spoken man in his late thirties. he would be the first to admit that he was not a great pulpit orator. But he was an effective pastor because, in his public and private ministry, he spoke the truth from the heart.

From Day 1 of Fausto's captivity, he came daily to call on the Buchelis. At first, when the activity in the home was so frenetic, he didn't stay long. But later, as the need arose for empathic company, he would often remain for several hours.

Pastor Crocker's effectiveness stemmed not from his ability to provide answers to unanswerable questions, nor from a superhuman kind of faith that produced the miracles for which everyone longed. He never preached; he seldom read the Bible—though he knew it well and spoke of certain passages from time to time. He didn't do "religious" things. Yet the comfort that he transmitted was almost tangible.

One major reason for his impact was the fact that he was a fellow-sufferer. And on this particular night he chose to divulge his private burden to Rita. They were sitting in the family room—Rita curled up in her chair, Don on the plaid couch opposite her. Rita was feeling especially low and was having difficulty verbalizing her feelings. Don didn't press for conversation. Instead he asked a question.

"Rita, do you know what leukemia is?"

"Yes." she looked up, puzzled. "It's cancer of the blood, isn't it?"

"Yes, it is," he replied.

"Well, why did you ask?"

"Because I have it," he said softly.

Rita stared at him in disbelief. "That can't be!" she responded.

"That's what I said when the doctor first told me that several months ago," he replied. "But the fact of the matter is, it can be. I do have leukemia."

Rita shook her head. "But surely God will heal you!"

"He may!" Don agreed. "I have certainly asked Him to—many times. My family is praying fervently that I will be made well."

Rita was waiting for a concluding statement. "Well?"

Don shrugged. "I still have leukemia."

Rita was grieved. "Oh, Pastor Crocker, I am so sorry to hear that! Does it . . . uh . . . hurt . . . uh . . . bad?"

Don smiled. "No, right now it's not too bad. I'm able to work all right, though I tire out much sooner than I would like. But God has been gracious to me in giving me strength for each day."

Rita was becoming angry. "But it's not fair!" she protested. "You are still so young. And you have a family. And you are a pastor."

"And why would God let something so awful happen to someone like me?" he said, completing her line of reasoning. Rita nodded. "Well, you're right! It isn't fair! But then there are few things that are. We don't live in a fair world. We live in a world that is polluted by sin. We live in a world where young, healthy people are struck down by deadly, obscene diseases, and where good people get victimized by wicked people."

Don stopped talking for a while, and Rita remained silent. "Rita, it's all right to ask the questions. It is not sinful to want to understand."

She accepted his invitation. "Then why hasn't God answered your prayer? Why doesn't He make you well? Why doesn't He *do* something?"

"To be honest, Rita," Don responded after a time, "I don't know the answers to those questions."

Rita looked perplexed. "You don't?"

Don almost laughed. "Not fully!"

"Then who does?" she questioned.

"I don't think anyone does, apart from God Himself."

"Then what good does it do to ask?"

"Oh, it does a lot of good!" said Don. "For one thing, asking whatever questions come to mind helps us to face reality and to be honest with our feelings. We only hurt ourselves when we deny that we feel angry, or sad, or hurt, or whatever. By turning to God with our griefs and our fears, we begin to come to grips with the real world. And that is vital if we are to cope with our crises."

"But isn't it sinful to be angry with God?" wondered Rita. "I mean, wouldn't He be upset with me if I talked to Him like that?"

"I think He would far rather have you be honest with Him. After all, He already knows how you feel—He knows everything about you. So there isn't much point in trying to hide anything from Him."

"But doesn't He give any answers?"

"Oh yes," Don said, "He does. It's just that He doesn't often give them all at once. And sometimes they are rather surprising. After all, He is God and He doesn't think or act like we do. And I rather suspect that He waits until we are ready for the parts of the answers that He intends to give us—for our own good."

"Pastor Crocker—" Rita began. Then she hesitated.

"Yes, Rita!" he probed. "What is it?"

"Are you going to die?" she blurted.

"Of course I'm going to die!" he replied. "Unless Jesus comes back first, we're all going to die."

"Of course, I know that. What I mean is, will you die from the leukemia?"

"I knew that's what you meant," he said, smiling. "But I answered the way I did because it puts the whole issue in perspective. Frankly, I don't know whether the leukemia is 'terminal.' I'm not interested in dying 'before my time.' The Lord has put me on this earth for a purpose, and I don't think He's going to take me out of here until I've done that job. But I don't know what God is going to do about my leukemia. He is not . . . uh . . . predictable."

"Well, even though it makes me sad," said Rita, "I'm glad you told me about it. But I can't help but wonder why you did it tonight."

"I guess I just wanted you to know that I know something about how you feel. I have been where you are. In some ways, I am still there. I have my ups and downs, my highs and lows. But I am closer to the Lord than I've ever been before. I have found Him to be utterly trustworthy."

"And," he continued, "I want you to know that my wife

and I, and the people at the church, will see you through this situation, whatever the outcome. I'll try not to give you glib answers to hard questions. I'll try to keep my mouth shut when you don't want any talking at all. I'll do my best to help."

The conversation was interrupted by the ringing of the telephone. One of the girls answered it, but soon called Rita to come. "Mama, it's Father Ross calling from Fort Wayne!"

When the family lived in Berne, Rita commuted to St. Francis College to get her teaching credential. The Catholic school mandated three religion courses of all students as a graduation requirement. Father Ross had been the professor for Rita's classes in theology and Old Testament.

"Hello, Father Ross!"

"Hello, Rita!" he replied. "I'm sorry it's so late, but I wanted you to know that I am going to be conducting a special Mass for Fausto and your family at twelve noon tomorrow in chapel. I know that you cannot be there, of course, but I wanted you to know that we will all be with you in spirit."

"That is so kind of you!" said Rita, emotion evident in her voice. "I appreciate that very much."

"Well, I won't keep you," said the professor. "I just wanted to let you know that all of your friends here are praying for Fausto's safe return, and your comfort. Good night!"

"Good night!"

In the next two days Rita received several other calls, the first from Sister Arilda, telling her what a beautiful service had been conducted on their behalf. Though such communications did not eliminate her pain, they softened its impact. She had never known such an outpouring of love.

13
Under House Arrest

Day 9 *(Saturday, 29 September)*

DAYS 7 AND 8 WERE unremarkable apart from the worsening of the rash and a slight improvement in the condition of my hands.

On Thursday the increasing discomfort of bedsores prompted me to request some kind of pad to lie on. I didn't hold out much hope for a positive response—an expectation that seemed to be confirmed as the hours passed.

On Friday I was given more water with which to rinse my body. I did not remember a great deal about the biblical character Job from parochial school, but what I did recall seemed to correspond to my condition—right down to the sores that covered my skin.

Saturday could have been Christmas, but a more unlikely group of Santa's helpers could scarcely be imagined. I was initially frightened by the abrupt arrival of all three hooded chiefs. Yet I could not have been more surprised when they produced not only the pad I had requested, but a pair of aqua-colored briefs. I immediately donned the shorts. No article of clothing has ever felt so good. "Thank you, *señors*," I said, over and over again. My gratitude knew no bounds. I had been absolutely naked for one full week.

The pad was of foam rubber, about an inch-and-a-half

thick, such as one would use on a cot. It transformed my pallet into a bed at El Camino Real. Of course, neither the pad nor the briefs produced a cure for my various symptoms, but they did wonders for my devastated spirits.

When I lay down again in my assigned position, Señor Glasses said, "You must be a very important man, *gringo!*"

I was still absorbed with my newly acquired sense of decency and the luxury of my cushion. "Why do you think that?" I asked, satisfying his expectations.

"The ambassador from Ecuador has taken out an advertisement in the newspapers of San Salvador begging for your release!" These men were obviously pleased with the response they were getting to my kidnapping.

"That's nice!" I replied, not knowing what else to say.

"They said we should release you because you are a family man with a father and mother, brothers and sisters, and a wife and children." Señor Glasses paused. I said nothing. "They should send that ad to Hartell," he concluded. "They are the ones who have the power to set you free." The three chiefs left the room.

I hardly knew how to react to what had happened, what had been said. Their triumphant attitude argued for the truth of what they had told me. That would indicate, at least, that my parents knew about the kidnapping and were trying to do something to help. I just hoped that their efforts wouldn't backfire. If the kidnappers tried to extract ransom from my family as well as from Hartell, I could remain a hostage until the real Christmas.

◪◻

Day 10 *(Sunday, 30 September)*

JUAN ORTEGA and Kelly Johnson, a former FBI agent, were dispatched from Miami to San Salvador by Fred Rayne. Their mission: Set up a base of operations for negotiations.

Phone calls, one per day, had been received at various times from the kidnappers. With all of the contacts coming to the Chapman residence, Linda had found it prudent to leave. She emigrated with her two children to Guatemala, where they stayed for about a week before relocating permanently with

Bruce's parents in Southern California. Ortega and Johnson arrived at the house before the Sunday call came.

"Boy, am I glad to see you guys!" said a greatly relieved Raul. "The PRTC leaders are growing very impatient!"

"Have they made any new demands yet?" Juan asked.

"Only that they be put in contact with Fred Rayne."

"They must have gotten his name from Bruce."

"I'm sure that's true," Raul agreed. "And every day that Mr. Rayne is not here, the angrier they become. I'm very glad that you are here to talk to them. I'm not sure I could have stalled much longer."

"Well, you've done a good job!" commended Juan. "We'll take it from here. In fact, if you want to go back to the plant, that would be all right."

Johnson attached a suction cup microphone to the telephone receiver and plugged it into a cassette tape recorder. "We're all set!" he announced.

"We'll take the recordings you have already made," Juan explained to Raul, "and re-record them on this master tape." He pointed to the larger reel-to-reel machine that Kelly was setting up. "We'll add each new incoming call," he continued. "That way, we'll have a complete recording that contains every conversation in one place. We'll also translate all of the transactions into English for the people at Hartell."

"That could turn out to be quite a book!" Raul observed.

Juan nodded. "We'll just have to hope that it doesn't get too long," he said.

"And that it has a happy ending," Raul added.

The telephone rang. "Do you want to listen in?" Juan asked Raul.

"Sure!" he replied. "I'll grab the extension in the kitchen."

There was a second ring. Juan activated the record button of the tape recorder and waited a few seconds for the tape to advance past the leader. The phone rang a third time. Juan picked up the receiver. "Hello!"

"Is this Fred Rayne?" a man asked.

"No!" said Juan. "My name is Juan Ortega. I was sent—"

"Where is Fred Rayne?" the irate voice interrupted.

"He is still in the United States," Juan explained. "I work—"

A string of obscenities cut him off. "If you are not Fred Rayne," shouted the man, "then we have nothing to talk about! And you can start planning two funerals!"

"Please, listen to me!" Juan responded calmly. "I work for Mr. Rayne. He sent me down here to speak for him because I speak Spanish fluently. I am authorized by Hartell Industries to receive your conditions for the release of their employees. We are prepared to negotiate."

There was no immediate response from the spokesman. After a few moments of apparent consultation, the man returned to the line. "If you are authorized to act for Mr. Rayne, our first demand is that you obtain rooms at the El Salvador Sheraton Hotel. We will see to it that a special telephone line is hooked up between our headquarters and yours. That will prevent the murderous government officials from putting a tap on this phone. Also, the Sheraton is in a more residential area than El Camino Real where your people have been staying. You will be able to come and go with less chance of being noticed by the police."

"No problem!" replied Juan. "Is there some way we can contact you when we have made the move?"

"You *never* contact us!" ordered the man. "We will call you!" The line went dead.

Juan hung up the receiver as Raul reentered the living room. Juan shrugged and smiled. "Well, it was worth a try!"

Day 11 *(Monday, 1 October)*

For the first time since he began staying with the Buchelis, John Pike brought some concrete news to Rita. This morning he delivered the letter Fausto had written, which Raul had picked up in the restaurant. The Crisis Management Team had already gone over it to glean whatever information it might reveal. But since it was addressed to Rita, it was ultimately passed on to her.

The children were not around when Pike arrived, so no one else was present to witness Rita's weeping as she read the note. It was clearly Fausto's handwriting that covered the soiled page—though the effects of physical stress produced observable irregularities in his normally precise lettering. What was equally clear was that the words were *not* those of her husband—at least the first part of the letter. But the letter was the first tangible evidence to Rita that her husband had survived the initial violence of the kidnapping and was undoubtedly still alive.

"Do you think I should send a reply?" asked Rita presently.

"The company thinks that a letter from you would be appropriate," John replied. "It might not make any difference at all. But then again, seeing a letter from the wife of one of their captives might engender some feelings of sympathy within the kidnappers. If you can handle it, we're inclined to pursue any opportunity we can."

"All right," she replied, "But I don't want the children around when I am trying to write. I'm going over to Gert's to compose my letter."

She didn't wait for a response from John. She simply picked up Fausto's letter and walked out the front door.

After showing the message to Gert, Rita decided to pen a brief reply. The less she said, she reasoned, the less were the chances that she might unintentionally anger Fausto's captors and turn them against him even more. So she wrote:

Dearest Fausto,

I got your letter today. I know that the people who have you there must not be bad because they let you write to me. Some of them probably have wives and children, so they know what it is like for us to have you away from our home.

We send all our love. I hope that this love will surround you until the time that you come back to us. It will be soon. God bless you, Fausto. I love you.

Your Rita

Having been unable to secure rooms immediately at the Sheraton Hotel, Juan Ortega and Kelly Johnson spent their first night in El Salvador at the Chapman home. In the morning, as they were preparing to put their gear in Raul's car for the ride to the hotel, the phone rang. "Probably from California," Juan said as he picked up the receiver. "Hello!"

"Señor Ortega!" said the now-recognizable voice of the PRTC spokesman. "I have called to repeat our demand to speak to Fred Rayne. Mr. Chapman does not know who you are. The only name he knows is Fred Rayne. We must speak to him!"

"I realize that Mr. Chapman does not know me," replied Juan. "We have never met. But as I told you yesterday afternoon, I am Mr. Rayne's representative. He sent me here to open the negotiations."

"Well, we will only speak with Señor Rayne!" The man was adamant. "You tell him that! You tell him that if he wants these two men back alive, he better come to San Salvador!" The man hung up.

"I guess," Juan said to no one in particular, "that it's time for Fred to make his entrance."

† † †

Day 12 (Tuesday, 2 October)

MY ABILITY to recall details from the first few days of captivity stems in part from the macabre aspects of my circumstances. The contrast between my new experiences as a hostage and the relative normality of my life until now made my initiation days memorable, to say the least.

By the second week, my captivity was no longer an adventure. It is not that I didn't long for a return to my former, comparatively undramatic lifestyle from the outset. But during the second week the tension of not knowing what was going to happen next was replaced by the stress of monotony. The daily pattern became so routine that my system received virtually no stimulation from external sources whatsoever. The daily routine of three feedings (and one wall-marking) made me feel like a creature in a zoo—without benefit of animal lovers to stare at. Between the advents of bananas were great empty stretches of time. I was too determined to read, too depressed to reminisce much, too distraught to sleep. Boredom was steadily prying loose my grip on sanity.

What almost killed me, though, was fright. I lived in mortal fear of the submachine gun. The murder of Luis Paz became a perpetual nightmare from which I could not escape. My greatest anxiety came at night, for I was always afraid that the guard would fall asleep and pull the trigger by reflex or an accident. It was like one continual game of Russian Roulette, only it was always my turn. I could turn my back on that barrel, but I could never evade its one-eyed stare.

One night during the second week, my greatest fear was fulfilled. As I lay semi-conscious on my back, I was jolted awake by a blow to my chest. The guard had fallen asleep, and the gun had slipped from his hands. The cold steel of the barrel jammed into my left breast.

I instantly realized what had happened, and my heart rate must have tripled all at once. Incredibly, the guard did not wake up, and I lay there paralyzed for several moments, the submachine gun balanced on my chest. It dawned on me that this gun could be my ticket to freedom. But almost as quickly I realized that if I attempted an escape in my weak condition, the weapon would be my ticket to a bloody death.

Carefully and silently I moved the barrel off my chest and onto the pad on which I lay. Then I reached over and tapped the guard on the leg. *"Señor,"* I whispered. *"Señor,* wake up!" The guard jerked upright, staring wildly about the room. I pointed to the gun. "You dropped that!" Immediately he picked up the weapon and pointed it at my head again. I smiled at him. He never said a word. I shrugged and rolled over. The shakes returned.

$$\boxed{}\boxed{}\ulcorner$$

WITH THE blessings of Hartell Industries, Juan Ortega and Kelly Johnson set up their post in a suite at the plush El Salvador Sheraton. The first order of business was to organize the electronic recording equipment. The machinery was not ultra-sophisticated, but it was compact and efficient. Most important, the components were compatible.

The two men had already transferred all the recordings of telephone conversations onto the big master tape. Then they had transcribed these dialogues and wrote translations of them into English. Once they were moved in and set up, they settled down for their next responsibility: waiting for the phone to ring.

Kelly looked out the window at the spectacular view commanded by this largest of San Salvador's hotels. "This isn't a bad location!" he noted. "We can see most of the city from here."

"Yeah!" Juan agreed. "And the scenery is nice too! I don't think I've ever been this close to an honest-to-goodness volcano before." He surveyed the slopes of the mountain crater named for the city over which it stood watch. "I understand you can hike right down into that thing!"

"Some people can!" replied Kelly. "But I suspect that this is as close as we're going to get to it!"

The telephone rang. "You are undoubtedly right!" Juan said as he depressed the record button on the tape machine. He picked up the telephone receiver. "Hello!"

"The telephone you are using now is connected to a special line with our headquarters," a man said. "Don't use it for any other calls. When we need to talk to you, we want your man to be there. Understood?"

"Understood!"

"Now let me talk to Fred Rayne!" said the man.

"He isn't here yet," Juan said. "He will be here soon!"

'Let me tell you how soon!" the man said. "If Fred Rayne is not at this telephone in twelve hours, the first body will come out. You people have not been taking us seriously. You will find out just how serious we are! Twelve hours!"

As the days of Fausto's captivity stretched on with no apparent sign of change, the Bucheli children returned to school. It took real effort to try to establish a "normal" environment, to be involved in things that would occupy their minds and divert them from the tragedy. To a certain degree, the strategy worked.

Helen and Tina, who were in grade school, had supportive, understanding teachers. The girls' classmates were not fully aware of their father's circumstances, so they were better able to submerge themselves in the world of school. There would be times, of course, when thoughts of their dad could not be derailed. Tears would come, and there would be a trip to the school nurse or counselor. But on the whole, school was a good place to be, and life went on.

Hilda and Fausto Jr., the two high school students, found life at school more awkward. They had been in the new system for only a few days when the abduction took place, so they hadn't had time to form close friendships. Then they were out of school during the first few days of the captivity, awaiting word on the fate of their father. So when they returned to classes, they felt isolated. Most of their classmates didn't know them; those who did, now identified them as "the kids whose father was kidnapped in Central America." Few knew how to relate to a person who is experiencing an ongoing crisis. So it took longer for Hilda and Fausto to regain a sense of comfort and routine.

Veronica, the eighth-grader, came by new friends a little more readily than her older siblings. But her emotional distress was intensified by the incredible insensitivity of her fourth-period English teacher. At the beginning of class he looked over at her and said, "Hey, Veronica, tell us the exciting news about your dad!"

She looked at him numbly, wondering what he could possibly mean.

"You know!" he prodded. "How he was kidnapped and all—tell us all about what happened!"

Veronica broke into tears. A friend, Caleb, stood up and said, "Hey, man, don't you have any feelings?" Others in the class voiced their disapproval of the teacher's remarks. Caleb said to Veronica, "Come on, let's get out of here!" He walked her to the counselor's office.

The next day Karen Pike came to the school and confronted the teacher, berating him for the inappropriateness of his questions. But though he never said another word about the matter, the damage had been done.

However, the greatest thorn in the side of the children was John Pike. In the one area where they wanted information, he never said enough. There was virtually no news coming from Hartell—nothing about the state of their father or what steps the company was taking.

On other matters he said and did too much. He essentially tried to take over the Bucheli household. But his personality did not fit with this family. For one thing, profanity had never been permitted as a means of expression. But John resorted to it frequently—especially in his clumsy attempts to discipline the children.

In his efforts to prevent "news leaks," he tried to control where the children went outside the home. When Gert came over to talk with Rita alone, John wanted them to stay in the family room where he could monitor every conversation. Gert felt as if she had to pass an examination every time she wanted to come into the house.

The conflict was greatest between John and Fausto Jr. Aged sixteen, Fausto had accepted the responsibility to look after his sisters; in fact, they accepted him as the authority in the home. During the times when Rita was indisposed by grief, the girls turned to Fausto for permission to visit friends or whatever. The role that Fausto adopted was the position John wanted to occupy. Fausto viewed John as a usurper.

This conflict came to a head over an incident involving a local newspaper. A reporter came to the high school attended by the two older children and attempted to interview Fausto. Sensitive to the delicate nature of the negotiations for his father's life, Fausto offered no new information. But the remarks he made, which were repetitions of previously reported news, were quoted that evening in the *Chino Champion*.

Even though Fausto's statements were innocuous, John viewed those comments as being a violation of his order not to speak to the media. In retribution he not only castigated the boy, but also cut him off completely from any new information that might have come in about his father. Fausto Jr. was placed under a news blackout.

Thus the ironic effect of John Pike's presence in the home was that the wife and children of Fausto Bucheli were also being held hostage against their will. The only reason Rita tolerated his continued obnoxious attempts to govern their existence was that he was her only link to the company and whatever information might be forthcoming from them about Fausto.

As it turned out, Pike's contribution to the situation was almost entirely negative. While Hartell had gotten the very best team to negotiate Fausto's release, it could be argued that the firm put the worst man possible in the position of family liaison. It was probably an oversight, perpetuated by preoccupation with the negotiation process. But the company's insensitivity to the family's need to know what steps were being taken ("We're doing everything we can" is meaningless) and the antagonistic presence of a heavy-handed dictator served to intensify the emotional stress of the family. Even the friends who provided the constructive support needed by the Buchelis were unanimously appalled at the way the family was treated throughout the crisis.

A further irony is that, through Ginger Martin, Fred Rayne's fiancé, Linda Chapman was routinely kept informed of what was transpiring in El Salvador. Ginger did not contact Rita because they had never met; she assumed that the Crisis Management Team was keeping Rita apprised of developments.

14
This Is a Test

THE TENSION WAS mounting in the Sheraton hotel room as the clock ticked closer to the 10 A.M. deadline. Juan Ortega sensed that the kidnappers viewed their ultimatum, and Hartell's response to it, as a test of strength and resolve. If they felt that Fred Rayne was disregarding their threats, they would have to do something drastic to prove themselves. They would *have* to execute one of the hostages or abort the whole operation. There was little doubt in Juan's mind which alternative the kidnappers would choose.

Juan's immediate problem was that Fred Rayne was not going to meet the twelve-hour deadline. The phone was going to ring in a matter of minutes, and the wrong man was going to have to answer it. He hoped he would be dealing with reasonable men. He formulated the wording of his first statement. If he failed to communicate concisely and persuasively in the first few words, he might not be given the chance to recover.

The phone rang. Juan activated the recorder and picked up the receiver. "Fred Rayne is in Guatemala," he declared without preamble. "He is on his way here right now. He will be in this room in two hours."

There was silence on the other end of the line. Juan considered adding other reasons why the PRTC should not kill either of the hostages, but checked himself. He didn't want to plead. So he kept quiet and let his message sink in. At last the man spoke.

"All right!" he said. Juan resisted the impulse to expel a great sigh of relief, but he did give a thumbs-up sign to Kelly. "We will call back in three hours," promised the spokesman. "Your man better be there!"

Juan hung up. "They've given Fred three more hours," he reported. "We better pray he doesn't hit any more snags!"

Fred Rayne did not hit any snags. He arrived at the Sheraton on schedule, accompanied by his two bodyguards. He had been fully briefed by Juan and Kelly by the time the next call came at one o'clock.

Juan turned on the recorder. Fred picked up the receiver and spoke in Spanish: "This is Fred Rayne. To whom am I speaking?"

The caller was momentarily startled. "We don't give out our names!" came the reply. "All you need to know is that we are the PRTC!"

"Listen!" said Fred. "If we are going to be doing business, I want to know the name of the man I am dealing with! We are both human beings. I will treat you with respect, and I insist on being treated in the same way. Otherwise, we cannot trust each other."

After a pause the man said, "My name is Carlos."

"Thank you, Carlos!" said Fred. "Now I think that you will agree that it is very important that we understand each other. You can also tell by now that my Spanish is not perfect. To avoid running the risk of miscommunication, I would like to have Señor Ortega speak for me and deliver your messages to me. Is that all right?"

Again there was silence as the spokesman consulted with others at his end. "All right!" said Carlos. "As long as you are the one who does the negotiating."

"I will speak to you personally at the beginning of every conversation," Fred assured him. "Now I am going to give the phone to Juan." Fred continued to talk, pausing from time to time to allow Juan to deliver the Spanish message. "As you can readily understand," he said to the kidnapper, "I must be able to assure my clients that you do in fact have custody of our men, that they are the men that you claim that they are, and that they are alive and in good health." There was no objection from Carlos, so Fred continued. "We will be prepared to consider your terms for their release when we are satisfied on those three counts. Accordingly, I must ask you to provide us with evidence of their identity and well-being. Specifically I would consider a tape recording by each of the men reading from today's edition of *La Prensa Grafica* to be of value. Also, I will ask you a list of questions about each of the men. If you are holding Señors Chapman and Bucheli, you will have no difficulty securing the answers. I will give you a chance to write them down."

Fred dictated the questions he had prepared with Rita's help.

Then Carlos responded. "We will call you when we have collected the proof that you have requested. Good-by!" The conversation was over.

"Well!" said Fred. "We seem to be open for business." He walked over to the king-sized bed, lay across it, and went to sleep.

† † †

UNLIKE THE first few days of the second week, Wednesday was eventful. My emotional exhaustion was so complete after the incident of the falling gun that I didn't even move when the three hoods returned for their fourth visit. This time they brought with them a cassette recorder, a camera, a grimy T-shirt, and a large banner.

Señor Skinny immediately set about attaching the banner to the wall opposite the nonwindow.

"Get up, *gringo!*" ordered Señor Mustache. "We have some work for you to do!"

With great effort I managed to sit up.

Señor Mustache directed the guard to leave the cell. he moved the chair next to the five-gallon can. Señor Glasses tossed the T-shirt to me. It belonged to one of the guards, and it smelled worse than I did. "Put it on!" commanded Señor Glasses. I held my breath as I pulled the damp fabric over my head.

Surely it had not been washed in the history of the world.

"Stand up!" declared Señor Glasses. I tried to comply, but my legs wouldn't work. I had not stood for over a week. They had become rubbery from disuse and inadequate nutrition. Señors Skinny and Mustache stood on either side and hoisted me to my feet. Once upright, I was able to stand unaided.

They moved me into a position in front of and to the left of the banner. I looked back at it over my right shoulder. It displayed the large, circular emblem of the PRTC with a five-pointed star in the center. Señor Mustache handed me the front page of a San Salvador newspaper. Across the top in bold letters was the headline: U.S. ARMADA IN CARIBBEAN.

"Hold it up in front of you!" directed Señor Glasses. The newspaper would establish that it was October 3. It also confirmed the accuracy of my row of boxes—it was Day 13.

Señor Glasses snapped the shutter, and the flash momentarily blinded me. Señor Mustache returned the chair to its original place, approximately in front of where I had been standing, and told me to sit down. Señor Skinny took the newspaper from me and gave me a standard-sized sheet of paper with Spanish words written on it. He also handed me my glasses. Señor Mustache picked up the tape recorder.

"We are going to have you make a recording now," he explained. "If you do a good job, it will help get you out of here. First, you must read the words that we have written on that sheet of paper. Then describe in your own words the articles and pictures we have circled on the first and fifth pages of the newspaper."

I read over my script. I was about to lie about the excellence of my health, my conditions, and my captors.

"Are you ready?" asked Señor Mustache. I nodded. He turned on the recorder.

I read the words as a novice news announcer might quote wire-service copy over the air. Anyone who knew me would recognize that I do not normally speak in that manner or with that vocabulary. They would know that I was reading something written by someone else. It was important to me that the recipients be aware that I was not a willing participant in this affair.

After reciting the paragraph they had written, I spoke

briefly about the newspaper report of a delivery of food and towels for the elderly poor folks in a Salvadoran village. Finally I described a photograph of Pope John Paul II printed on page 5. He had just addressed the United Nations General Assembly in New York.

My managers were satisfied with my performance.

"Now one more thing!" said Señor Glasses. "I am going to ask you some questions which you must answer truthfully and accurately. Be very careful how you respond," he warned, "for your life may very well be at stake in your answers."

The veiled threat was so melodramatic that I might have been tempted not to take it seriously. What prevented this was my awareness that these men took *themselves* seriously—always. It may have appeared that we were all playing roles in a poorly written movie, but they were not kidding around. I assured Señor Glasses that I would do my best.

The questions were all about me—where I went to high school, who my supervisor was at C.T.S. in 1973, what the annual earnings of B & K Enterprises were, how much my monthly housing allowance from APLAR was, where I went to church, what my favorite books were—questions seeking details that were obscure enough to make me have to think hard to remember.

As I formulated the answers, it dawned on me that these riddles were for purposes of identification. My captors had to prove to someone that the man they had kidnapped was, in fact, Fausto Bucheli. My answers, the picture, the tape would all establish that I was alive and being held hostage by these particular men. Something was happening out there! Who, I wondered, had made up those questions?

When we were done, Señor Skinny pulled the T-shirt back over my head. The removal of the perspiration-soaked shirt was a relief. I was told to return to my mat, and the guard was brought back.

"Please, *señors!*" I pleaded. They turned to me. "I must talk to you about this guard. Listen, I am not a violent man. I have not given you any trouble. I am very weak and very frightened." They could see this was true. "All day, all night, the guards point that gun at me. It is killing me! Please, could you tell them not to point their guns at me? I won't cause you any trouble! I just want the guns pointed someplace else!"

"We'll talk it over, *gringo*," replied Señor Mustache, "but don't get your hopes up."

They left the room taking all of their props with them, but leaving my glasses with me. The guard sat down and pointed the submachine gun at my head again. I began to shake.

Suppertime brought another surprise. In addition to the standard fare of fried bananas, my captors had provided a special entrée—the toughest piece of beef in El Salvador. It hurt my teeth and gums to chew it, and I had to be careful to keep it on the right side of my mouth. Nevertheless, the flavor was different from bananas and it was a welcome change—even if I eventually had to spit the unpalatable leather into the toilet.

When Ocho returned to collect my tray, he was accompanied by Señor Mustache. The *señor* did not say a word. Rather, he signaled the guard to leave the cell, picked up the chair and removed it as well, and left me alone in my own little world. For the first time in almost two weeks I was by myself—no guard, no gun, no nothing. Solitary confinement never felt so good.

In a few hours the light went out. The cell was totally dark, like the interior of an underground cave. It was the first time since I had been taken hostage that I was permitted to experience night as night. I think I even slept a little.

Day 14 *(Thursday, 4 October)*

My introduction to Thursday morning was novel—the light was turned on in the cell. In contrast to the blanket of total darkness I experienced through the night, the little forty-watt bulb seemed much brighter than it had before.

The light was followed by Ocho and breakfast. As he went through his routine of servicing the can and refilling my water container, I nibbled on a few pieces of banana. When he came to pick up my tray, I said, "My friend, we are alone. There is no guard in here now. Will you tell me your name?"

He hesitated. Then he whispered, "Ocho." ("Eight.")

"Ocho?" I repeated, startled that someone would have a number for a name.

He nodded.

"Do you remember, Ocho, that I once asked you to request a Bible for me?"

Again he nodded. Then he whispered, "I was afraid that if I asked them for that book, they would hurt you even more."

"Thank you, my friend!" I said softly. "But I would still like to have a Bible. I do not think they will hurt me now. They have done some nice things for me. Please ask them again."

Ocho nodded and left.

My request was born of a sense of urgency. I realized that without something wholesome to occupy my eyes and my mind, I would go crazy or suffer a complete breakdown. I was not at all certain that having a Bible would make any difference at this point anyway, but it was the only hope I had. I did not have enough control over my mind, without something to read, to channel my thinking in healthful directions.

Within an hour Señors Mustache and Skinny were back in my cell. "We understand that you have asked for a Bible," began Señor Mustache.

"That's right!" I replied. "I would like to have one if I may."

"Have you finished reading the books we gave you to read?" he questioned, pointing to the stack next to my head.

I phrased my answer carefully. "I am finished with them. Thank you very much. But now I would like a Bible."

Señor Mustache launched into a diatribe: "Do you know who makes that Bible? The *gringos* write that book to keep the poor Salvadorans down. The Yankee imperialists use it to step on the poor people, to keep them under subjection. That is where our people have always been, and the *gringos* use that book to keep people poor and oppressed."

"That may be true," I replied, "but I think it would be interesting to read it."

Neither of the chiefs said another word. They turned and stormed out of the cell, slamming the door behind them.

The remainder of the day passed uneventfully. What this means is that with each passing hour, I became increasingly uncomfortable—make that miserable. Anyone with my assortment of maladies should have been in a sterile hospital room under the best medical care. When one is beset with agony, and there is no mental diversion, all there is to think about is how bad things are and how much one hurts and how remote are the chances of release from either the pain or the confinement. Before my captivity I would have been totally incapacitated by a bad toothache *or* dysentery *or* chronic insomnia *or* a full-body rash *or* psychosomatic tremors *or* confinement in a filthy, cockroach-infested, hot, humid, dark closet *or* absolute monotony. Now I suffered all. Despite the niceties bestowed upon me by my captors by the end of my second week, I was in the worst physical, emotional, and mental condition of my life.

It was precisely at this point, coinciding with supper on the fourteenth day, that Ocho showed up with a Bible. It was actually a Gideon New Testament, Spanish edition, which had been stolen no doubt from a nearby hotel. It was blue and bore the Gideons' seal, a golden lamp within a circle of gold, embossed on the front. I meekly held it in my hands and stared at it as I absent-mindedly ate my banana.

When Ocho left for the night, I opened the little book and began reading from the very first pages. From the special introduction I learned that the Gideons are Christian business and professional men from 125 countries. By the time this edition of the New Testament had been published in the early seventies, the Gideons had placed more than ninety million Bibles and New Testaments in public places around the world. *These little books have probably ended up in strange places,* I thought. *But whoever would have thought that another businessman would end up reading one in such a hole as this!* I read these words:

> We are pleased to present you with this copy of God's precious Word and trust that you will enjoy reading it daily.

Without knowing why, I felt tears welling up. I knew that these very same words were probably printed in 89,999,999 other Bibles. But at this moment it seemed as though someone had addressed them to me. I had written one letter and made a tape; this was the first "mail" I had received myself.

I wiped the tears from my eyes and turned the page. There I read two paragraphs describing the values of the Bible. Two sentences in particular seemed to jump out at me:

> Read it to be wise, believe it to be safe, and practice it to be holy. It contains light to direct you, food to support you, and comfort to cheer you.

As I read these words, the forty-watt light bulb was turned off. I was through reading for the night.

I pulled the Bible to my chest as a child would clutch a teddy bear. I thought about those words: "Light, food, comfort." Light, food, comfort. If I couldn't have freedom, then above all else I needed light and food and comfort. Could any book deliver on such a promise? I intended to find out. I closed my eyes and waited for the rooster.

THE CONCENTRATION being devoted to a novel, a crossword puzzle, a game of gin rummy, and a Spanish-dubbed television rerun of "Bonanza" was disrupted by the ringing of The Telephone.

"This is Fred Rayne!"

"This is Carlos!"

"Just a moment!" said Fred. "Here is Juan!" He handed the receiver to his associate.

"Hello!" said Juan.

"We have obtained the information and evidence required by Mr. Rayne," said Carlos. "Do you know where the McDonald's Restaurant is?"

"Yes," said Juan. He didn't really know, but he figured it would be easy to find.

"Go into the men's restroom," directed Carlos. "You will see two mirrors. Behind the one on the right you will find two packages. In one envelope is the tape recording you asked for as well as answers to all of the questions about the hostages. In the other package is a manifesto that we have prepared. Our first demand is that Hartell publish that manifesto, according to our specifications, in all of the newspapers listed on the attached sheet. Our declaration must be published in the Sunday editions of those papers."

"This Sunday?" asked Fred Rayne, when Juan had relayed the message to him.

"Yes, October seventh," replied Carlos.

"Carlos!" said Fred. "I don't know if that is possible. We will do our best, but we'll have to see what's in the packet before we can guarantee anything."

"I suggest that you find a way to succeed!"

"I need to talk to you about something else," Fred said, changing the subject. "You have done a good job of arranging for the security of our negotiations. But I am concerned that the local authorities might still be able to monitor our conversations. I don't think they have had time to tap this line yet; but before they do, I would like to set up a code for us to use to ensure the secrecy of our transactions."

Carlos conferred briefly with someone else before responding. "What do you suggest?"

"When my man picks up the packages you have left for him, he will deposit an envelope for you to retrieve from the same location. In it you will find a list of vocabulary words that we can use to get us started. More precise communications can be carried out through the same kind of drops you have set up this time. And we can use the drops to add words to our telephone vocabulary as the need may arise."

"We want to see the list before we are prepared to commit ourselves," replied Carlos.

"That's fine with me!" said Fred.

The discussion was over and both men hung up. The communications system was now in place. To maintain continuity, Fred designated Juan to be the courier for all drops and pickups in San Salvador.[1] A chauffeur was drafted from among the APLAR employees. Although he was very nervous about his assignment, his familiarity with San Salvador would prove to be indispensable in the days ahead.

So the pattern by which the negotiations would be carried out was established. Fred prepared an elaborate glossary which, with some practice, became an almost natural way of talking for the respective negotiators. Among the code words and their equivalent terms were the following:

Bruce = "Jack"	Guatemala = "Mountains"
Fausto = "Jill"	Dollars = "Bananas"
Rayne = "El Maestro"	Airplane = "Horse"
Reynolds = "The Judge"	Suitcases = "Shoes"

---

[1]When his assignment in El Salvador was completed, Juan Ortega would complain that he knew the layout of every public restroom in San Salvador. The other side seemed to have a penchant for toilets.

Juan was transported to a busy McDonald's Restaurant, where the pickup and drop were executed without incident. He returned to the hotel and turned the two packages over to Fred.

From the matter-of-fact attitude evidenced by the PRTC spokesman, Fred fully expected the parcel with the tapes and "answer sheet" to be complete. They could wait. He carefully opened the other envelope to see what his first major assignment would be. He removed several pieces of paper, some photographs, and a larger sheet of paper, folded several times to fit into the package.

He looked first at the texts of the manifesto that Hartell was to publish. There were two of them. The one in Spanish was addressed TO THE PEOPLE OF CENTRAL AMERICA. The English version was headlined: TO THE PEOPLE OF THE WORLD. The basic message of the proclamation was contained in the revolutionary rhetoric of the three-paragraph "Introduction," which read:

> The publication of the present proclamation is a conquest of our party through the operation GLORY TO OUR FIGHTERS FALLEN IN BATTLE: DAVID, JAIME AND RAUL ANTIM! VIVA NICARAGUA SANDINISTA! executed in San Salvador the 21st of September 1979; said operation consisted in the capture of two top North American executives in the transnational North American [Hartell Industries, Inc.] that has a subsidiary in El Salvador the company, APLAR of El Salvador.
>
> The development of our party, its growing vinculum and growth of its popular basis, in particular with workers and having acquired the necessary combative experience and resources, has implemented our operative capacity to the level of having been able to carry out successfully the operation we mentioned.
>
> The choice as objective of a transnational North American company is a clear expression of our policy that defines as a fundamental enemy of the Central American revolution the North American Imperialist who support [sic] the system of "free zones" as a new modification to make more effective a cruel and voracious exploitation that our people are victims of at the hands of the North American companies. In order to realize their economic projects, the interference in the internal politics of our countries, promoting lackey dictatorships, sustaining oppressive and bloody regimes (with a pretended democratic mask included) and maneuvering with the utopian purpose of stopping the develop-

ment of the fight for liberation it is urgent that our people sustain heroically against exploitation and anti-popular violence and counter revolution.

Fred skimmed the rest of the text, which he estimated to run about two thousand words. The majority of the proclamation consisted of documentation of allegations against the Romero government's "brutal repression" of the poor in general and political opponents in particular. The manifesto concluded with an apologetic for a popular revolutionary war to overthrow the current regime. It was dated September 30, 1979.

There were three photographs. They were black-and-white glossy prints of the gory remains of mutilated human beings— alleged victims of government-inflicted atrocities.

There was also a professionally prepared ink drawing of the PRTC emblem, camera-ready for reproduction.

Fred unfolded the larger sheet and spread it over the end of a bed. It was a tissue layout showing how the kidnappers wanted the ads to appear in the newspapers. This work was also professionally done. The quality wasn't good by North American standards, but the kidnappers' intentions were clear. A layout artist would have no difficulty following their format.

Finally Fred turned to the page of instructions. As he read the directions, he spoke for the first time. "Uh-oh! We're in trouble!"

"What do they want?" asked Juan.

"We have to publish facing two-page ads in, let's see, thirty-two newspapers." He paused as he did some more calculations. "And those papers are in twenty-eight countries in South, Central, and North America—and Europe."

"Europe?" Juan was amazed.

"Europe." confirmed Fred. "They are to be printed in red, black and yellow. I guess those are their official colors."

"Can it be done?" asked Kelly Johnson.

"Not by Sunday!" replied Fred. "We may not be able to meet some of these specifications at any date. I just hope these guys don't get belligerent over these details!" He turned to his two bodyguards. "Regardless of what they say, we need to get moving on this! I want you men to charter a flight to L.A. and deliver these materials to Reynolds at Hartell as soon as possible. Then stand by to deliver the finished product. One of you will need to take the English ad to the *New York Times* just as soon as it is off the press. The other one will return the Spanish version to me here. We will disseminate them from here."

As the two men gathered their belongings for their flight to the States, Fred opened the other package containing two cassette tapes and several sheets of paper. He skimmed the contents of the pages. They contained written answers to his "identity quizzes," and they were accurate enough to assure him that the men in custody were Bruce Chapman and Fausto Bucheli.

It did not take him long to listen to the recordings. They too apparently complied with his instructions, although the people in Fullerton would have to verify the voice prints. "Put these on the master tape," he instructed Juan. "Then we'll send this package to Hartell along with the other one."

When the couriers left with their precious cargo, Fred Rayne sat down next to the other telephone in the room. He placed a call to Fullerton, California. He scarcely put down the phone the rest of the day.

Reunited. Rita and Fausto Bucheli accept a check from Hartell Industries during Fausto's rehabilitation after his ordeal.

TO THE PEOPLE OF THE WORLD

PROCLAMATION OF THE REVOLUTIONARY PARTY OF CENTRAL AMERICAN WORKERS

PRTC

Demands. This revolutionary manifesto (above) was published at the terrorists' demand; a picture of Fausto reading a Salvadoran newspaper was required by the negotiator.

Support. Vital support for Rita in the ordeal came from (below) her son, Fausto Jr.; (left) neighbor Gertrude Verhoeven; and friends David and Pauline Solano.

Free! Fausto (left) disembarks from his freedom flight out of El Salvador, with his colleague in captivity, Bruce Chapman, right behind him.

Safe. Still enduring trauma, Fausto tells negotiator Fred Rayne (right) his story minutes after arriving in California on his flight home from El Salvador.

15
A Matter of Time

Day 15 *(Friday, 5 October)*

IT WAS MORNING when The Telephone rang in Fred Rayne's suite at the El Salvador Sheraton. He answered it personally, then turned it over to Juan.

Carlos was the first to report. "We picked up your package, and we agree with your suggestions."

"We also picked up your packages," replied Fred, "and we have some problems."

"Problems?" asked Carlos, perturbed. "What problems?"

"I haven't heard from the company yet as to whether they are willing to comply with your requirement. And even if they agree, I doubt if we can meet your deadline."

Carlos exploded. "You tell those imperialist pigs that they have six hours to meet our demands!" He slammed down the phone before Juan even finished translating to Fred.

"I hope he cools down in the next six hours!" said Fred. "This hardly qualifies as negotiating!"

† † †

THE ROOSTER announced the beginning of my third week in captivity. It was not a good day. It took all my strength to draw the diagonal line through the third box on the wall. I was so ill

166

that the Bible reading I had anticipated a few hours before was out of the question. I knew that if I did not receive medical attention soon, I was a dead man.

I did not move when Ocho brought breakfast. I did not have either the appetite or the strength to force down another banana. I just lay there. When I did not respond to Ocho's encouragement to eat, he leaned over and whispered, "*Señor, are you all right?*"

"No," I murmured, "I'm not all right! I need to see a doctor!"

Ocho retreated with the undisturbed fruit, and I probably lapsed into delirium. Presumably time passed. At some point in the day, my cell was invaded by Señor Glasses. Others may have been with him, but I didn't bother to take roll. Señor Glasses was angry again. And again I did not know why. Nor did I care. I just waited for the outburst that was sure to come.

"That stinking, imperialist company of yours doesn't care whether you live or die!" he cursed. "Our first condition for your release is not so impossible! But they are not taking us seriously!" He stormed about the cubicle. "If they do not comply within six hours, they will learn that we mean business! Yours will be the first body we throw out of here, you miserable traitor!"

He opened the door, then turned back for a Parthian shot: "You better prepare to die, *gringo!*" The door slammed so hard it made the light bulb swing.

Prepare to die? Earlier I had concluded that death was probably a matter of time. Under the circumstances, it mattered little how it happened: I did not want to die. But neither did I want to live—if my present condition constituted living. If it had been Señor Glasses' intention to terrorize me further, he failed. I was beyond that. He had been beating a nearly dead horse.

IT WAS three o'clock in the afternoon when the second call of the day came to Fred Rayne's headquarters.

"Listen, Carlos!" Fred began. "If we're going to get anywhere, you are going to have to give me some room to do my job!"

"Then do your job," replied Carlos, "and publish our manifesto."

"We will!" promised Fred. "We will do everything we can to meet your specifications. The problem is that you have not given us enough time. It is simply impossible to publish the proclamation in Sunday's papers. I couldn't do it if I had all of the resources of the State Department—which I don't."

These statements were met with a silence that indicated another conference. "When can it be printed?" asked Carlos.

"Possibly by Wednesday in the American papers," replied Fred. "A few days later in the other countries."

"Why later?" asked Carlos.

"Several reasons! One is distance. It simply takes time to travel as far as we have to go. In London, there is a strike by advertising workers in the television industry, so the newspapers are overwhelmed with orders. I called *The Times* and told them I wanted a two-page ad in Sunday's edition, and they told me to come back in February.

"Then there are political problems," Fred continued. "The governments control the press in some of these countries. And there are some regimes in this part of the world that aren't exactly sympathetic to your cause.

"And besides all that," he concluded, "it will take all weekend just to get the proofs printed up and ready for delivery to the papers." Fred rested his case.

"All right!" Carlos acquiesced. "We will agree to a deadline of Wednesday, October tenth, for the American newspapers. Now listen, Rayne!" he continued. "Within one week, by Wednesday, October seventeenth, we want copies of every manifesto. You have to prove to us that you have done as we have demanded."

"All I can promise," Fred replied, "is that we will do our best."

"October seventeenth," reiterated Carlos.

"October seventeenth," said Rayne grimly.

"Now, one more thing!" added Carlos.

"Go ahead!"

"Our second condition for the release of your men is the release from Salvadoran prisons of five freedom-fighters. You will write down their names."

Juan Ortega transcribed the names as they were dictated.

Fred responded: "If I try to secure the release of those prisoners, we may jeopardize the whole negotiations process. So far, I've been able to keep government officials out of this. But things could get very sticky if I have to start working with embassy officials and government agents. They could even expel us from the country—or arrest us for trying to undermine their authority."

"You are a very resourceful man, Señor Rayne," replied Carlos. "You will think of something!" He hung up.

"I've already thought of several things," Fred said to the others in the room. "But none of them get our men out alive." He sighed. "The plot thickens!"

† † †

ONCE AGAIN, the amount of time that passed was indeterminable. Ocho came in with some meal—I had lost track of which one—but when I still expressed no interest in food, he lowered his head to my ear and whispered, "Señor Bucheli!" I was startled to hear my name. "They are not going to kill you!"

Who is to say? I thought. I had no response for Ocho. He left the cell.

Not long after, Señor Glasses returned with his two cohorts. "You are a lucky man, *gringo!*" he announced.

Wonderful! I thought. *I've won the national lottery!* Gallows humor.

"Those capitalist pigs in California have decided to meet our terms!" he boasted. "We don't have to kill you! At least not now!"

"But you *are* killing me!" I protested weakly. It didn't seem that I had much to lose by protesting.

"You will be all right!" replied Señor Mustache. "Tomorrow we will bring a doctor to give you some medicine. You will see that we are not cruel people."

You are not cruel, I thought, *and I am not sick. And this is all just an obscene joke.*

The "Three Stooges" took their act someplace else.

Day 16 *(Saturday, 6 October)*

The first thing I noticed about him was his hands—they were very soft. But they were more than soft—they were tender, almost sympathetic in the way they touched and probed my tortured anatomy. Hairy, remarkably thin arms guided the hands over my body.

Slowly my clouded mind recognized the presence of an individual whom I had not seen before. The white, short-sleeved shirt, the white pants, and the beautiful, gold wrist watch were the additional features that confirmed the man's identity. A doctor had come to examine me.

He was talking to me, but his softly spoken words were so muffled by the obligatory pillowcase that it took me awhile to discern what he was saying. "You're going to be all right now!" I heard him say. "Just relax. That's good. Everything is going to be fine." It was doctor talk—the kind of rambling that physicians engage in when they are dealing with an emergency patient.

He even had a black bag, and from this he extracted all the instruments one normally encounters in a routine physical exam. His hood kept getting in the way, but he utilized the tools of his trade with the skill of an experienced professional.

Finally he pronounced, "Your biggest problem is your nerves." He looked about the cell. "And that is certainly understandable." He looked back at me. "You have been under tremendous stress over the past few days, and your nerves are in bad shape. You should try to relax your mind and your body. These people will not hurt you if you do what they tell you. You must try to think about other things. Like your family. Do you think about your family?"

"Yes, oh yes!" I replied. "I love my family! I think about them all the time." I started crying. "Doctor, what have I done to deserve this? Why has this happened to me?"

"I can imagine how you feel, *señor*," he tried to comfort me. "I'm afraid I can't do anything about what has happened. But I can help you to relax." He reached into the black bag and pulled out a bottle of tablets. He gave me a pill. "Here, take this! It will help you to sleep." I found my canister of water and took the pill.

Then he opened the bag again and withdrew a syringe.

"I'm going to give you an injection now," he announced. I've always hated shots, but I lay motionless as he plunged the needle into my arm. "Now relax and try to get some sleep" was the last thing I heard. I didn't even hear the doctor leave the room.

IN FULLERTON, the Crisis Management Team gave quick approval to the kidnappers' demand to publish the manifestos, making every effort to comply with the directions as fully as possible.

The first step was to obtain translations of the text from Spanish into English and the various languages required for Europe. A personnel director combed the files and called in Hispanic clerical personnel who were multilingual. The translation work began.

Hartell's advertising agency, Ayer Jorgensen Macdonald of Los Angeles, was notified of the need to produce the ads in a form suitable for insertion in a variety of newspapers. The senior vice-president of the agency suggested to the Crisis Management Team that AJM should take over the whole production process. Hartell agreed.

Even though it was the beginning of a three-day holiday —Columbus Day—AJM mobilized a team consisting of media and traffic personnel, the art director, the production supervisor, and technical experts who researched the mechanical requirements for the various publications. Agency executives telephoned the American newspapers that evening to apprise them of the situation and arrange for publication on Wednesday. In every case, the head of the advertising departments of the newspapers agreed to withhold the story about the proclamations from their editorial staffs. They accepted the rationale that premature news coverage could endanger the lives of the hostages.

The around-the-clock effort made by AJM personnel, along with a crew from John Adams & Son—the engravers who printed the ads on Sunday—made possible the completion of the project within less than forty-eight hours. The couriers dispatched the finished products to the *Los Angeles Times,* the *New York Times,* and Fred Rayne in San Salvador.

Rita, Veronica, Helen, and Grandma were home when John Pike arrived Saturday morning. The two girls made themselves scarce. When John didn't volunteer any information, Rita asked the perfunctory question: "Have you heard any more news from Hartell?"

"As a matter of fact," he said, putting his briefcase on the kitchen table, "I have!" With the flair of a magician producing a rabbit, he withdrew from his briefcase a cassette tape. "A couple of our men just flew in from San Salvador, and they brought this with them!" He handed the plastic box to Rita.

For a moment she just stared at it. A wide array of emotions swept over her. She was jarred into action by John's words: "Well, aren't you going to listen to it?"

To his amazement and chagrin, Rita turned away from him and hurried down the hallway to the back bedrooms. She found Veronica, Helen, and the tape recorder in their room. The three of them went into Rita's room and closed the door.

The girls sprawled out across the king-sized bed, and Rita turned on the recorder. After an eternity, they heard a familiar voice speaking in Spanish:

"My name is Fausto Bucheli. I live in the United States and I work for the Hartell Company. I am in good health. I am fine. The people here treat me very well. They give me everything I need. I have no reason to feel wrong toward these people. I am treated very well. They are very decent people."

The three listeners began to cry. There was no question that it was Fausto's voice. He was still alive! The tears were, in part, tears of relief. But the sound of the voice brought a lot of pain as well. It was a forceful reminder of reality—that Fausto was being held hostage in God-knows-what conditions. From the manner in which he spoke, it was obvious to them that he was reading something written by someone else. And the one thing they could count on was that none of the statements about his well-being was true. There was entirely too much emphasis on how "fine" he was. He didn't *sound* well at all.

The remainder of the tape didn't make much sense to them. He read from a newspaper, and what he read was of no significance to them.

Rita rewound the tape and played it again. Then she sent the girls to round up the rest of the family and to bring Gert

Verhoeven. Again the clan convened behind the closed doors of the master bedroom. This was a family matter: John Pike would have been an intruder.

Rita played the tape one sentence at a time. As each statement was heard, Rita hit the pause button and translated it for Gert. When the message was complete, they all talked together about what they had heard—how Fausto sounded, what the tape meant, how good it was to hear his voice, how painful it was to imagine the circumstances in which the tape was made. It was probably the first time the family had really talked together about what they were going through and how they felt.

Eventually everyone drifted back into the family room. One of the girls put an album by Elvis Presley on the stereo turntable. It was her dad's favorite record. Somehow it seemed like the thing to do.

The appropriateness of her choice was confirmed as they listened to the last song on the side: "It's a Matter of Time." Each member of the family was absorbed in his or her own thoughts; yet each was intensely aware of the presence of the others. It was a poignant scene—one that would remain sharply focused in each memory for a lifetime. The rendition was vintage Elvis; the song belonged to Fausto.

> It's a matter of time before I go back there,
> A matter of time before I go home.
> I have been away from her for a long time,
> And I've lived a life as I thought that it should be.
> It's a long, long way from "now" to "maybe sometime,"
> And the waiting 'round is really killing me.
> It's a matter of time before I go back there,
> A matter of time before I go home.
> It's a long way, I know, and the goin' ain't easy;
> She'll see me again—it's a matter of time.

As John Pike was preparing to go home that evening, Rita asked him, "John, do you know where Fausto's suitcases are?"

"Why, I think they are still in his room at El Camino Real."

"Do you mean that they are still paying for that room even though he is not there?" she questioned.

"Yes, I guess so!"

"Do you think you could have them sent home to me here?"

"Are you sure that's what you want?"

"Yes, I'm sure," Rita answered.

"Then I'll see what I can do," he said as he walked out the door.

"I would really appreciate that," she said. "Good night!"

† † †

Day 17 (*Sunday, 7 October*)

WHEN I awoke, I found myself lying in a pool of sweat. I became aware of the presence of a guard. My first thought was: *How did I get so wet?* The second was: *If I am waking up, I must have been asleep!* It was the first time since my kidnapping that I experienced the sensation of real sleep.

The guard must have come to check on me. I spoke to him: "How long have I been sleeping?"

He shrugged. "Maybe twenty-four hours! I don't know—a long time!" He left the cell.

My body had a washed-out feeling, the way one feels the day after a severe bout of flu. My muscles were very weak, as though I had just completed running a marathon. But the sleep had done me good. I could tell that, on the whole, my condition was not nearly so dire as it had been.

Ocho entered the cubicle bearing two cans of water and a towel. As I rinsed myself off, I noted that my rash was not as severe as it had been. Ocho took my water canister to refill it and returned with a helping of fried bananas. I ate a little and drank a lot. During the meal I surveyed my cell and noticed that the population of cockroaches and spiders had all but disappeared. Either the encroachment of humans on their habitat had driven them into hiding, or the guards had succeeded in stomping them into extinction. In any event, I was encouraged by their disappearance.

After Ocho removed the remains of Sunday dinner, I penciled two marks on the wall—one of them to account for my long sleep. Satisfied that I was caught up with my record-keeping, I picked up the New Testament and attempted to read the first chapter of the gospel of Matthew.

I was too weak to read. I put down the New Testament and fell back to sleep.

16
The Divine Defendant

I HAD NEVER READ the Bible before. It seems that all my life I have been surrounded by religious people. I went to parochial school as a youngster and was taught the catechism of the Roman Catholic Church. I had heard sermons and had engaged in discussions about God.

But I had never read the Bible itself for myself.

At last I had the opportunity and the strength to begin. During my third week in captivity I read through the New Testament for the first time.

As a means of occupying my mind in a constructive enterprise, it was a positive undertaking. But in many ways it was also difficult. For one thing, there was a great deal that I did not understand. This was certainly due in part to my lack of background knowledge. The New Testament was written nineteen hundred years ago in a different cultural setting. Another difficulty stemmed from contradictions between what I was reading and what I had been taught. As a child I had not paid a great deal of attention to the subject matter of my religion classes. Yet much that I had retained did not harmonize with what I found in the New Testament. This was confusing.

More disturbing, however, were the conflicts between what I was reading and what I had experienced in the spiritual

175

realm. I was subject to such a mixed bag of positive and negative influences over the years that I had long since despaired of ever sorting out "the truth." Yet I was reading a book that claimed to tell the truth about a person who called himself "The Truth." Questions that I had repeatedly suppressed were raised again and again by this book. I realized that if I was going to continue reading, I would have to wrestle with issues I had steadfastly refused to confront.

Among the host of influences that produced tension as I read were my parents.

My father had a saying that he repeated often enough to make a strong impression on me: "The only god you will ever need is in your pocket." He was what one might call an atheistic materialist. He was a good man who worked hard and earned everything he acquired. He never had use for formal religion. He figured that if there was such a place as heaven, a person could buy a ticket to gain entrance.

My mother's beliefs could hardly be more opposite my father's. She was born and bred Latin American Roman Catholic. Her parents were patrons and benefactors of Catholic institutions throughout Ecuador. My aunt became a mother superior; one uncle was an archbishop; another became a parish priest. Everyone on my mother's side of the family hoped that I, as the eldest son, would continue the tradition by becoming a high-ranking clergyman in the Catholic Church. Some of my relatives even told me that if I didn't follow in the family tradition, I would go to hell when I died. That really scared me when I was small.

In such matters, my father's influence ultimately determined my attitudes. He conceded that religion was all right for women, but he didn't want his sons to have any part of it. When my mother pressured him to enroll me in a parochial school, he gave his consent only because he was persuaded that I could get the best overall education there. But he continually resisted the influence of religion in my life, counteracting the effects of religious instruction with long walks among the eucalyptus trees during which he taught and argued for his philosophy of life.

One incident in particular seemed to confirm thee validity of his contempt for religion. By the time I became a teen-ager, I shared my father's disdain for ritual. I faked my way through catechism, but I frequently skipped Mass altogether. For this infraction I had to endure the discipline of a whack on the back of each hand with a twelve-inch wooden ruler. After experiencing this form of punishment a few times, I learned that if I lowered my outstretched hands just before the moment of impact, the force of the blow was lessened and the pain diminished.

The priest who administered this discipline was no less observant than I, and he began to compensate for my predictable flinches. On one occasion he over-reached and caught my forehead with a corner of the ruler. The wound bled and he panicked. After stanching the flow of blood with tissue paper and pressure, he performed cosmetic surgery, covering the scratch with rubber cement and pulling strands of hair down to camouflage the injury.

I said nothing about the incident when I got home, but my father noticed that my hair was combed differently. When he asked about it, I told him what had happened. My father stands five-feet-eleven and must have weighed 250 pounds. When he became angry, he was terrifying. And he was angry.

He grabbed me by the hand, pulled me out to his big Chrysler sedan, and went roaring down the road to the monastery. The car came screeching to a halt right in front of the iron gate at the entrance. A small man in a priest's garb peered out at us from the other side of the metal bars. *"Buenos dias, señor!"* he began. But my father shoved the big gate open, pushing the little man aside, grabbed me by the hand again, and pulled me along after him.

My father rampaged across the courtyard. We came upon a group of monks who were walking, hands folded and heads bowed, in a solemn procession. Father stopped the first two priests dead in their tracks and demanded to know the whereabouts of my assailant. As they stood there in stunned silence, another man came running up to us, pleading, "Please, *señor*, these men are in complete seclusion! They cannot speak to you!"

"Then you tell me where my son's teacher is!" my father demanded. The frightened priest directed us to the room. We mounted a flight of stairs two at a time, and father pounded on a door. When the unsuspecting instructor opened his door, my father grabbed him by his robes, hoisted him back into his room, and pinned him against the wall.

"Why did you hit my boy?" he yelled.

"He m-missed the Mass!" stammered the priest.

Father reached back with his right hand and hit the man on the jaw. "If you ever even look cross-eyed at my son," he warned, "you will never see him in your school again! But you can expect to see me!"

He let go of the teacher and stomped from the room. "Come on!" he ordered me. "Let's get out of here!"

I couldn't believe it! My father actually punched a priest!

As I read through the New Testament in my cell and reflected on the things my mother taught me and the things I learned in school, I realized how much of my religion was grounded in fear. Perhaps the reason my father impressed me so much was that he was not afraid. Nevertheless, most of my concepts about the nature of God, the person of Jesus, the status of the Virgin Mary, and the character of religious experience had their roots in that childhood exposure to Catholicism.

I did not fare much better, as a young adult, in my experiences with Evangelicals. I had to admit that I carried a built-in hostility toward anything religious into my relationships with these people. I resented the place of priority that Rita gave to her faith in Christ. On the whole, the way the evangelicals presented and represented God was far more positive than anything I had previously encountered. Moreover, missionaries Doug Hodges and Paul Erdel, who founded Light and Liberty Christian School and were very close to Rita, proved to be good friends in spite of my spiritual delinquency.

Once again, however, a single experience confirmed my prejudice against pious-sounding people and soured me on Rita's alternative to Catholicism. The incident occurred two-and-one-half years after we were married, and it could not have happened at a worse time.

Just before Fausto Jr. was born in May 1963, I lost my job at F.A.S.A. over a dispute I had with another pilot. I couldn't find another job. That summer the school at which Rita taught reviewed the contracts of all the teachers. Rita not only had the highest degree of any of the teachers, but also a nationwide reputation as one of the most innovative teachers of young children. She had no reason to suspect that her position in the school was in jeopardy. In fact, there had been some discussion about her becoming the principal.

But a national pastor, taking advantage of the absence of Paul Erdel who was in the United States on furlough, persuaded the young missionary left in charge of the school that Rita's contract should not be renewed. His stated basis for dismissing her was that she was married to an unbeliever and thus in violation of the principles for which the school stood. His reason became evident later.

A letter was drafted and delivered by the missionary to Rita informing her of her termination. The emotional shock to Rita was so great that our nursing infant became violently ill from drinking her spoiled milk. The scene that I happened upon as I returned home from an unsuccessful search for work was beyond comprehension. The baby was screaming, Rita was crying, and I could not figure out what was wrong. All I could get from Rita at first was "How can they do this to me after all that I've done for that school!"

Finally Rita showed me the letter, and I flew into a rage of my own. "They cannot do that to you!" I shouted. "It is against the law for them to fire you for that reason! I'm going to have that school shut down!"

"No!" she screamed as she tore the letter from my grasp. Helplessly I watched her rip it to shreds. "That school is for the children, and it belongs to the Lord. He will take care of what has happened."

That wasn't satisfactory to me. I called the State Superintendent of Schools and told him what happened. he said, "If you give me the letter of dismissal, I will close down the school." But I didn't have the letter, so he could do nothing.

I went to see the missionary. "What kind of Christians are you?" I asked him. "I thought you were supposed to be different! You knew that I was out of work! Now Rita doesn't have a job! And you have the gall to kick her out after all that she has done to get that school started in the first place!"

He said, "I understand how you must feel. I'm really sorry." I almost hit him.

Instead I said, "Well, don't look for us in church! And it

would be a good idea for you not to walk in front of my car in the near future!" And I stormed out of his house.

Someone immediately wrote to Paul Erdel in the United States to inform him what had happened, and he cut short his furlough to return to Esmeraldas.

In the meantime, within three days Rita got another teaching position in a government school. I got some satisfaction from the fact that her salary was tripled, the assignment was more prestigious, and the hours were reduced. She was glad for the job, but her heart had been in Christian education.

When Paul arrived in Ecuador, he came to see us right away. "I am so sorry about what has happened!" he apologized. "The whole thing was a terrible mistake."

"Mistake?" I protested. "It was one of your missionaries who delivered the letter to Rita!"

"That's true!" he agreed. "And he probably should have done more to prevent it from happening. But it was the Ecuadorian pastor who insisted. We have since learned that he just wanted to obtain the position for his wife. There isn't a great deal that we can do about them because they are no longer with us."

"What do you mean?" asked Rita.

"They took all of the money in the school's account and disappeared. We don't know where they are! I'm just sick about the whole thing."

"I'm really sorry to hear about that!" consoled Rita.

"I've come to ask you to forgive us, Rita," said Paul, "and to formally request that you consider returning to your position at Light and Liberty."

I didn't give her a chance to answer. "She can't do that!" I said. "She has a contract with the government school. It's too late for her to change what she is doing now." Then I added, "And even if she could, I wouldn't let her."

"Fausto," said Paul, "it grieves me that these things happen in the Christian church. I deeply regret that you and Rita have been hurt by all of this. I just want you to know that I love you, and I still want to be your friend—if you will permit that. And I hope that some day the pain in your heart will be healed."

It did take time—a long time—for healing to come to Rita's

wounded spirit. Her faith was in no way shaken, but it wasn't until we had lived in Berne for a few years that she fully participated again in the ministry of a church.

I had mixed emotions over the entire affair. On the one hand, I was saddened by Rita's pain. But there was a part of me that secretly rejoiced over the whole debacle. In my "righteous indignation" I could point the finger of judgment at the Evangelicals. They had had the audacity to say I was a "sinner," but they had proved themselves to be no better than I. With the spotlight focused on the church's one glaring failure, all the pressure that I had been feeling to participate in church life simply evaporated.

For his part, Paul Erdel remained true to his commitment to us. Four years later, when Rita became ill in Detroit, it was Paul who made arrangements for us to come to Indiana—a move that proved to be a turning point for our family.

During the period of our transition to life in America, I generally succeeded in putting spiritual matters on a shelf. Survival—getting work, learning a new language, adjusting to a different culture—demanded most of my time and energy. Rita didn't push so hard for church attendance, mostly because she couldn't understand or speak English.

With the move to Indiana, several things happened that changed our direction. The month that we stayed with the Erdels rekindled the desire within Rita to have fellowship with other Christians and to nurture her spiritual life. So when we found a home in Berne, we began visiting various churches. I even went with her for a time because I knew of no other place, besides work, where I could make new friends and find acceptance in the community.

I don't know how the people of Berne regard that time now, but for us it was very difficult. To put it bluntly, the people seemed cold and aloof. It may well have been that they weren't sure what to do. They may have felt awkward with people who spoke English falteringly, or hardly at all. But it disturbed us that few seemed to reach out to us. As far as I was concerned, that behavior reflected poorly on their Christianity.

The one undeniable exception was another missionary: Gerald Stuckey. Home on furlough from his regular assignment in Colombia, Gerald worked as an associate to the pastor of the

Mennonite church. He was a frequent visitor in our home. His knowledge of Latin American customs and his willingness to speak with us in Spanish, which he spoke fluently, endeared him to Rita. It took him longer to overcome my antipathy for missionaries in general, but his genuine warmth and concern for our well-being won me over eventually. I believe he probably helped other people in the church to know how to relate to us as we learned how to live as Americans.

Gerald was the first person with whom I felt comfortable discussing God and spiritual issues. Much that he told me I had already heard from Rita, Doug Hodges, and Paul Erdel. But Gerald was able to interact with me. For the first time I asked questions because I really wanted to know. It wasn't enough for me to hear what someone believed; I wanted to know *why* he accepted those things.

Eventually I talked with Gerald of my resentment toward those who professed to be Christians. "How can these people preach about love all the time and yet be so indifferent or even cruel to others?" I challenged. "How can I believe in what they are telling me when they seem to live like everyone else?"

Gerald was silent for a while. Finally he said, "Fausto, in all of the universe there is only one perfect person. There is only one person who lives perfectly, loves completely, never hurts anyone. There is only one God.

"I don't say that to excuse the behavior of God's children," he continued. "But the fact of the matter is, we are people. We are sinners. Receiving Christ as one's Savior does not keep a person from ever doing anything wrong again. I love you very much. I don't want to ever hurt you as others have. But I could. The point is, the fact that there are imperfect Christians, or perhaps people who claim to be Christians but aren't, does not make the gospel invalid."

"But if it doesn't change the way people live, then what good is it?" I questioned.

"If it doesn't change the way people live," he replied, "it isn't any good at all! To say that we don't become perfect is not to say that there is *no* change. God wants us to become like His Son, Jesus. Part of His provision for that is forgiveness of our past sins. And part of His provision is a changed character that makes it possible for us to grow in holiness.

"Unfortunately," he continued, "we tend to remember the damage that people inflict on us. We often don't see the quiet growth in positive qualities—especially if we're looking for the bad, which non-Christians often do." He really jabbed me with that point. But for some reason I didn't get upset.

"Let me ask you a question!" he said. "Do you know any people who profess to be Evangelicals whose lives are consistent with their beliefs?"

I didn't have to think very long. "Yes, I do."

"All right," he responded, "how are you going to determine the legitimacy of the Christian message? Are you going to count the number of professing believers who, in your judgment, don't practice what they preach and compare it with the number of Christians that you deem to be consistent?"

I thought about that.

"Wouldn't just one Christian whose life consistently reflects the attractive effects of walking with God argue forcefully for the truth of the Gospel?" he reasoned.

"To tell you the truth, Gerald," I replied, "I haven't looked at it that way before. I'll need to think about it some more."

"In the final analysis, Fausto," he concluded, "the truth of Christianity has to be weighed on its own merits. The issue is not Christians, but Christ. You should not believe in Him because I say you should, but because you are convinced that what the Bible says about Him—and you—is true. You have plenty of excuses to disregard Jesus. But if you will take the trouble to look, I think you will find compelling reasons to turn to Him."

In fact, I had already done some personal research into the historic founder of Christianity. Not long after we moved to Berne I purchased a set of *Encyclopedia Britannica*. Out of curiosity I looked up and read articles on several historical figures: Thomas Edison, Shakespeare, Dr. Faustus[1] (my namesake), and Jesus Christ. The material on Jesus was impressive. For one thing, fifteen pages were devoted to His life and subsequent impact on history. For another, He was treated as a historical figure, and the accounts of His life were regarded as being reliable.

[1]The historical Faustus is a shadowy figure, Johann Faust (c. 1480-c. 1538), a German astrologer, alchemist, and magician who has been immortalized in literature and legend since his death.

At the end of the article was a list of resources for further study. I bought a couple of the books and read them. They spoke highly of the integrity of the Bible as a record of God's dealings with men.

When I took breaks from reading my Spanish New Testament through the days of my third week of captivity, these thoughts and recollections swirled in my mind. The mental images and records of conversations did not appear in the neat chronological order in which I have just presented them. Sometimes they were triggered by what I was reading; at other times they intruded upon my attempts to digest the meaning or ramifications of a particular passage. Some great debate always seemed to be raging in the courtroom of my soul.

The one question that loomed in the background and overshadowed all the others concerned my present situation. From time to time it would break through to the forefront, and I would push it away. But at last it demanded my attention. In its simplest form, it could be expressed in two words: "Why me?"

It could also be expressed in more than two words, and with great feeling: "What could I possibly have done to deserve such horrible treatment?". . ."I don't belong here! I wouldn't even be here if I hadn't decided to put my family ahead of my business. Is this the reward I get?" . . . "What great crime have I committed? Is it so wrong to try to help these people?" . . . "If you are a God of love, a God who answers prayer, why haven't You done something to get me out of here?" . . . "Don't You at least care about my family?"

When it all came pouring out, I suppose I raised all the philosophical questions that a person victimized by tragedy and evil shouts at heaven. But for me, the questions were not academic.

It was somewhat frightening when I suddenly realized that I was putting God on trial. I was demanding that He answer to me for His failure to perform as I thought He should. Scandalized, I tried to retreat from that stance; but I knew that I could desist from my prosecution only at the expense of honesty. I had nothing to gain by ignoring the problems, and nothing to lose by asking for answers. If God was the defendant, so be it. His Bible would be His testimony. As Gerald Stuckey had said, the case would stand or fall on its own merits.

I ceased shaking my fist at the Almighty. Instead I prayed:

> God, if You are there, and this is Your book, help me to understand what I am reading. I just got confused the first time, and I can't afford that now!

With sober determination I started through the Divine Transcripts a second time.

WITH THE copies of the terrorists' manifesto in his possession, Fred Rayne began the distribution. The Crisis Management Team in Fullerton was handling the American newspapers. Rayne would orchestrate delivery of the ads to the other thirty papers.

To do this, he recruited nine couriers to take the proclamations to the specified countries of Central and South America. Each man was instructed to do whatever it took to get the manifesto published in the designated newspapers. Each courier was to remain in place until the document was printed. Then copies of each newspaper were to be purchased and returned to Rayne in San Salvador.

Rayne himself took the manifesto to Europe. He hired an advertising agency in Switzerland to place the ads in the continental newspapers. He dealt with the London newspapers himself. The *London Times* refused to cooperate in the publication of terrorist propaganda, and the persistent Rayne was finally expelled from the premises. He did succeed in placing an ad in the *Daily Mirror* and the *Evening News*.

17

A Matter of Timing

Day 20 *(Wednesday, 10 October)*

ACROSS THE FRONT-page of the *Register*, a major newspaper of Orange County, California, ran the bold, black headline: KIDNAP DEMANDS. Beneath it in red letters was a subheadline: "[Hartell] to Pay for Ransom Ads." Smaller explanatory headings read, "Company Hoping to Save Workers" and "Two Were Abducted Last Month." The article by staff writer Kim Murphy said in part:

> Fast-paced negotiations over the weekend produced a pair of two-page newspaper advertisements that [Hartell Industries] officials hope will be the key to saving two of their employees kidnapped last month in El Salvador.
>
> Wednesday editions of the New York Times and The Los Angeles Times carry what El Salvador's Revolutionary Party of Central American Workers calls a "revolutionary proclamation" which party members said may be the only ticket to freedom for two Orange County-area businessmen abducted Sept. 21. . . .
>
> Advertisements appearing today in two American newspapers and slated for publication later this week in Central American and European publications represent the first ransom demands issued by the leftist guerrilla organization that kidnapped the two businessmen and killed their Salvadorian bodyguard, Jose Luis Paz Tratara. . . .
>
> "To ensure the safe return of its two employees [Hartell] is

complying with the PRTC demands," said president [Russell Shannon]. "The company expects the safe return of its employees after the advertisements have appeared."

Company officials have been assured that [Chapman] and Bucheli are in "good condition," [Shannon] said. . . .

[Hartell] officials, who have consistently declined to comment on the kidnapping, would not confirm one U.S. State Department official's report that the company flew an employee to El Salvador this weekend to negotiate with the kidnappers.

"I'm not going to jeopardize the lives of those two men by talking about it," said [Shannon]. "We're doing what we were asked. We're trying to save our people."

The combined cost for the two two-page ads was slightly more than $62,000.

Day 21 *(Thursday, 11 October)*

Almost one week after he brought the first tape from El Salvador, John Pike arrived at the Bucheli home with Fausto's suitcases. As before, Gert was immediately sent for. Rita could not bring herself to act until Gert was there.

Once again the group went into the bedroom, secluded from John Pike. As Fausto Jr. opened the suitcases, the girls broke into sobbing. All Gert, uncomprehending, saw was clothing—shirts, slacks, underwear—neatly folded and carefully set in place. She looked bewildered.

"It's just him!" Rita exclaimed. "That's how he packs! He is the most meticulous man I've ever seen. Everything has to be folded just so and placed just so." As she looked at the clothes, she too began to weep.

Fausto left the bedroom. It was still difficult for him to display emotion in the presence of others; but the suitcases had the same effect on him as on the others. In his room he grieved silently. When he felt in control of himself again, he picked up the telephone.

"Pastor Crocker! This is Fausto Bucheli. The company my dad works for just brought us his suitcases. Seeing them, you know, without him being here . . ." His voice trailed away.

Don Crocker was quick to grasp the situation. "I'll be right over, Fausto."

When Pastor Don arrived, Fausto met him and they joined

Rita and Gert in the bedroom sanctuary. Fausto picked up an airlines ticket from one of the suitcases. "There are some things in here, Pastor Don, that are puzzling. Some of these things—his pens, this notepad, the plastic pocket protector—he always carried with him. They shouldn't be in the suitcase if he was kidnapped before he got back to the hotel."

"Rita and I have been talking about this!" Gert offered. "It doesn't add up. When Fausto is at work, he always has those things with him. How did they get into his suitcase?"

There was no answer.

After a moment Don asked Rita, "How are you feeling?"

"I guess I'm about as low today as I have been since the first night."

"Why do you think seeing these suitcases has hit you so hard?"

"Because they're here,"—she started to weep again—"and he's not!"

Gert put her arm around Rita, whose face was buried in a pillow. "It's been like a funeral here ever since that luggage arrived," Gert said. "It's as though those bags held his ashes."

Rita raised her head and blurted, "Well, that *is* all that remains of him—as far as we're concerned." She buried her face in the pillow again.

There was silence. Then, when Rita's grief was spent, she sat up and wiped her eyes. "What I can't figure out, Pastor, is this," she said at last. "If God can return Fausto's suitcase to us, why can't He get Fausto back home?"

"You are right about the one task not being any more difficult for Him than the other," Don replied quietly.

"Then it's a question of 'why,' isn't it!" she reasoned. "*Why* did God return the suitcases without Fausto? Are we being punished for something we've done?"

"Those questions I understand, believe me!" said Don. "I promised you, Rita, that I wouldn't offer superficial answers to deep questions. But I can share some insights that I believe the Lord has given to me.

"First of all, it is not a matter of punishment. According to the Bible, as I understand it, punishment is reserved for those who reject God and rebel against His rule. God doesn't punish His children—those who trust in Him as we do. He does see fit to discipline us from time to time, but we have been exempted from punishment by Jesus Christ."

"I don't see any difference between punishment and discipline," replied Rita. "They both hurt—and this hurts."

"I'm not sure how critical the distinction is between the two," responded Don. "I just know that it has helped me to realize that my leukemia is not a curse from God to judge me for my wickedness. It is something that has come upon me because I live in a sin-infested world. It is true that God has allowed the disease to infect my body. And He hasn't told me why I am sick any more than He ever explained Job's boils to him. But I know that He loves me, and He intends for this difficult circumstance to discipline my life—to help me to trust in Him more, and to equip me to serve Him better."

Don paused to let his explanation sink in. "For what it's worth," he resumed, "it has had that effect on me. Having a 'terminal illness' has helped me to sort out what is really important in life. As I told you the other day, it has made me more open to learn from the Lord and to accept what He has for me."

Rita said nothing, but it was apparent to Don that the issue was far from resolved within her. "Look!" he said, "I realize that it isn't really fair for me to compare my situation with yours—they are two different circumstances."

Rita interrupted him. "Oh no, Pastor Crocker, that's all right! I appreciate what you are saying."

"It's just that sometimes you wonder how long it's going to be before the Lord says, 'Enough is enough,' right?" Don took a stab at mind-reading.

Her eyes widened in acknowledgment. "Right!"

"It seems to me," he ventured, "that in many of these situations, the question is not so much 'what' or 'why' as it is 'how long.' Frankly, we don't know what is going to happen. You are feeling today as if Fausto is never going to come home. But you don't know that he is not going to be released. You just can't figure out why, if God is going to set him free, He is taking so long to do it."

"I guess that's right!" Rita agreed.

"Well, that's a question God never answers ahead of time!" Don said. "All I know is that He doesn't operate according to our schedules. We get all upset if things don't happen the way we want them to when we want them to. For us, everything is instant. He tends to take longer. That's one abiding impression I get from the Bible: God is never in a hurry."

Rita looked at the suitcases. "It seems as if it's been forever. I don't know how long I can go on like this."

"He does!" Don assured her. "That's the other thing about the Lord's timing. He may not be in a hurry, but He's never late either. He knows just how long it is going to take to accomplish His purposes. Believe me, Rita," Don added, "you don't want to change that about God. If you could, and you did—if you changed God's timing—you would deeply regret it. He knows what He's doing."

Rita rose from the bed and very deliberately closed the suitcases and moved them to the far side of the room. Then she turned to Don and said, "I guess we won't have you officiate Fausto's funeral today. I will wait and see what the Lord is going to do. But I sure hope, when this is all over, that He lets me know what He was waiting for."

Don smiled. "Maybe He will."

18
Setting a Prisoner Free

WHILE THE PRTC proclamations were being placed in the European newspapers by the Swiss agency, Fred Rayne flew back to the United States for consultations with the Crisis Management Team in Fullerton. Then he returned to his Sheraton Hotel command post in San Salvador to monitor the efforts of his Latin American couriers.

Carlos called again during the morning of October 12. The conversants used the agreed code. "Did our manifesto run in the two American papers?" he asked.

"Yes!" replied Juan Ortega. He didn't elaborate.

"Good!" said Carlos. "Then you can pass on to Señor Rayne our final demand."

"Señor Rayne is here," replied Juan. "He is standing by to receive your proposal."

"Once we have received all of the copies of our manifesto, on schedule, we will be prepared to sell your men back to you," Carlos offered.

"How much?" Fred Rayne asked.

Carlos quoted him an astronomical figure—in the millions of dollars.

"That's preposterous!" Fred exploded. "I've been in this business for years, and I have never heard a more absurd offer!

Hartell would never agree to pay such an outrageous price—
especially after what they have paid to have your propaganda
spread all over the world!"

"Don't lecture me, Señor Rayne!" Carlos responded. "We
are discussing the lives of two human beings. They are of great
value to you! But to us they are expendable! If we kill them—
which you know we are prepared to do—we will just get more
money for the next capitalist pigs we kidnap!"

"Well, you won't get it from us!" Fred declared, standing
his ground.

"I think," rejoined Carlos, "that you had better deliver our
demand to your people in California. We will give you six hours
to give us an affirmative reply."

"That's not long enough!" Fred protested. "Consideration
of a ransom demand requires the convening of the entire corporate board. I can't give you an answer in six hours."

"Ten hours, then!" said Carlos. And the line went dead.

† † †

MY THIRD full week in captivity would have to be rated as
better than the first two. That is like saying that a formerly
"critical" patient has been upgraded to merely "serious" condition. But my reading project made life infinitely more bear-
able, even if I hardly felt up to it physically. In addition, with
the guards no longer posing a constant threat to my life, I was
beginning to get some sleep each night.

In the meantime, if I may put it crudely, God was acquit-
ting Himself remarkably well as I read through His "defense" a
second time. By the time I had read through the Gospels again, I
had read the story of Jesus eight times. I still didn't understand
everything, but some definite and surprising impressions were
beginning to emerge.

For one thing, I began to perceive Jesus as a compassionate
human being. This was a corrective to childhood images de-
rived from Catholicism. The Jesus I was exposed to as a child
was a statue. Often He was portrayed in agony on a cross. But
always He was distant, cold, aloof, untouchable. The countless
representations of Him in paintings and carved figures seemed
to evoke feelings of guilt by design. Invariably Jesus was as-

sociated with death—rarely with life. He was at best the object of ritualistic devotion, to be approached only through the mediation of priests.

The Jesus I met in the New Testament was entirely different. What I came to appreciate most was His care for hurting people. Everywhere He went He set people free from bondage to illness, evil spirits, and even death.

On the other hand, Jesus often expressed indignation over hypocrisy in no uncertain terms. It was revealing to see that Jesus was more concerned with religious play-actors than even I was.

There were other things, however, that puzzled me. It was obvious that this Man had great power—He could multiply fish and bread, walk on water, and calm raging storms. And He also evidenced a great love for people. He could have become the greatest human ruler the world had ever known—and there were people who wanted Him to do precisely that—but He never used that power to overthrow oppressive governments. He didn't even bring physical healing to all who were sick—He restored only those who came to Him for help. I would have expected that anyone with such powers would do more to correct or overturn the evils of this world.

One incident in particular really seemed to bring these observations into focus for me. Jesus once read a prophecy from Isaiah that He applied to Himself:

> The Spirit of the Lord is on me; therefore he has anointed me to preach good news to the poor. He has sent me to proclaim freedom for the prisoners and recovery of sight for the blind, to release the oppressed, to proclaim the year of the Lord's favor (*Luke 4:18–19*).

I especially identified with the references to "freedom for the prisoners" and "release" for "the oppressed." Yet, just prior to the occasion of this reading, Jesus' forerunner, John the Baptist, had been imprisoned by a King Herod. And Jesus never did anything about it. John was beheaded. Given the twin realities of Jesus' ability to set John free and His stated mission of releasing the oppressed, I couldn't help but wonder at the outcome. What were the ramifications for my own situation?

I was impressed by the amount of attention given by the

gospel writers to the events leading up to and following the
crucifixion of Jesus. As I read the details four more times, several things struck me as significant. One was the terrible injustice of the whole process that culminated in His execution. Related to this was the extreme indignity and pain inflicted upon
Him. Yet he could have prevented any of that from happening.
He even said so more than once.

But Jesus deliberately subjected Himself to that torture. He
told His disciples that He would be killed, then raised again on
the third day. At one point He explained: "For even the Son of
Man did not come to be served, but to serve, and to give his life
a ransom for many" (Mark 10:45). Though I didn't yet understand what that statement meant, the word *ransom* leaped from
the page. It was obvious from the gospel accounts that Jesus
intended to die on the cross and that He perceived of this death
as a kind of sacrifice on behalf of others.

I had been asking why God didn't do something about my
situation. His answer, through the New Testament, was that
He *had* done something about it. I had thought that an
omnipotent God should point His finger and erase all evil and
pain and injustice from human experience. But He didn't do
that. Instead He chose to endure that evil and pain and injustice Himself. I did not then, and do not now, understand all
the ramifications of this. But after witnessing the crucifixion of
Jesus eight times in a single week, I believed that God had
done something about our situation and that what He had
done was significant.

My second exposure to the Book of Acts was also an exciting adventure. For one thing, the followers of Jesus were continually being thrown in prison: and again I identified with
this. For another, I could see the effects of faith in Christ in the
lives of His disciples.

In some ways the Book of Acts affected me even more than
the Gospels had. Certain events held special interest to me. Like
the time that two of Jesus' disciples, James and Peter, were
imprisoned by another King Herod. James was executed. But
God sent an angel and miraculously set Peter free. Why did God
allow James to die and yet intervene so that Peter might live?
The Bible doesn't say. But it does say that not long thereafter,
God struck down King Herod because of his wickedness.

What I began to see was that, according to the New Testament, God is actively involved in the affairs of mankind. Sometimes He deems direct intervention to be appropriate; at other times He seems to let matters run their course. But He apparently has reasons for what He does and does not do. And they are not always revealed. God reserves the right to act without giving an accounting of His behavior to anyone other than Himself. In short, He reserves the right to be God.

As I reflected on my own captivity and compared my experiences with those of whom I was reading, a glaring contrast became evident. I had been an "innocent bystander," as it were, caught between two warring factions, neither of which had any real claims on my loyalty. But these people in the Bible were being persecuted for a reason over which they had control—namely, their allegiance to Jesus.

If I had reason to ask "Why me?" surely they had even more cause. I had been kidnapped while going about my own business. But they were arrested, beaten, and thrown into jail for going about God's business. Yet they never asked "Why me?" They did not challenge God's integrity; they never insisted that he do something constructive to prove Himself and relieve them of their unjust affliction. Quite the contrary! They rejoiced over the privilege of suffering for the cause of Christ. On one notable occasion, two Christians were arrested, flogged, and imprisoned far from home with their legs in stocks. Their response? At midnight they were serenading the guards and other prisoners with hymns to God!

One of those men was Saul of Tarsus, who later became known as Paul the Apostle. He probably influenced me more than any other man. I identified strongly with him. Before he became a Christian, he was a man of position and influence in his community. He was intelligent and well-educated. He was, if I may put it this way, a gentleman from the upper class of society. He was hard-working, aggressive, and persistent in the pursuit of his goals. And while I thought of myself as being an essentially good person, Paul could claim to be genuinely good. He was scrupulous in his obedience to the laws of God. He was, in fact, proud of his achievements as a religious man.

But when confronted by Jesus Christ, this good man bowed before the Lord and acknowledged that he had been fighting against Him. He was converted from a persecutor of Christians to one of their leading spokesmen.

Subsequently Paul endured great hardship for his Savior. Most of the references to imprisonment are about him. The things he endured, I noticed, were more severe than the sufferings I had encountered.

All this knowledge helped me to see my own situation in a different light. I realized that perhaps I should ask "Why me?" from a different perspective. For instance, why was I born in Ecuador to affluent, upper-class parents instead of, say, in El Salvador to a peasant family? Why had I been granted the opportunities of self-advancement in America when I could have been one of four million poverty-ridden people locked into the oppressive Salvadoran system? Why me, indeed?

There is something perverse about us that makes us think that if good things happen to us, it is because we deserve them; but if evil befalls us, we cry about the injustice of it all. I had formed a good deal of my image of myself on the basis of favorable comparisons with others whom I felt were "below" me. And so, in my conversations with Rita, for instance, I was absolutely sincere when I spoke of myself as being "better than some people." On these grounds I had felt that refusal to associate with the lower-class people in her church was justified. By the same token, when I was labeled a "sinner"—first by Rita, then by others in the church—I was able to defend myself on the basis that there were thousands of people who were much worse than I was who really deserved such a designation. In fact, when I witnessed duplicity on the part of Christians, I felt morally superior to them, in spite of the fact that I had been less than honest with Rita in order to gain her hand in marriage!

There in the cell, as I read the New Testament and observed the spiritual pilgrimage of Paul, I recognized that I had been comparing myself in the wrong direction. Witnessing the eightfold crucifixion of Jesus, who gave His life for "sinners," and looking on as Paul, a better man than I, acknowledged his need of a Savior, I came to understand the nature of my sin: selfishness.

I said that I was kidnapped while "going about my own business" in contrast to "going about God's business." Well, I had *always* been going on about my *own* business. I lived my life totally for me. In the final analysis, I followed my father's religion all the way.

But I came to see that, not only is there a God, but He deserves to be worshipped and served. I also saw that those who responded in faith were remarkably happy, even though they got into trouble for it. When their whole reason for living changed, their values changed too. They were no longer citizens of this world only, but members of the kingdom of God. For them the reward of God meant more than the esteem of men. For them death held no terror.

I am not able to recall to what degree these thoughts had crystallized by the twenty-second day. But my personal response to them was brought to a head by the return of Señors Glasses and Skinny. This time they brought the disheartening news that Hartell was balking at their demand for payment of ransom. They had finally gotten around to talking money, and the irresistible force had met the immovable object.

"They don't want anything to do with you, *gringo!*" spat Señor Glasses. "They say, 'You can go ahead and kill that traitor, because we're not going to pay any money!' [I could just imagine these words on the lips of Carl Reynolds!] So we told them that they have ten hours to meet our terms. If they do not change their minds, yours will be the first body we ship out in a box. If they remain stubborn, fifteen minutes later they'll have another one. All that money and two corpses—that's what they'll have if that's what they want!"

Bruce. He was still alive at least! I wondered how he was faring.

Señor Glasses didn't let me wonder for long. He was more grim than angry. "From the way they were talking, you better do some praying. We are not joking about the ten hours. That could be all you have!" The bearers of bad tidings went their grisly way.

When I worked for C.T.S. in Indiana, some of the other employees had posters that read "T.G.I.F."—Thank Goodness It's Friday. Ordinarily I shared that sentiment. But three of the last four Fridays had been life-threatening for me. I was kidnapped on the first one; I was given six hours to live on the third one; and now I was given ten hours to prepare for my end.

My reaction to this death warning was different from the

former one. The first time, I was in such terrible shape that I didn't greatly care what they did to me. I hardly knew whether to take them seriously. But this time, for whatever reasons, I believed that the end of my life was at hand. And I did care.

I began making some rather specific preparations. First I picked up the tablet and pencil and wrote a letter to Rita. I told her how much I love each one of the children and what she means to me. Then I informed her about my insurance policies, instructing her to use the money to pay off the mortgage on the house. I also told her to go to Hartell for financial help and assistance in securing the education of each of the children. If the company couldn't get me out of that pit alive, the least they could do was see to the well-being of my family.

That is, in fact, what I told Hartell Industries in a second letter. I argued that because they were responsible for what had happened to me, they were morally obligated to do what I would not be able to do: provide for my family. I submitted a bill, in advance, for the college education of my children.

Delivery of the two letters posed a major problem. If I merely left them in the cell, I couldn't expect my executioners to mail them out of the kindness of their hearts. If I held on to them or tucked them into my briefs, they would probably be discovered and destroyed. With an ingenuity born of desperation, I rolled up the papers together and inserted them into my rectum like a suppository. My only hope was that somehow an autopsy might be performed on my body. In that way I could in effect deliver the letters myself.

With my last will and testament filed away, I picked up the blue Bible and began "preparing to meet my Maker," as the saying goes. The time for leisurely contemplation had expired. It was time to transact business. God was no longer on trial—I was.

I knew what I needed to do to get right with God. I needed to confess before Him the one thing that I had always tried to deny—that I was a sinner. I needed to throw myself upon the Lord for forgiveness. I needed to bow before Jesus and declare my trust in Him as my Savior.

There was only one problem.

The problem was not doubt. The issue of the validity of faith in Christ had been resolved as I was reading the Bible. My questions had not all been answered fully, but they had been answered sufficiently. God had answered my prayer for understanding.

The problem was not an unwillingness to repent. This had been the bottom-line obstacle all my life. I hadn't turned to God for the simple reason that I didn't want to. But once I gave God my undivided attention, so to speak, I began to see my life from His perspective. Eventually I, like my friend Paul the Apostle, came to adopt that perspective myself. True, Jesus' words to Paul—"It is hard for you to kick against the goads"—could have been addressed to me. But when I stopped kicking, I really wanted to give my life to Him.

And *that* was the problem. I had nothing, really, to give. I was backed into a corner. I was on my deathbed. Under such circumstances, could any confession of faith possibly be legitimate?

This was no small question, and I wrestled with it for a long time. The gravity of the issue was magnified by the fact that I had long been critical of people who turned to God only in times of crisis. He was, for such people, the great Cosmic Crutch. And yet there I was, in my very own foxhole, ready to make a deal with God.

I could see Rita's face as clearly as if she were there. "You see?" she seemed to say. "When you really need Him, that is the time that you turn. You have had so many chances, but only now do you respond."

And it was true. But I couldn't turn the clock back. I couldn't change the past. The only thing I had was the present, and likely not much of that.

I sat up on my mat and got on my knees. I was facing the wall opposite the boarded-up window. I hugged the New Testament to my chest with my left hand and placed my right hand over it on my left breast. Then I spoke, softly but aloud, to God:

> Lord, I don't know the right way to pray. I will just say the words in my heart. I know that You are God, that You are the Lord of Lords. You are the Lord that Rita has told me about so many times.
>
> I admit that I should have come to You sooner. I have done many wrong things in my life, and I am truly sorry that I have not lived for You. I have read about Your Son Jesus, and I want Him to be my Savior and Lord. I want to give my heart to You.

I don't know what is going to happen to me. Maybe I will die soon! If I do, I want to come to be with You. But if I live longer, if You get me out of here, I want to live the rest of my life for You.

Lord, You know that it bothers me that I have not come to You sooner. You know what is in my heart. I am as sincere at this moment as I know how to be. I really mean what I am saying. For whatever remains of my life, You are the Commander-in-Chief.

At that moment something happened that is very difficult to describe. I felt as though someone had placed his hand on top of my head. There seemed to be a "presence" in the cell. I did not see anyone else; but the feeling was very strong, profound.

From the top of my head a wave of coolness flowed down through my body. In that hot, humid cell, I felt cool—I felt good for the only time during the entire captivity. My various ailments and weakness seemed to be replaced with a surge of energy.

I saw myself running free, soaring effortlessly across desert sands. I was in wide-open spaces, without the oppressive heat, unhindered by fatigue.

I do not know what caused these sensations, nor do I recall how long they lasted. At the time I thought that the Lord Himself had come to visit me, that He was with me—and He certainly was. I had already experienced a measure of hell; perhaps I was being given a taste of heaven. Or maybe the angel who escorted Peter from Herod's prison had come to encourage me. In any case, I was convinced that God had heard my prayer. He put a strong sense of hope in my heart and took away any fear of death.

19
Reprieve

Day 22 *(Friday, 12 October, continued)*

FRED RAYNE UNDERSTOOD the Latin American system of bartering. His response to the figure first suggested by the PRTC as a ransom price for the two captives was carefully calculated. He knew that he would get a similar response from them when he made an equally unacceptable counteroffer.

He notified the Crisis Management Team in Fullerton of developments in San Salvador. There was not a great deal to discuss. The team had surmised earlier the options that they could expect. Fred knew what ransom payments had already been made by multinational corporations in similar and recent circumstances. He knew the extent of Hartell's insurance coverage. So he and the executives of Hartell had already agreed on a "target amount" to aim for and an "upper limit" that they would be willing to pay. Fred had been right when he told Carlos that the final approval of any ransom payment would have to be made by the board of directors. But if the final demands remained within the preestablished limits, they would pose no difficulty.

Fred's only worry, waiting for the ten-hour deadline to arrive, was that these particular kidnappers might not be bartering. Moreover, their ransom demand was far above the "upper limit" Hartell was willing to pay.

The call came.

"Well," asked Carlos, "is your company ready to meet our price?"

"Of course not!" replied Fred. "You know your demand is not reasonable. But I am authorized to make a counteroffer."

"What is it?"

Fred stated the figure, in hundreds of thousands of "bananas." The expected outburst of obscenities and revolutionary clichés followed on cue. "I don't understand why you went to all the trouble of publishing our manifesto when you obviously don't care about the lives of your Yankee hirelings!" scoffed Carlos. "Your people spent thousands of dollars for our cause, and they won't get a single thing in return! You are even more stupid than I thought!"

Fred smiled to the men in the room. *Carlos had not hung up. The terrorists were bartering.* The tirade served to benefit whoever was listening to Carlos's side of the conversation in the PRTC headquarters.

"We do care about the lives of our men!" Fred replied when Carlos's harangue ran out of steam. "We are businessmen. We are prepared to pay a fair price for the merchandise you have offered for sale."

"Then get serious about your offer!" said Carlos.

"Is anyone else listening to our conversation on an extension at your end?" Fred asked.

"No!"

"I would suggest to you," said Fred, "that you and I are in the same position. We both have to convince those we represent that we have made the best possible deal, and that we have made the other guys come out on the short end? Am I right?"

"I'm listening!" said Carlos.

"O.K.!" said Fred. "I don't believe that you people really want to kill our men. After all, it is that kind of cold-blooded murder that you claim is characteristic of the government. If you do what they do, it will cost you dearly in international support. World opinion will be much more favorable to your cause if you are viewed as being more humanitarian than the present regime.

"From our side," he continued, "we are willing to pay generously for the safe return of our men. I guarantee that the

PRTC will be well financed by what you receive from Hartell. What we need to do is come up with a figure that we can both sell to our people."

"I am glad to hear that you are finally prepared to be reasonable about this!" said Carlos.

Fred made an offer that was one million dollars below his target.

"You are at least three million too low!" replied Carlos.

"Truthfully, Carlos," said Fred, "you are still above what I can get this company to pay. I will come up another million."

"Make it one million more," answered Carlos, "and we will consider making the sale."

"I don't know if the company will go for that!" replied Fred. "But I think they will consider it. Give me the weekend at least, and I should have an answer for you."

"Good-by!" said Carlos.

† † †

WHILE I was still on my knees, Ocho entered the cell. I was as surprised to see him as he was to see me in that posture. He wasn't due to make a banana delivery for some hours yet. Somewhat nervously he went over to the corner and looked into the can, as though to determine whether it needed to be emptied. He had serviced the toilet just a few hours before, and he never did it more than once a day. As he made to leave the cell, he looked at me and whispered, "Do not worry, *señor*, they are not going to kill you!" Then he left.

I said, "Thank you, Lord, but I don't know whether to believe him. He is only a boy. I am still prepared to die."

I sat back down on my pad and resumed my reading.

Sometime later, hooded figures carrying submachine guns came into the cell. My heart began to beat faster. This was either the end or the beginning: I didn't know which. "You are the luckiest man I have ever seen, *gringo!*" announced Señor Glasses. I gave a sigh of relief. It took awhile for my heart to stop pounding. "Your people changed their minds. They are going to pay for you after all. So we are going to let you live!"

"That was not luck, *señors!*" I replied.

"What?" said Señor Glasses.

"I did what you told me to do," I explained. "I prayed!"
The hoods exited laughing.

"Thank you again, Lord!" I said when they were gone.
"Now I will have a chance to make good on my promise."

I removed the two letters from their hiding place and proceeded to tear them into tiny pieces. I did not want those letters
found now. Some of the pieces I put in the can. Others disappeared down into cracks in the cement. There was no shortage
of secret compartments.

If I had dared, I would have sung a hymn—even if my feet
weren't in stocks.

◻◻◻◻⌐

A PICTURE of Fausto Bucheli appeared in *La Prensa Grafica* on
October 12. He was standing soberly before a large emblem of
the PRTC. In front of him he held a newspaper with a bold
headline: U.S. Armada in Caribbean.

The accompanying article read:

PICTURE OF THE KIDNAPPED

Together with a communiqué from the clandestine group
"P.R.T.C.," there arrived last night at LA PRENSA GRAFICA a
picture without identification—which could be that of the North
American [Bruce Chapman] or Ecuadorian Fausto R. Bucheli, both
of whom were kidnapped and are in the power of the above-
named subversive group.

In the text of the communiqué, it was put on record that both
of the kidnapped men found themselves in a good state of health;
and that they fell into the power of this still little-known group
last September 21 in an action carried out by a commando force of
that clandestine group.

The communiqué adds that from the moment of the capture
of the two executives, every attention has been given to care for
their health.

The text beneath the picture read as follows:

KIDNAPPED. A photograph received last night at this daily
paper, together with a communiqué from the "P.R.T.C.," that
corresponds to one of two [men] kidnapped by this clandestine
group on 21 September. The photo arrived without identification;
therefore, it is not known if it is Mr. [Bruce Chapman] or Fausto R.
Bucheli, Ecuadorian.

† † †

Day 24 *(Sunday, 14 October)*

NEITHER THE euphoria that followed upon my "conversion" prayer nor the relief occasioned by my reprieve from death was permanent. As the hours passed I came to understand that, as far as my captivity was concerned, the situation had simply returned to the status quo. My cell was stifling, my physical disorders continued to be painful, and my emotional state was still susceptible to great fluctations. Negotiations were going on, and I was still a hostage.

Nevertheless, there was a change in me. I firmly believed that the transaction I had made with God was genuine. I was now on His side and, what was more germane to me, He was on mine. What that might mean in terms of my release from physical captivity I had no idea. After all, although the apostle Peter was set free, James was put to death. I was convinced that my life was in His hands. Even though I no longer had the physical sensation of another "presence" in my room, I knew that God was with me.

That conviction held immeasurable comfort. I considered that the Lord might want to use my story to encourage faith on the part of others. This thought raised my hopes for release. But even when subsequent circumstances seemed to reduce the likelihood of my eventual freedom, I was still sustained by my confidence that God was with me and would accomplish His will in my life. I was buoyed by the gift of added days to prove the authenticity of my faith beyond the extremity of the foxhole.

My continued reading of the New Testament strengthened both my faith and my understanding of God and what it means to live for Him. As I read through the section of Paul's letters to the churches for the second time, I was seeing God's truth through new eyes. No longer was God proving Himself to me; now He was revealing His character and His ways to me. Though there was much that I still did not grasp, I found that the mind of faith comprehended much more than did the mentality of skepticism.

Especially encouraging to me were many of the words of my new friend, the apostle Paul. Much that he wrote was penned in prison. I found his attitude in the face of death remarkable. He expressed this in several places, but the verse that I decided to adopt as my personal goal is found in the letter to the Philippians, "I eagerly expect and hope that I will in no way be ashamed, but will have sufficient courage so that now as always Christ will be exalted in my body, whether by life or by death" (1:20).

This is not to say that I always lived up to that goal or that I was continually calm and serene in my spirit from this time on. In a matter of hours, new upheavals would dispel any illusions I might have had that I had become emotionally whole. I still chafed at my imprisonment. I still craved freedom from my confinement, relief from my pain. In short, I continued to experience much of the trauma of a human being who has been brutalized in his body and debased in his personhood. I did not always remember that God was with me; my faith was not unwaveringly strong.

But I was not the same person I had been. I had a new sense of my humanity. I had hope. I experienced times of incredible tranquility. And when that blessing was disrupted, either by external circumstances or the specters that still lurked in my twisted imagination, God always had ways to return me to a healthier perspective on my experience of reality. As often as not, reading the Bible was my most effective exercise for restoring and promoting mental health.

On this Sunday I rather enjoyed walking through the day with Rita and the children in my imagination. I computed time differences and determined (more or less) when they would be in Sunday school and then at worship. During those hours, though they didn't know it, we went to Sunday school "together" and worshiped "together." This gave me great encouragement. Rita had prayed for my salvation for so long, it hardly seemed likely that God wouldn't let her know, at least eventually, that I had come to faith.

Day 25 *(Monday, 15 October)*

THE HISTORIC events of October 15, 1979, were chronicled for *Newsweek* magazine by staff writer Steven Strasser under the headline: Coup in El Salvador.

Rumors of an impending coup had circulated through El Salvador for days. The country's dictator, Gen. Carlos Humberto Romero, hurried home from Miami and stayed up all night waiting for the attack. It never came. At dawn, Romero relaxed, dismissed his staff and went to bed. He was more than a little startled when a crisp junior officer telephoned him at 8:30 A.M. to inform him that mutineers controlled five military posts and fourteen regiments. The messenger politely gave Romero a few hours to leave the country.

In a last attempt to save his two-year-old Presidency, Romero sent his press secretary, Rafael Flores Lima, to negotiate with the coup leaders. When Lima decided to join the rebels, Romero meekly flew to exile in Guatemala. For weeks, Salvadorans had predicted gloomily that Romero would be replaced by an even harsher right-wing dictatorship—or by left-wing anarchy. Instead, the new regime proved to be surprisingly and reassuringly, moderate.

ACCEPTANCE: The two obscure officers who led the bloodless coup were not even troop commanders. But Col. Adolfo Arnoldo Majano, 41, a military-college administrator, and Col. Jaime Abdul Gutiérrez, 43, an engineer, had the support of El Salvador's military rank and file, which had chafed at Romero's inability to control political violence from both the left and right. The coup also won the cautious acceptance of much of El Salvador's powerful business Establishment.

The two colonels quickly named a predominantly moderate five-member junta composed of themselves and three civilians: Román Mayorga Quiroz, former rector of the Central American University; Guillermo Manuel Ungo, a leader of the National Democratic Union, and Mario Antonio Andino, a liberal businessman. The junta promised free elections "within a reasonable period" before 1982 and declared an amnesty for political prisoners. In a gesture to the left, the junta also announced plans to recognize Cuba and said it would investigate the disappearance of more than 400 persons during Romero's rule. "I believe that the people of El Salvador will very soon see the differences between this and the last government with respect to human rights and honesty," predicted Mayorga.

NIGHTTIME CURFEW: The most powerful leftist guerrilla group, the People's Revolutionary Army, indicated it would support the junta. But several other leftist organizations said they still opposed the new government. So far, El Salvador's revolutionaries lack the training and cohesion of successful guerrilla movements like Nicaragua's Sandinistas. But they made trouble enough last week. One rebel band in San Marcos set up roadblocks and passed out weapons to university students. Other leftists invaded radio stations to broadcast communiqués and fought running battles with soldiers in San Salvador. Dozens of rebels died, and late in the week the new government was stunned by the loss of one of its own: the army's inspector general, Col. Tadeo Martell, was shot and killed in an ambush as he left home for work. The junta suspended constitutional rights for 30 days and imposed a nighttime curfew.

The U.S. was an interested bystander. The Carter Administration had pushed Romero to make liberal reforms, and it declared his ouster "encouraging" only three hours after the coup occurred. Privately, U.S. officials said they had advance word of the coup, but they insisted that Washington had done nothing to either stop it or encourage it. They said the U.S. preferred the moderate officers only to the alternatives: the far right or the far left. "We don't want to be in the business of endorsing coups," said one official. "But we are in the business of facing reality."

CAUSE FOR OPTIMISM: There was also talk in the Administration of resuming U.S. aid, which had been cut back because of Romero's human-rights violations. "If the new leaders act as they say they are going to act, we'll do everything we can to help them," said one insider. "We'd be foolish not to." Despite the flurry of leftist opposition, there was some cause for optimism. As the junta's policies unfolded, many Salvadorans preferred to tune out the bulletins and martial music on government-controlled radio and turned instead to television, which was broadcasting the last game of the World Series.[1]

As was often the case these days, the Buchelis first heard news about the happenings in El Salvador from the media. Along with millions of others in Southern California, they learned of the overthrow of President Romero by watching the eleven o'clock news on television. Their response was fear and anger—fear for what the coup might mean to Fausto's well-being, anger toward Hartell for keeping them so much in the dark.

The Verhoevens heard the news at the same time. Gert didn't even call next door, but put on a housecoat and walked straight to the Buchelis' sliding glass door. Fausto Jr. let her in. No one was surprised to see her.

The television was off, but Gert could tell that the family had been watching the news.

"I don't know what upsets me more," Rita said, as though they were in the middle of a conversation. "The news about the government in El Salvador, or Hartell's refusal to tell us what's going on."

Fausto Jr. spoke. "Ever since we got the suitcases, we've known that the company wasn't telling us everything. We asked John about the pens and paper that Dad always carries with him—you know, the ones that came back in his bags—and he just shrugged it off."

"And we're always finding out stuff from the news that Hartell hasn't told us about!" Hilda added.

"Rita, if you want to go in and talk to the president, or somebody," Gert suggested, "I'll take off work tomorrow and go with you."

"Yeah, mama," said Fausto, "and I'll go too. I think we deserve to know more than they're telling."

Rita agreed. "All right, first thing in the morning we'll go see Mr. Reynolds. He seems to be in charge of this operation. Maybe he'll give us more information than John has been offering."

"Don't hold your breath!" muttered Hilda.

20
The World's Most Expensive Notebook

Day 26 *(Tuesday, 16 October)*

GUNFIRE—SINGLE SHOTS from rifles and pistols interspersed with the rat-a-tat-tat of an occasional machine gun—shattered the relative calm of my cell and my soul. Unseen antagonists were shooting at each other somewhere in the world outside my six-by-ten bunker. The debilitating effect of the noise of war on my nervous system was caused by several factors: at age forty-one, I had never been in war—my only exposure to guns had been through television; the effects of the kidnapping and the continual threat of death with which I lived for two weeks at the business end of a submachine gun continued to haunt me; even in the absence of a visible guard, the nightly ritual of weapon-cleaning carried out in the adjacent room made me shudder; and to make matters even worse, my program of Bible reading had taken me through the Book of Revelation, with all of its cataclysms, a second time.

Without benefit of explanatory commentary from a newscaster to soothe my fears, my terror-ridden imagination formulated the most gruesome of scenarios to account for the furor I was hearing. Of all possible causes for the gunfire, two emerged as most likely: Either this was indeed the end of the world, or President Carter had sent in the U.S. Marines to rescue me by force (A variation on the second option placed government-sanctioned Salvadoran troops in the role of would-be rescuers.) In either event, the prospects for my survival were not good. I may have had "nothing to fear but fear itself," but fear was indeed an overwhelming enemy that reduced me to the condition of a child in the clutches of fantasy's most hideous monster.

It was Ocho who delivered me from this fate worse than death. Before I knew for certain who was opening the door, his routine delivery of bananas prompted great fright. As recognition of his boyish frame brought relief to my beleaguered nervous system, I whispered, "Ocho, what is happening out there? Why all the shooting?"

"The army has overthrown President Romero," he explained succinctly. "He has fled the country."

"Then why are they still shooting?"

"Some of the popular revolutionary groups are trying to bring down the new government before it really gets established," Ocho said. That was all the conversation he would risk. He withdrew from my cell.

My worst fears had not been realized. The shooting that I was hearing had nothing directly to do with me. But the consequences could certainly have a bearing on my situation. Who would rule El Salvador? Would the new government expedite or hinder my release? Would civil war erupt? Would prolonged fighting interrupt the negotiation process? Were my captors involved?

My thoughts returned to the question of sovereignty. Who would govern the country? I thought of the towering statue of Christ—El Salvador del Mundo (The Savior of the World)—that overlooks downtown San Salvador. El Salvador is the only country in the world that is named for deity. And in the heart of the capital, where most Latin American countries have erected a monument to honor their nation's greatest hero, stands a likeness of the Man for all the nations—Jesus Christ. Would that Jesus did rule in the hearts of all Salvadorans!

I was glad that He had come to rule in my own. Though I still flinched with each sporadic exchange of gunfire, my jangled nerves were soothed by my assurance that whoever might govern temporarily in El Salvador, Christ was my Commander-in-Chief. He and He alone would determine my destiny.

I am convinced that "El Salvador del Mundo," the Savior of Fausto Bucheli, preserved me from a nervous breakdown.

◻◻◻◻◻|

FROM ALL over the Western Hemisphere, Fred Rayne's couriers returned to San Salvador bearing the evidence of the success of their mission. Their task had not been easy. Customs officials in Mexico City, for instance, had intercepted one of the manifestos at the airport, snarling it irretrievably in governmental red tape. A second courier had to be dispatched. He succeeded in eluding detection, and the proclamation was published within the allotted time.

Not all of the agents' efforts were successful. The newspapers of Ecuador refused to cooperate on the same grounds as *The Times* of London. The constitution of El Salvador itself prohibited compliance on the part of the local press. In all, Fred Rayne and his associates were able to place the ads in twenty-five of the thirty-two publications named by the PRTC.

Fred himself had returned to Europe via Concorde supersonic jet to retrieve the tear sheets from the newspapers on the Continent. The tardiest of the publications included the ads in Tuesday's edition—one day before the deadline established by the kidnappers. The French and German papers in particular finally relented—but only with much editorial kicking and screaming. Fred was still in Europe when the terrorists called the Sheraton command post on Tuesday evening. Juan Ortega answered the phone.

"Ortega!" he announced.

"Do you have the manifestos?" asked Carlos.

"We will have them by tomorrow, as you prescribed."

"Good! Now I will give you instructions for their delivery. Bind all of the samples in a notebook. Then take it to a funeral home opposite the University of San Salvador. It is on Autopista Norte, northeast of El Camino Real. On the grounds of the funeral home, there is a courtyard, and in the center of that courtyard is a statue. Put the notebook in the opening in the base of the statue. Then leave. Do you understand?"

Juan repeated the instructions to Carlos' satisfaction. The conversation was over.

The Bucheli fact-finding team was not expected at Hartell Industries that morning, and startled expressions and raised eyebrows followed Rita as she marched past the receptionist and led Gert and Fausto Jr. into Carl Reynolds's inner sanctum.

"Would you please tell Mr. Reynolds that Mrs. Bucheli would like to speak with him," Rita directed the surprised secretary.

"I—uh—believe that he is in a—uh—meeting right now!" the woman stammered.

"Please notify him that we are here!" Rita insisted.

"Would you like to have a seat while you wait?" suggested the secretary, recovering her composure.

"No, thanks!" replied Rita. "I don't plan to be waiting that long. I'll stand." Gert and Fausto stood too.

The secretary activated the intercom. "Mr. Reynolds! I'm sorry to disturb you but—uh—Mrs. Bucheli is here to see you!" There was no reply from the desk speaker, but within seconds Carl Reynolds emerged from his office. A surprised John Pike followed close behind.

"Mrs. Bucheli!" greeted Mr. Reynolds, extending his hand. "How are you this morning?"

"I'm pretty upset, thank you!"

"Why don't we step into the conference room and talk a bit?" Reynolds suggested.

"I think that is an excellent idea!" said Rita. Reynolds was about to show Gert and Fausto where they could wait, but he never had a chance. Rita grabbed Gert by the hand as she led the entourage into the conference room. Fausto took the cue from his mother and followed her. Reynolds had to scramble to reach the door to open it for the women. John Pike brought up the rear and closed the door behind them all. He glared at Fausto Jr., but said nothing.

Once inside, Rita introduced Gert. "Mr. Reynolds, this is my next door neighbor, Gert Verhoeven." The vice-president was not happy to have her in the room. But he was polite.

"Happy to meet you, Mrs. Verhoeven."

"And this is my son, Fausto Jr."

Reynolds nodded toward the boy. "Fausto," he acknowledged. He offered a chair to everyone.

"Mr. Reynolds!" said Rita. "My friend, Gert, has been my

closest friend ever since Fausto was kidnapped. She listens to me when I need to talk, and she doesn't tell anyone else anything she knows. She and my son are here because I want them in on this conversation."

"I see!" said Reynolds. Then, in an effort to regain some initiative, he said, "We were stunned, as I'm sure you were, to hear the news about President Romero."

"I was stunned," retorted Rita, "that I had to hear that news from the News."

Reynolds understood her. "Mrs. Bucheli, we only learned of the coup a couple of hours before it hit the North American wire services. We wanted to try to find out what it might mean for your husband and Mr. Chapman before contacting you. We didn't want to alarm you unnecessarily with incomplete information."

Fausto entered the conversation. "So have you found out anything about my dad and Mr. Chapman?"

"No," admitted Reynolds. "We have been waiting for some contact from the kidnappers, but they haven't called since Romero was overthrown."

"It seems to me," asserted Fausto, "that you people are continually determining what *you* think would be best for our family to know. And as a result, you don't tell us anything! We don't know what you are doing, we don't know how things are going. Hey, that's *my* dad down there; he's *her* husband! We find out more from watching television than we do from personal briefings by John here!"

"That's even true when Hartell is the source of the media's information!" added Rita. "When I was here before, Mr. Reynolds, you promised to keep me informed. And I got a letter from Mr. Shannon telling me to let him know if I felt like anyone here was falling down on the job. Well, I'm just that far,"—she held up a thumb and a forefinger—"from taking him up on that offer!"

"Mrs. Bucheli!" replied Reynolds, trying to calm her down. "I'm sorry that we haven't been able to pass along more information. But really, there hasn't been very much hard news to tell you. What information we do have, we have to guard very carefully."

"That's exactly what I was talking about before!" Fausto

interjected. "The heart of the problem is that you don't trust us. You think that we are going to blab everything we know to reporters—that we are too stupid to protect our own flesh and blood."

"You are hardly in a position to be making such statements, young man!" retorted John Pike. "You're the one the reporters got to!"

"Now look, John!" Fausto was angry. "You know I didn't give them anything they didn't already have. I was just getting them off my back. You guys have way overreacted to that whole thing."

"Don't you think maybe you're overreacting a little bit today?" suggested Reynolds.

"No, Mr. Reynolds, I don't!" replied Fausto. "I think we've been very patient for a long time. We've talked this over several times at home. But up 'til now, we've just put up with it. And then we hear that the government of El Salvador has been overthrown—on television, for goodness' sake—well, we're not putting up with it any more!"

"Listen!" began Reynolds. "I can understand how you feel—"

"You *don't* understand how we feel!" Fausto insisted.

"At least let me finish a sentence!" Reynolds returned hotly. He took a deep breath, then turned to Rita. "Mrs. Bucheli, this whole thing is very sensitive, and we are *all* under a lot of pressure. Our primary concern is to get your husband out of El Salvador alive!"

"That's very commendable!" Rita replied. "No one appreciates that more than I do. But as far as I'm concerned, that's the least you can do. It's your fault that his life is in danger today."

Reynolds was losing patience. "Now just a minute!" he protested. "We had no way of knowing he would be kidnapped. We took every realistic precaution to prevent this sort of thing from happening!"

"Listen!" Rita shot back. "I had a better picture of how dangerous it was down there than you did. You people were acting like ostriches with your heads stuck in the sand. I *begged* Fausto not to go! I was so upset with him for going . . ." A lump growing suddenly in Rita's throat choked off her words, and her eyes filled with tears. The room became deathly quiet. Finally she whispered the rest of the sentence: ". . . that I didn't even kiss him good-by!" She broke down completely. Gert put her arm around her and gave her a hand-kerchief. Everyone waited while Rita struggled to regain her composure.

"I realize that you didn't know that Fausto and Mr. Chapman were going to be kidnapped. But you knew there was a risk. And you did nothing—nothing to prepare Fausto for that eventuality. Tom Elliott told me that Fausto had prepared a report on conditions down there. He said that Fausto was angry that the company had placed him in such danger. He wasn't going back!"

At the mention of Tom Elliott's name Reynolds stiffened, but he said nothing.

"Did you tell Fausto what to do if he was kidnapped? Did you warn him that it could happen? Did you tell him that you would take care of his family if he didn't make it back? How is he supposed to know what is happening to us while he is stuck down there?"

Rita had vented three-and-a-half weeks' worth of anger and frustration in a matter of a half-hour.

Reynolds made no effort to answer her questions or defend the company. All he said was, "Mrs. Bucheli, I'm so sorry this has happened! All I can promise you is that we'll continue to do our best to make things right—and to get your husband home safely to you."

"I would appreciate being informed of what is happening from time to time," she requested, wiping her eyes with Gert's handkerchief. "Perhaps a phone call a couple of times a day would be a better arrangement than the one we have."

"We'll see what we can do!" said Reynolds. "For what it's worth, I am flying down to Guatemala tomorrow to meet with Mr. Rayne and review the situation with him. I'll let you know anything I can as soon as I return."

There was no more to be said. The two men escorted Rita, Fausto, and Gert from the conference foom.

"Do you think we accomplished anything?" asked Fausto when they were out of earshot of the executives.

"Probably not!" said Rita, sighing. "But I feel better."

Day 27 *(Wednesday, 17 October)*

John Pike did not favor the Bucheli family with his presence that day.

In fact, for the duration of the crisis, Pike came to the home only to deliver Fausto's paycheck or any other items that were related to his captivity. For all intents and purposes, from the standpoint of Hartell Industries, the family became incommunicado.

As Rita became aware of this, it bothered her at first. But when she realized that the situation was not materially different from what it had been before her visit to Reynolds, she decided that the easing of tension brought by Pike's absence was for the good: The guard had been removed from their cell.

As he was being chauffeured to the designated funeral home, Juan Ortega pondered the macabre choice of drop site. He wondered whether the kidnappers were trying to emphasize the consequences of any failure on his part to complete the delivery of the manifestos.

At least he had no trouble finding the place. One previous drop had almost met with disaster because Carlos's Salvadoran word for "mattress" was the same as Juan's Honduran word for "pillow," and Juan couldn't figure out the directions. But after a few tense hours and not a few angry words, the two negotiators had gotten everything straightened out. Both became more precise in their communication after that.

What Juan discovered when he arrived at the funeral chapel distressed him. The courtyard was being used as a park by university students, and the place was much too crowded for comfort. But there seemed to be no acceptable alternative. Juan decided that the best way to be inconspicuous was to approach the statue directly—as though it was his job to maintain it. He found the described opening and inserted the notebook with no trouble. Then he walked away from the statue, found a cement bench nearby, and sat down. He knew that he had been directed to leave. But he was afraid that a curious student might investigate the statue and make off with the hidden treasure.

Mulling the situation, Juan realized that as long as he remained in the courtyard, there was no way that a PRTC courier would expose himself by making the pickup. The PRTC knew what he looked like, but they guarded their own identities carefully. In fact, it was likely that one or more of the proximate "students" *was* his counterpart.

In any event, he could do nothing to protect the notebook. His presence could only serve to block delivery. So he returned to the car and rode back to the Sheraton Hotel.

Day 28 *(Thursday, 18 October)*

Juan Ortega did not sleep well the night of October 17. His anxiety over the fate of the notebook increased with each passing hour that the telephone did not ring. Fred Rayne maintained that completion of the transfer was the responsibility of the PRTC, and they were probably just going over the contents of the ads.

Fred's concern was over what the kidnappers would find in the notebook, or would not find. This concern proved to be justified.

Juan answered the belated phone call.

"This is Ortega! Did you get the notebook?"

"Yes, we got it!" replied Carlos. Juan began to relax. "But we're not happy with what we have! You people did not follow our instructions!"

"We *did* follow your instructions!" replied Fred Rayne. "But some of the details were impossible to carry out. If you have any questions, I'll be happy to explain to you what happened."

"There are only twenty-five manifestos here!" complained Carlos. "Where are the other seven?"

"There were seven newspapers that would not print your proclamation at any price," explained Fred. "In your own country, it is against the law. There were several other papers that didn't want to print it, but we persuaded them to anyway. I think we did rather well, all things considered!"

There was an interlude in the phone conversation as Carlos relayed Fred's explanation to his comrades. "We don't approve of your company's efforts to save money at the expense of our instructions!" scolded Carlos when he returned.

"I don't know what you mean!"

"We ordered three-color ads! We were very explicit: red, yellow, and black. One of these papers, the one from Los

Angeles, is in red and black. The others are all in black. You disregarded our directions!"

"No, that's not the case!" Fred said. "We had to choose between meeting your deadline and having all of the colors. The machinery limitations of the newspapers themselves prevented us from meeting the color specifications."

"Well, you misrepresented our message in the way you translated the manifesto in the European editions!" Carlos charged.

Fred was becoming angry. "Listen, Carlos!" he countered. "If you wanted those declarations translated a certain way, you should have done it yourselves! Our people did the best they could with the time they had. We busted our backsides running all over this planet to put together the most expensive book in existence. I doubt if anyone else could have pulled it off as fast and as completely as we did!"

"Well, I guess it will have to do," said Carlos at last.

"Have to do!" muttered Fred to the others in the room. "Those guys are impressed out of their socks!" He turned back to the phone. "By the way, Carlos. We also met your second demand."

"You did what?"

"Those five men that you wanted released from prison— they are free now! The new junta cut them loose."

"You didn't have anything to do with that!" scoffed Carlos. "The army kicked out that traitor Romero!"

"Now how do you suppose those officers knew they could pull that off without intervention from the United States?" Fred queried.

Carlos was silent.

"Stay in touch!" said Fred. Juan hung up the phone, and the Americans exploded in laughter.

21
On Hold

SATURDAY WAS A low day for me. Even though the noise of firing weapons had abated, I remained disturbed by the uncertainty of what was happening, or not happening, in the outside world. My captors did not communicate with me about the coup, the negotiations—anything.

My only human contact during the week was Ocho. And that was not pleasant. When he came to do his chores one morning, I could tell he was distraught.

"What is the matter, Ocho?" I asked.

He said nothing.

"Ocho!" I repeated. "Is anything wrong?"

"Yes, *señor!*" he finally responded. "There is something wrong!" In the dim light of the cell I could see that he had been crying. He was on the verge of tears as he spoke.

"What is it, my friend?"

He took a deep breath. "Last night there was a raid on my village! Many were killed!" I anticipated his next pain-racked words, but they still hit me like a sledge hammer. "My whole family was slaughtered!" He fought a desperate battle against breaking down completely.

"Who would do such a horrible thing?" I couldn't help asking.

220

"Our enemies." For all its obviousness, his simple answer was an eloquent summary of the world in which Ocho and I were living. "The man on the radio called it an operation to root out leftist guerrillas who are trying to destroy the government." He shook his head in despair. "It was a massacre!"

"Ocho, I am so sorry!" We were both weeping when he left the room.

The gloom that Ocho's tragedy cast over my soul was accentuated on this last day of the week by the routine activity of drawing the diagonal line through the sixth box on the wall. Thirty days I had been in this hole. Who would have thought that I could survive for a whole month under such conditions? Yet I did.

I was not in the best frame of mind when my three hooded tormentors made their first appearance in more than a week.

"Hey, *gringo!*" remarked Señor Glasses. "Your stupid imperialist bosses seem to need some more encouragement to pay for your release!"

A quick inventory of the paraphernalia being set up by his two accomplices told me that I was going to provide the "encouragement." We were going to produce another audiovisual spectacular.

"The man who is doing the negotiating on behalf of Hartell is Fred Rayne," explained Señor Glasses. I had never heard that name before, but of course, there were hundreds of employees whose names I would not recognize. "We want you to talk to him on this tape and tell him how badly you want to get out of here. You may decide what words to use—the way you want to say it. Just don't say anything stupid, or we will simply erase the tape and do it again!"

I did as they instructed. At that point I really wanted release from confinement. I was prepared to do virtually anything to gain it. I rambled on for a few minutes, asking Mr. Rayne to do what he could to help my family and me. I'm not sure how coherent I was, but the director and the technicians were satisfied with my performance.

They also took another picture, then they left me alone again.

They also left me with something new to think about. I now knew the name of the man who was trying to accomplish my release. "God bless Fred Rayne," I prayed, "and help him to do his job right."

◫◫◫◫◫◫

FRED RAYNE would need all the help he could get.

The change in the El Salvadoran government, though applauded by the U.S. State Department, created headaches for the negotiator. Essentially there was but one condition that remained to be fulfilled to secure the release of the hostages—the payment of ransom. But it was not easy to bring millions of dollars across national boundaries. If the cash were brought in through conventional channels, it would have to be done with government permission. Yet the purpose for which the money was designated was hardly in the best interest of those in power. The alternative of smuggling the ransom into the country was fraught with even more difficulties. And apprehension by the authorities would be disastrous.

All these obstacles were made more imposing by the fact that for several days no one in the American embassy was sure who was in control. It was expectedly taking a while for the new junta to get a secure grasp of the reins of government and to keep the leftist opportunists in hand. Once official power was consolidated, American diplomatic pressure could be applied to secure the new regime's cooperation in this hostage case—Fred hoped.

Fortunately Fred had secured the support and the practical assistance of the U.S. State Department. Moreover, embassy officials agreed to play a behind-the-scenes role in extricating the American citizens from captivity. It was hoped by all involved that once the new junta was really in control, its desire for the good will of the Carter Administration would outweigh its antipathy to the leftist cause.

In the meantime, though Fred was working hard to set everything in place for the final transaction, the negotiations were definitely on hold—along with the hostages.

Day 35 (*Thursday, 25 October*)

As the days of her husband's captivity stretched into the second month, Rita Bucheli was torn by conflicting emotions.

The words once spoken by a distressed father to Jesus—"I do believe; help me overcome my unbelief!"—could well express her sentiments.

There were some heartening elements to her daily existence. Of no small encouragement was the expert help of Gert Verhoeven in managing financial matters such as depositing pay checks, paying bills, and so forth. Fausto had handled these details ever since the family came to America. So Rita was totally unprepared to cope with this aspect of his sudden departure from the family scene. But Gert, a bookkeeper by profession, soon taught Rita the basics of finance. As a result there was no disruption of services, no overdrafts on checking accounts, no shortage of cash to buy groceries.

Rita's employment situation improved also. She had tried returning to her job in the shipping department at Hartell, but it was too hard on her emotionally. Staying at home all day was also depressing. The solution came when her Indiana teaching credential was accredited in the state of California. She applied for a position as a substitute teacher—primarily for Spanish classes—and was hired immediately. She was able to devote almost every day to the mind-absorbing task. She could also get home from work sooner, which benefited the rest of the family.

The Christian community provided on-going comfort to Rita. The family's friends in Berne continued to call and write faithfully. At one point they even organized who-was-going-to-call-when so that Rita wouldn't have to repeat the information. As the number of calls tapered off, Rita was afraid her friends were beginning to forget about Fausto and her. But as she later learned, they were just trying to be sensitive to her situation.

Locally Rita made it a point to attend every church service she could. At one Wednesday evening prayer meeting, Pastor Crocker invited requests for a favorite hymn. Rita requested "Sweet Hour of Prayer." The lyrics, especially for the first verse, became an admonition, and she found herself singing the words frequently during the gloomy times:

> Sweet hour of prayer, sweet hour of prayer,
> That calls me from a world of care,
> And bids me at my Father's throne
> Make all my wants and wishes known,

> In seasons of distress and grief
> My soul has often found relief,
> And oft escaped the tempter's snare,
> By thy return, sweet hour of prayer.

Prayer took on a different character for Rita as the days passed. Never before had she gone to God with such "distress and grief"; but often the things that she felt like saying to the Lord didn't seem appropriate. One of Don Crocker's services to Rita was to help her express her innermost feelings to her heavenly Father without fear of reprisal. He showed her from the Psalms how David and others poured out their hearts to the Lord, expressing themselves in ways that sound shocking to the ears of modern, Western Christians. Rita began to learn that expressing even negative emotions to God is neither an act of rebellion nor a sign of disrespect—it is rather a manifestation of faith that Someone who cares is really listening. Sometimes such gut-wrenching wrestling with God is necessary in order to escape from the "slough of despond" and see reality from the standpoint of God's perfect character.

Nevertheless, there were times when, as Rita told her pastor, "it seems that the sky is made of iron, and my prayers just bounce back to the earth." At such times God had His own ways of breaking through to Rita from the other side.

On one occasion Rita was questioning God's care for Fausto and herself and the family. As she drove to the grocery store in a distracted state of mind, she ran a stop sign. Cars approaching the intersection from both the right and the left swerved and screeched to a halt. She was jolted from her preoccupation to realize how close she had come to causing a potentially serious accident. But there was no collision, no harm done. "Thank you, Lord!" she murmured as she continued, now alert, on her way to the store. "And thank you for taking care of us all."

As the crisis continued, the cumulative effects of the stress took their toll of Rita physically. She began to experience sharp, stabbing pains in her chest. When they persisted, she submitted to a physical examination. Her doctor prescribed medication to control the pains, but he warned her that the symptoms could not be expected to pass until the level of tension and pressure was reduced.

The stress level did not go down—it went up. On this Thursday, the additional strain came through none other than John Pike. He was not the cause of the additional grief—merely the courier. He brought to Rita Fausto's second tape.

Again Gert was summoned to accompany Rita through the valley of the shadow. Rita played the whole message through once nonstop in the privacy of her bedroom.

Gert could understand only a few of the words spoken in Spanish. But it was clear that this recording was not like the first one. The message was not read—it was delivered extemporaneously. Moreover, one did not have to understand Spanish to hear the pain in the voice. The man was half speaking, half crying as he repeated his appeal to "Señor Rayne" to do something—anything—to secure his release.

What Rita heard almost broke her heart. The rambling, broken sentences were difficult to translate for Gert. But Rita managed to repeat the substance of Fausto's message in English:

> I'm doing fine. They treat me fine. I spend every hour, every moment thinking about when I'm going to get out, when they will let me go. I would like to say to Mr. Rayne to please look at this situation. Especially my case. In my situation, it was a matter of accident that I arrived here. I shouldn't be here.
>
> My wife, my family, my children haven't been told where I am and the situation in which we find ourselves. Especially the way the situation is for myself. I have no home, I have nothing—especially being brand new in the state of California.
>
> I am under extreme pressure not knowing how my family is being cared for, having no idea who is providing food and support for my family. Mr. Rayne, you understand my situation. There is no way that I can take care of them with myself being here.
>
> Anything can happen, especially in my situation. I beg of you to please do something for us, for myself—help me out of this situation. I beg you because I want to go home. I have no reason for being here. I miss my family. I need to see my family. I should not be here. I was sent here—I don't know why. I have a family. I have responsibilities and obligations. I don't know why I am here.
>
> At present, I would like you to do me a favor, Mr. Rayne. I would like you to send a message to my family. Tell my wife and my children that I am fine, that I find myself in good health. I find

myself well—not to worry about me. Also to change the license plates on the car. And make sure you change the name on the insurance policy and that the payments are kept up or else they will just take them away from us . . . and as poor people you understand we have to keep these things going. That my wife and children take care of themselves, take care of anything and everything because here in California we have nothing. There is no way that I can help.

I am under extreme pressure of finding something for me to provide for myself with. There is no way that I can take care of the situation at hand, so I am begging you to please take care of this situation as soon as possible because I want to go home.

I have spoken enough. Maybe we will see each other later. Thank you very much, Mr. Rayne.

The images of Fausto conjured up by this latest communication haunted Rita's mind as she went to bed that night. For several hours she tossed and turned, sleep eluding her completely. Finally, about three in the morning, she put on a robe and went outside. She opened the iron gate at the entrance to the pool area and walked in. She sat down on a green lounge chair, and—as the cool night breeze swept across her, sending involuntary shivers up her back—she tried to think.

After several minutes, she spoke aloud: "Lord, take him!" She paused. "We've reached the limit of what we can endure. If You are not going to bring him home to us, then take him home to Yourself." She sighed deeply. "And let us get on with living."

Weariness descended on her body and her mind. She returned to the house and collapsed across her bed. Within seconds she was asleep.

God did not take Fausto, but He heard Rita's prayer. The next day her chest pains disappeared. It was not yet time for the crisis to end, so He gave her more strength.

† † †

Day 38 (*Sunday, 28 October*)

MY FIFTH and sixth weeks in captivity made no lasting impression on my memory. At some point during that span of time, I finished reading the New Testament for the third time. But most of the details from those days were lost in the unrelieved tedium of waiting. It appeared likely that the kidnappers were intent on marketing me for hard cash, but the delay in accomplishing it seemed interminable. Day after day I ate, drank, read, slept—and waited.

The only exceptional day in that entire fortnight was Sunday, October 28—and I would have gladly exchanged the excitement of that day for some manageable boredom. The day began with a bona fide ground-shaking, bone-rattling, panic-causing earthquake.

I was lying on my mat not long after Ocho had made his morning rounds when the ground began to shake. I could have sworn that the cement walls of my cell were flexing. Dust cascaded from the ceiling, and the boards beneath my pad began knocking together. The tremor lasted for several seconds, and its effects on me were compounded by the severe pounding in my chest. Again, it didn't help that I had recently read the Book of Revelation. My fearful mind had no trouble believing that the end of the world was at hand.

When the tremors ceased, the only thing moving in my cell was the light bulb that continued to swing eerily from the center of the ceiling. Its continued motion amid the absolute stillness of the room confirmed that I hadn't been imagining the seismic convulsions.

I went to my hands and knees and crawled to the door. With some trepidation I knocked, then crawled back to my pad. I had never knocked on that door before.

I was surprised to get a response, but the guard in the next room opened the door. "Don't you think we should go outside?" I asked with genuine concern. I was convinced that our lives were in danger from the collapse of the structure. My will to live was still strong.

"Don't worry about it!" the guard responded. "We get earthquakes like that one all the time, and"—an aftershock hit with such force that the guard pitched against the wall and had to hold onto the door to keep from falling. I sat up and covered my head with my hands and arms. When the rumbles died away, he finished his sentence as though nothing had happened—"they are over right away."

I was hardly convinced, but it didn't matter. He had his

orders, and I was not to leave that cell come quake or high water. It was of little consolation that he proved to be right. There was no more action for the remainder of the day, and that was fine with me.

I couldn't help but wonder what else I could possibly undergo by way of terrifying experiences. Then I recalled from my reading the similar episode endured by the apostle Paul in the jail at Philippi. This was the time when he and his companion Silas were singing hymns at midnight. Their concert was interrupted by a terrible earthquake that simultaneously freed them from their shackles and left the prison in rubble. Though they could have escaped, they remained captive voluntarily because they believed it was God's will for them to be there. But before long, they were released.

I marveled at how many similar imprisonment experiences I shared with those first-generation Christians. Incredibly, God used the earthquake to strengthen my hope of release. The comparison between my situation and the apostles' helped to bolster my sagging confidence that God remained in control of my life—and would free me at the right time.

22
"Bananas" in Honduras

Day 41 *(Wednesday, 31 October)*

JUAN ORTEGA WAS suffering from an acute case of cabin fever. His job was to talk to the PRTC spokesman. To do that, he had to be "on call" virtually twenty-four hours a day. He had been staring at that telephone for days. But he could not will it to ring.

Fred Rayne did not have the same problem. There had been plenty of action to keep him busy. His negotiations did not involve only the kidnappers; he had to negotiate the ransom settlement with Hartell and an agreement of cooperation with the newly formed government of El Salvador. Both of these had been accomplished, but not without considerable effort and several plane trips. In all Rayne landed at Ilopango runway fifteen times.

So when the phone finally did ring, Fred was ready—and Juan was positively jumpy.

"Do you have the 'bananas'?" asked Carlos, speaking in the vocabulary of their special code.

"We have access to the money!" Fred replied. "We are awaiting your instructions for delivery."

"Good! This is what you must do. The money is to be delivered in two stages. Put half of the ransom in a single, large suitcase. On Friday take the suitcase to a construction site." He

229

gave Juan directions to a remote residential area on the outskirts of San Salvador where a home was being built. "In front of the house, right out by the street, you will see a mattress. Drive by the site and drop the suitcase on the mattress. Do not stop the car! Throw out the suitcase as you go by—then keep on going! Do you understand?"

Juan repeated the directions and the instructions. It made him sweat just to describe the process, because he knew he would be the one who would have to pull it off. The whole thing sounded like a scene from a gangster movie.

"Now," continued Carlos, "the second half of the ransom is to be delivered to Honduras."

"What?" Fred esclaimed.

"You heard me!" Carlos retorted.

"What in the world for!"

"That's none of your business!" snapped Carlos. "You just do as you're told."

Fred made a reply to the other men in the room, but Juan didn't repeat it to Carlos.

"Are you still listening?" Carlos asked.

"Yes, we're still here!" Juan replied. "Continue with your instructions."

"All right! Fly the money to Tegucigalpa by noon on Saturday. When you arrive, place a call to this phone number." He gave Juan a number. "Ask for Jorgé. He will give you the final instructions for the drop."

Juan repeated the directions

"Don't foul up!" warned Carlos. "Not if you want your men out alive!"

"Carlos," interjected Fred, "when we have delivered half of the money, we want you to turn over the passport of Mr. Bucheli. We're going to need this to get him out of the country."

After a pause Carlos replied, "Fair enough! Where do you want it?"

Fred designated a simple restroom drop and grinned at Juan. When his spokesman hung up the phone, Fred said, "Nixon had his 'plumbers,' I have mine."

† † †

Day 43 *(Friday, 2 November)*

IT OCCURRED to me, as I made the forty-third mark on the wall, that all over Latin America, shops and businesses would be closed down this day for the observance of *Dia de los Difuntos* (Day of the Dead), which is Memorial Day. My family in Ecuador would no doubt attend the special Mass that was said this day. For all intents and purposes, I qualified to be among the remembered: My life had ceased, and I was buried in an unmarked grave. Would the prayers that were sure to be offered on my behalf be effectual? Would I be resurrected from this living death?

After a wait of more than forty days, I was surprised at how quickly the answer came. After an absence of many days, Señor Mustache and Señor Skinny paid me a visit.

"Good morning, Señor Bucheli!" Señor Skinny greeted effusively.

"Good morning!" I replied. I was astonished by the apparent change in the demeanor of my captors. It was the first time I had been addressed by my name rather than my official titles: "Traitor," *"Gringo,"* "Pig," and some obscene ones. More surprises followed.

"We have some good news for you, Don Fausto!" announced Señor Mustache. I braced myself. "Your company is being most cooperative! Today they paid the first half of the ransom!"

I was stunned. There was no news that I more wanted to hear. But the change in the way these men were treating me was so drastic, and the wait had been so long, I didn't know whether I dared to believe them. I knew that if I allowed my hopes to be raised by information that proved false, it would crush me.

"That's nice," I said.

Señor Mustache didn't seem to notice my lack of enthusiasm. "The second half of the payment is to be made tomorrow," he continued. "If that delivery goes as smoothly as the first one, you will be a free man!"

I was stupefied. This man who had been so abusive to me for so long was acting like someone at a celebration. He was behaving the way I would expect a friend to react to good news. It was as if he wanted to rejoice with me.

"That's nice," I said again.

"Don Fausto," said Señor Mustache. "Before you leave us, there is one favor we would like to ask of you."

Now it was going to come out. Now I would find out what kind of game these sadists wanted to play.

Señor Skinny produced two spiral notebooks and handed them to me. "Señor Chapman has been writing some things in these books. We would like to know what he has written, but he wrote in English," explained Señor Mustache.

I opened the top notebook and began scanning the hand-written contents. It was a journal. Bruce had occupied his time by writing down everything that had happened to him since the abduction.

"We would appreciate it very much of you would translate those words into Spanish for us," requested Señor Mustache.

"Do you want me to write it out for you?" I wondered.

"Oh no," replied Señor Mustache. "There won't be enough time for that." He seemed serious. "My friend here will stay with you, and you can read it to him."

In my state of mind I was prepared to do almost anything I was told. I agreed to translate the notebooks. Señor Skinny brought in a chair and sat down, and Señor Mustache left.

I had been jolted many times by unexpected circumstances, and it happened again. As I read aloud to Señor Skinny, I could not believe what I was saying with my own mouth. Bruce Chapman hadn't been in captivity—he had been on vacation! He was being housed in his own room, complete with an operational toilet and a shower. He was given a full pair of pajamas —the right size—and a normal bed to sleep on. he was given three meals a day. In fact, he not only got to eat "real food," but was allowed to select his menu on occasion (including hamburgers and french fries). The kidnappers provided him with many of the creature comforts he requested: cigarettes, liquor ("booze"), a radio. He even got to watch the World Series on television! He received tapes and letters from his wife. The only inconvenience he experienced was that he wasn't allowed to leave—he was a captive, technically. The only thing he asked for that he was denied was a woman.

It is difficult to describe the enormous sense of outrage I felt as I read the journal. Strangely enough, I was angrier with

Chapman than I was at the perpetrators of this outrageous inequity. As a victim of the so-called Stockholm Syndrome, I had developed a kind of love-hate relationship toward my captors. I held them less responsible for this situation than I did Chapman. That he could live in such comfort while knowing of my conditions (as he apparently did, judging from his comments in the journal) was almost more than I could stand.

Nevertheless, I was in no position to give vent to my wrath. I had neither the physical stamina nor the opportunity to strike out at anyone. All I could do is protest. And I did. "Why am I treated so despicably while Chapman is enjoying all this luxury?" I demanded to know. It was my most assertive action in the whole ordeal.

Señor Skinny retreated from the cell and returned shortly with the other two hoods. However, someone opened the door prematurely, and and I caught a glimpse of their faces. They hastily covered themselves, but my heart sank. *I'm a doomed man!* I thought. *They'll never let me out of here alive now!*

Hoods in place, the three men filed into my cubicle. "You saw nothing, Don Fausto, am I correct?" prompted Señor Glasses.

"I saw nothing!" I agreed. "I know nothing!"

"Good!" he replied. I couldn't believe that he wasn't completely unnerved by their exposure.

"Now, I understand that you are a little upset about what you have been reading."

"You might say that!" I responded as my fear abated and my anger surged. "I just want to know why I have been treated so cruelly while Chapman's accommodations are first class!"

"Well, first of all," he replied, "you represent one of our greatest enemies—the North American capitalist, imperialist companies that exploit our people and prop up the puppet governments that keep the elitist landowners and industrialists in control of our country!" I would have protested such insanity, but my mind was so boggled by what I was hearing that I was literally speechless. Señor Glasses continued. "You, Don Fausto, were the target of our kidnapping operation. Show him the pictures!" he directed Señor Skinny.

His associate handed me a stack of black-and-white prints, about thirty in number. I was in every picture. I had been photographed in the plant, traveling to and from work, at the hotel. The terrorists had known every move I made. I looked up uncomprehendingly.

"We were planning to grab you on Wednesady of that week!" he went on. "But when the trap was set, Luis Paz was not with you. That murderer was number one on our execution list. So we waited until we could capture you and kill him."

"But that's not right!" I protested. "I only came down here to help!"

"But you are an executive with Hartell!" he countered. "And one of our objectives was to teach a lesson to the Yankees. It's just the first step in our plan to evict the North Americans from Central America forever!"

"Well, I don't appreciate being the object lesson!" I said, amazed at my temerity. "I didn't come down here as an enemy of your people, I came down to help—to straighten out the mess at APLAR so that your people would have jobs."

"That isn't what we understood!" he said. "We heard that you were going to shut down the plant. That's what most of the workers at APLAR believed."

"Well, it wasn't true!" I asserted. "And I still don't understand why Chapman was treated so well. He works for Hartell too."

"Ah, but he cooperated with us!" explained the spokesman. "And you didn't! You see, when you didn't answer our questions about your company, you only confirmed our suspicions about your opposition to our cause. But when we went to Chapman, he gave us answers to all of our questions. He even had a card in his pocket with the name of the man we were to contact to open the negotiations."

I had already been upset with Chapman. Now I was even angrier. Hartell became the object of my ire as well. Bruce had been prepared for this kind of situation. But Hartell sent me down here like a sheep to the slaughter. I was so mad I couldn't see straight.

"I couldn't have told you anything then even if I had wanted to!" I complained. "It wasn't fair for you to single me out for this kind of treatment!" I waved my hand to take in my surroundings.

For the first time since the kidnapping, I sensed a trace of sympathy from my captors. "Don't worry, Don Fausto!" replied Señor Glasses. "If everything goes as planned, this will all be over soon." They prepared to go.

"There's just one more thing that I'm curious about!" I ventured. They gave me their attention. "Why are you telling me these things now?"

"We know that you are not our enemy now!" answered the leader. "And we don't need to punish you any more. If you have any more questions, we'll probably answer them for you."

All three men departed, and I was left to ponder the revelations of this incredible day.

Day 44 *(Saturday, 3 November)*

FRED RAYNE was becoming increasingly concerned. It was 4:00 P.M. He had arrived with his two bodyguards in Tegucigalpa shortly after noon, barely missing his deadline. The afternoon was spent at Toncontín Airport fruitlessly placing calls every fifteen minutes to the number provided by Carlos. Finally Fred called the command post in San Salvador.

"We've got problems!" he said when Juan Ortega answered the phone. "We hit a heavy storm en route to Honduras, and the plane couldn't handle the head winds! We missed our deadline, and no one will answer the number we were given!"

"Well, you can relax!" Juan replied.

"What?"

"Whatever problems you may have encountered are nothing compared to the troubles our counterparts had!"

"What happened?" Fred asked.

"Carlos called a little while ago and filled us in. The details are a little sketchy, and some of it is hard to put together. But apparently the PRTC sent a team of about a half-dozen men and women to Honduras to make the pickup. They selected a less-trafficked road, hoping to be able to circumvent customs officials. They were dropped off about a mile from the border. They left the roadway and trekked on foot through the jungle. But when they had crossed the border into Honduras, they were stopped by a policeman on border partol. So they killed him and stole his jeep!"

Fred gasped. Such ruthlessness was common in this kind of operation, but he never got used to cold-blooded murder.

Juan continued. "They knew that before long, every law enforcement officer in the country would be on the lookout for the government vehicle. So before they got into the capital, they hijacked a school bus full of children!"

A chill went through Fred Rayne's body. "Did they do anything to any of those kids?" he asked through clenched teeth.

"Mercifully no!" Juan replied. "Apart from scaring them to death, no doubt! They commandeered the bus into the city still trying to complete the transfer of the money."

"Those people are insane!"

"But when they heard on the bus radio that the authorities were hot on their trail, they abandoned the bus, split up, and straggled back into El Salvador each man, or woman, for himself—uh—herself—whatever!"

"Nobody would believe this story!" Fred muttered.

"Carlos said they would call back tomorrow when the dust settles. They'll have new instructions then. I suspect we'll be making the delivery a little closer to home."

"I think," Fred replied, "that Murphy invented his law in El Salvador."

† † †

SEÑOR SKINNY returned to my cell with the notebooks on Saturday morning. But before he put me to work, he gave me a single sheet of paper. "This is for you!" he said. "We thought you might like to have it."

I opened the folded page and stared at the familiar handwriting. It was from Rita, and my heart leaped to my throat. It took awhile for the reality of it to register in my mind. It really was from her—it was in her own hand.

The note was too brief. I read it and read it and read it again. Then I saw the date: she had penned it in response to my first letter a full month earlier. Anger boiled up inside me, but I controlled the impulse to complain: it wouldn't do any good. Getting the note at all was probably a gesture of good will.

Señor Skinny sat silently in the chair beside me as I absorbed the message of the letter and wept a little. If he hadn't been there, I might have indulged my feelings more. Instead, I refolded the paper, tucked it into my Bible, and composed myself.

When he deemed me to be composed again, Señor Skinny handed me one of the notebooks. As I turned the pages we had already covered, I recalled my ruminations of the previous night. I considered then that this journal could be just one great, elaborate hoax hoisted upon me as the *coup de grâce*. That thought temporarily terrified me. But as I reasoned more clearly I realized the impossibility of such a deception. The handwriting belonged to Bruce: I had seen enough of his memos to recognize it. This was all the evidence I needed, but it was supported by the perfectly American prose. These people did not understand English, much less speak it. The more I read, the more it was confirmed that only Bruce could have written this specific content.

When I found where we had left off, I resumed translating. But now I was doing the work as much for myself as for them. So my education continued. Bruce had written down everything that was of personal importance to him. It was obvious that Bruce Chapman never intended for this journal to be read by others. His thoughts about APLAR, his wife, his family, his confinement—all were recorded. From this diary I learned about the manifestos. I asked about them, and as they had promised, the hooded men came and explained what the company had done to meet that first condition for our release. Hearing about the effort so many people had expended to meet that demand was encouraging to me.

Occasionally as I read, Señor Skinny would tell me to stop. He would leave the room and return with one or another of the leaders. Then they would have me translate a portion over again. Then we would continue as before. We worked on the diary, off and on, through most of the day.

Toward suppertime both Señor Glasses and Señor Mustache returned. Señor Glasses spoke. "Don Fausto, I'm afraid I have some bad news!" I waited for the roof to fall in. "We had some problems in Honduras, and we were not able to complete the transfer of the ransom money."

I asked him what had happened, and to my amazement, he

told me all about the border guard, the school bus, the whole event. It sickened me to hear about the death of a man who happened to be at the wrong place at the wrong time. I couldn't help but feel that I was partially responsible for his death. It wasn't a rational response, but that was my reaction.

"But don't worry!" said the leader. "We'll just set up something else. It will just take some more time!"

The three men exited, and I was left with the echo of the last statement. It brought to my mind a song recorded by Elvis Presley: "A Matter of Time." I took Rita's letter from my Bible and looked at it. Now I didn't see the words. I saw her. In my mind, I could see us sitting in our family room listening to that album. It was my favorite.

Maybe this would happen again. Maybe it really was just a matter of time.

◻◻◻◻◻◻◻◻

THE HOTLINE at the Sheraton command post did not often ring at night, but on this Saturday evening it did.

"We have new instructions for you!" Carlos said.

"All right!" Juan Ortega replied. "Mr. Rayne is not back yet from Honduras, but I can pass them along if you want."

"Just tell him that we are arranging for the drop of the rest of the money in this area."

"Fine!" said Juan.

"And we want half of the money in *colones*."

Juan exploded. "You can't be serious!" he objected. "Why, tomorrow is Sunday. There's not a bank in the country that will be open."

"We *are* serious," Carlos replied calmly. "We will call you Monday with the final instructions. Be ready!" He hung up.

"I sure hope Fred knows where we can come up with that kind of change!" said Juan to no one in particular.

Day 45 *(Sunday, 4 November)*

Fred Rayne had two options for converting dollars into *colones*. He could ask the people at the U.S. embassy to pull whatever strings were necessary to pry open a bank; or he could ransack the available cash registers of San Salvador and vicinity. The former alternative would require less energy, but it would raise more complications. Besides, most banks didn't hold the quantity of cash he needed. So he and his men hit the streets in a frantic treasure hunt for Salvadoran currency.

The one thing in their favor was that U.S. dollars were greatly prized by the Salvadorans. Whenever a North American visited the country, he was immediately besieged with requests to trade his dollars for some *colones.* It may have seemed strange to the natives to see well-dressed Americans initiating this particular trade, but restaurant managers and hotel clerks, among others, were happy to accommodate them.

The problem lay not so much in finding willing moneychangers. The problem was volume. The currency being exchanged was in such small denominations that a single transaction converted very little money. It took many transactions. What it took was all day.

Even as Fred Rayne and his aides fanned out across the Salvadoran capital, another band of unknown militant revolutionaries staged a dramatic demonstration halfway around the world. Protesting American protection of their exiled Shah, some five hundred Iranians seized the U.S. embassy in Teheran and held all captured Americans as hostage. Though no one knew it at the time, another man would be president of the United States by the time all those hostages were released.

23
Paid in Full

Day 46 (*Monday, 5 November*)

"THIS DELIVERY WILL be carried out in two stages." The terrorist Carlos was giving Juan Ortega his instructions for the "final payment" on the "account."

"First, you must provide us with a key to the trunk of the car you will be using to transport the money." He specified a drop site, and Juan wrote down the directions.

"Put the money in four medium-sized suitcases and place them in the back of your car. Leave the hotel at seven o'clock tomorrow night and drive to a phone booth just beyond the city limits." He gave Juan more detailed directions. "Go into that phone booth and wait. We will call you there."

"Am I to understand," Fred Rayne queried, "that when you have the final payment in your possession, you will release our men?"

"Yes, that is correct!" Carlos confirmed.

"Then I will set in motion our plans to take them home," Fred said. "All you need to do, Carlos, is take Bruce and Fausto to some place where there is a phone and give them this number. Is that all right?"

"That is fine with us!" he agreed. "We have taken care of them long enough—you can have them." Then Carlos added, "It's been a pleasure doing business with you!"

Fred Rayne replied, "No offense, Carlos, but I hope I never hear your voice again!" The other man laughed and hung up.

Day 47 *(Tuesday, 6 November)*

Rayne and his team spent the day making the final preparations to deliver the money and transport the two hostages to the United States. Four suitcases were purchased from a store in town, and the cash was "packed." However, since half of the ransom was in *colones,* there were more bills than could be contained in four bags. A fifth suitcase was bought and filled.

Fred called Fullerton and ordered two private jets to be flown to San Salvador—one for Bruce, Fausto, and himself; the other to transport his team back to Miami. The men packed their belongings and moved out of the suite.

Under the aegis of the State Department, Fred had requisitioned office space from the manager of Ilopango International Airport. The telephone line that had terminated in the Sheraton Hotel room was rerouted to that airport office. The junta was persuaded to provide a contingent of military police to guard the jets until they departed safely with their precious cargo. To enhance the security, the government directed airport officials to route the Hartell planes into and out of the presidential hanger.

The trunk key had already been dropped, and by 7:00 P.M., when Juan Ortega pulled out of the parking lot of the Sheraton Hotel, everything was ready.

As before, Juan was accompanied by the Salvadoran chauffeur from APLAR. On this occasion, however, Juan did the driving; the other man served as navigator.

They found the telephone booth with no difficulty, and two minutes later the phone rang.

"There is another phone booth about one-and-one-half kilometers down the road," said an unfamiliar voice. "Drive to it and wait for your next contact."

The line went dead. Juan never said a word. He got back into the car and drove to the next booth. As he opened the door, the phone rang. He picked up the receiver.

"Do you see the restaurant on the righthand side of the road?" asked the man.

"Yes!"

"Leave your companion there and tell him to go inside and wait for you."

"All right!"

"Then drive to the top of the hill. There you will come to the end of the road. Turn the car around so that you are facing down the hill. Park the car, but leave the engine running. Flash your headlights on and off four times. Do not look in your rearview mirror, do not turn around! If you see one of our guns, it will be the last thing that you ever see! Do you understand?"

Juan's heart was pounding, and he was perspiring heavily. He hoped his voice was not shaking too much when he said, "I understand!" End of conversation.

He drove to the restaurant and dropped off the chauffeur —who was happy enough to wait. Juan then proceeded up the hill, made the U-turn, stopped, flashed the lights four times, and waited. He did not have to wait long. From out of the shrubbery came three couples. It looked for all the world as if Juan had stumbled onto Lovers' Lane.

In seconds he heard a key being inserted into the latch. The hatchback door was raised, and three suitcases were lifted out. Someone slammed the door, pounded on the roof of the little car, and shouted, "Go!"

Juan looked over his shoulder and, to his great dismay, saw that two suitcases had been left sitting on the second seat. The guerrillas hadn't seen them. In all his years as a security agent, Juan Ortega had never experienced fear as he did at that moment. He had only split seconds in which to act.

He honked the horn, rolled down the window, and without looking back shouted, "Wait! You missed two suitcases!"

At the sound of the horn, the startled revolutionaries whipped around. Within seconds six handguns were trained on the gray compact car. Juan gripped the steering wheel with both hands; his knuckles turned white, but he remained still. Two of the men cautiously approached the vehicle. Once again the hatchback door was lifted. One man looked over the back seat, saw the two suitcases, and lifted the one on the right out of the car. The one directly behind Juan was wedged between the seats; it had prevented Juan's bucket seat from latching completely. When the man extricated the jammed suitcase, Juan's seat slipped into place with a sudden jerk and a loud click. It startled everyone. But no weapons were fired and Juan did not die of fright. "Sorry!" he hastily apologized. The rear gate was slammed shut.

In the almost-empty car, Juan made rocks and dirt fly as he accelerated down the hill. He lurched to a stop in front of the restaurant. The APLAR man was standing by the front door.

Juan waved at him and shouted, "Let's go!"

The man didn't move, didn't respond.

"Come on!" Juan repeated. "Let's get out of here!"

Still no response. The man seemed petrified.

Juan left the motor running, set the brake, and got out of the car, walked over to the Salvadoran, and took him by the arm. The man appeared to be in shock. Juan led him to the car and helped him into the passenger's seat. Then he returned to his place behind the wheel and sped off.

"What's the matter with you?" he asked his companion as they headed toward the airport.

The man spoke as in a daze. "That restaurant back there—everyone in there has a machine gun, or a machete, or hand grenades, or pistols! That place is a guerrilla camp!"

Juan's body began to shake. It was all he could do to keep the car on the road.

Day 48 *(Wednesday, 7 November)*

"This will be the first time I have ever failed a client," Fred Rayne muttered as he paced back and forth in his new head-quarters at the airport. It was three o'clock in the morning, and Bruce and Fausto had not been released. The pilots of the jets didn't have the nerve for this cloak-and-dagger stuff. They had flown out at midnight, glad to be out of a hangar guarded by soldiers carrying real guns.

Fred racked his brain to figure out what could have gone wrong. He had followed every instruction to the letter. He had developed a relationship of mutual respect with his adversaries, he was certain. Had he relinquished several million dollars only to get nothing but mockery in return—or two corpses?

An exhausted Juan Ortega tried to sleep draped over a couple of office chairs. But Fred was so upset, with himself and the impudent PRTC, that no one could get any sleep worthy of the word.

The mounting tension was broken by the ringing of the telephone at 5:00 A.M. Fred answered it himself.

"What's the matter with you people?" he demanded without preamble. "Where is our merchandise?"

"Your merchandise is still in good shape and in our care," said Carlos.

"All right, what's going on?"

"We had to count the money!" Carlos replied matter-of-factly. "And you are a hundred dollars short!"

Fred swore. "We gave you millions of dollars!" he roared. "Do you think I'm going to cheat you out of a hundred lousy bucks? You turkeys can't count! I want my men!"

"All right, all right, Señor Rayne!" said Carlos. "Don't get upset!"

"It's too late!" Fred fumed.

"Well, we can't release the hostages right now!" Carlos explained. "We'll have to wait until dark. You'll hear from them tonight."

"I'll believe that when it happens!" Fred said curtly, slamming down the phone.

Well now, at least we'll be able to get some sleep, thought Juan, as he sought a comfortable position on the chairs.

One of the advantages of not having John Pike come to the house every day was the certainty that when he did appear, he was bringing real news about Fausto. This morning was no exception, and Rita happened to be at home to meet him.

"I thought you would want to know," John began, "that we heard from Fred Rayne yesterday."

"What did he say?"

"That they have received Fausto's passport from the kidnappers—and another tape."

"His passport and a tape? What does that mean?"

"We're not sure!" he responded truthfully. "We are not getting our hopes up. The news could be very good—or very bad. We just don't know what to make of it."

"Well, I appreciate your telling me about it anyway," said Rita, showing John to the door.

"We'll be sure to let you know when we hear more," he assured her.

Rita sat down and tried to sort out what this information could mean. She didn't know what to think about the passport. But another tape could only mean that the negotiations were likely to drag on for more days at least. This was not encouraging at all.

She stood up and placed a long-distance call to St. Petersburg, Florida. When a woman answered the phone, Rita said, "May I speak with Truman Gottschalk?"

The man Rita was trying to reach was a pastor with the Missionary Church. When she was a little girl in Esmeraldas, he was one of the first missionaries she had met.

"He is not in just now," the woman said. "I am his mother-in-law. May I have him return your call?"

Rita was disappointed. "Yes, I would appreciate that very much. My name is Rita Bucheli, and my number is—"

"Oh, just a minute!" the woman interrupted. "He just walked in the door!"

After a silent pause, the familiar voice came on the line. "Hello, Rita!" he said. "How nice of you to call! We've thought so much about you during the past month."

"I am grateful for that!" began Rita.

"Do you have any more word on Fausto?" he inquired.

Rita told him of John's visit and the confusing information about the passport and tape. "I called you," she explained, "because I really need someone to pray for me—for us."

"Our whole church has been praying for you, Rita!" he assured her. "And we will continue to do so until Fausto comes home."

"Pastor Truman," said Rita, "I think I need some special prayer. I don't seem to be able to pray myself. The sky appears to be made of iron for me. What I need is a miracle."

"The Lord knows what you need," said the pastor. "I'll tell you what I am going to do. It's lunchtime here, and I may be able to reach some of our elders by phone. I'll gather as many of our people as I can find, and we'll get together this afternoon for a time or prayer. And we'll ask for your miracle. But Rita," he concluded, "the sky only *seems* to be made of iron. There are plenty of prayer-sized holes in it."

"Thanks!" said Rita. "I needed that!"

Ginger Martin had spent half the morning on the phone, working on what she hoped would be her last assignment in this case. Fred Rayne had awakened her with his call at 6:30 A.M. Florida time. He had sounded tired—he had every right to be after being up all night—but he was hopeful. He needed a six-passenger Learjet to come to El Salvador and transport him and the two hostages back to Los Angeles that night. He wasn't sure Fullerton would accede to such a request prior to the actual release of the men—not after sending two jets on a false alarm the day before. But neither did he want to stay in San Salvador any longer than he had to. So Ginger was to procure the needed transportation on short order. "Try not to use the word 'hostage' if you can!" he had warned. "Some pilots tend to get a little skittish when they think there's a chance someone might start shooting at their plane!"

But it was very difficult to avoid using the word "hostage," because the charter companies she called all wanted to know the details of the contract. Eventually the person at the other end would ask enough questions to decide that his or her company wanted no part of such dealings. "Why, our insurance company would drop us faster than a blind alcoholic if they found out we made that kind of run!" said one charter manager.

Ginger expanded the field of her search beyond Miami and finally made connections with one Harvey Hop who operated out of Fort Lauderdale. He wanted to know only one thing: "Who's going to pay for this excursion?"

"Our client is Hartell Industries in California, and they will pick up the tab," Ginger explained. "But if you want, I can meet you on the runway at the Miami airport and give you five thousand dollars in cash as a down payment."

"Naw, that's all right!" said Harvey. "You sound like a good outfit! I'll go down and get your men for you!"

Ginger smiled. Mission accomplished. And she did it without saying "hostage."

† † †

AS DAY 48 was recorded on my wall calendar, I continued to struggle with my emotions. My fear of having my hopes raised and then cruelly dashed made me extremely hesitant to believe that I might actually be released soon. Yet the change in attitude toward me was undeniable. During the past couple of days, I had been given coffee to drink—good, hot coffee! My keepers had offered me bread and other food, but my stomach couldn't handle anything else and I had no appetite. So I declined. It occurred to me that this generosity on their part might be a form of bribery to induce me to translate Bruce Chapman's journal. But I had completed that project the night before, and on this morning the coffee was still part of the breakfast menu.

In midmorning the hooded ones returned to my cell, and Señor Glasses made the one statement I had most wanted to hear: "Your ransom has been paid, Don Fausto! Tonight we will return you to your people!"

I hardly knew how to react. Some news can be so good one almost dares not to believe it. But the three men were jubilant: they had won their war of nerves.

"Don't you want to hear about it?" invited Señor Glasses. I nodded numbly. I listened—at first fascinated, then chilled as I understood how close the exchange had come to failure.

But for the PRTC, all that was past. They apparently had but one detail to discharge—setting Bruce and me free. This would not happen till after dark, they said. So many things had gone wrong before, I decided to just wait and see. I would have spent some more time reading my Bible, but the suspense was so great, I couldn't concentrate.

Lunch on Day 48 was like a banquet. The main course was the same, and I was again treated to coffee. But as I was finishing the last of the coffee, my three hosts entered the cell. I couldn't believe my eyes! Señor Skinny was holding an ice cream cone! "We appreciate your cooperation over the past few days!" announced Señor Glasses, as the ice cream man presented me with my reward.

I had never tasted anything quite so good. It was vanilla and cold and sweet. Throughout my captivity I had not really craved food. My illnesses were such that my appetite was poor—which was probably just as well in view of my rations. Most of my fantasies were about water. I would dream of lakes and rivers. I would imagine what it would be like to lie down in a stream and feel the water rushing over my body. But I was not

obsessed with food. The ice cream cone proved to be the ultimate happy medium. I devoured it rapturously.

My bemused benefactors watched over my "pig-out" like
parents at a child's birthday party. As I was licking my fingers,
Señor Mustache said, "Don Fausto, you are not like the others
we have had!"

"You can drop the *don!*" I said. "Just call me Fausto!" We
were becoming positively cordial. But I was curious. "What do
you mean I am not like the others?"

"We had another guy in this room before!" he revealed.
"He didn't last a week!"

"Oh!" I replied casually. But to myself I said, *No wonder
these guys are so good at breaking a man down—they've had practice!*

"That's right!" Señor Mustache continued. "We didn't
think you would be able to take it for so long. Why didn't you
crack?"

It was news to me that I hadn't. I knew I was still in serious
condition—both physically and emotionally. But it was also
true that I hadn't gone stark-raving mad. "I have a Friend who
has been watching over me!" I responded. "He is the One who
has protected me."

And *that* was news to *them*. "Who?" demanded Señor
Glasses.

"His name is Jesus Christ."

My answer was greeted with nervous laughter. Their security had not been breached. They had nothing to fear from the
harmless delusions of an impotent captive, religious or otherwise. So they chose to humor me and change the subject.

"We will be back later to help you get ready to leave,"
Señor Glasses informed me. The three men left to tend to other
business.

But Ocho, who had been standing just outside the open
door, came back into my cell to pick up my tray. "Señor
Bucheli," he said in a low voice. "My comrades don't believe in
anybody! But I believe in God!"

Somehow that confession didn't totally surprise me. "Good
for you, Ocho!" I replied. I picked up the New Testament.
"They tell me that I am going to leave today," I continued, "so
why don't you keep this book?"

"Oh no!" he recoiled as I held it out to him. "If I took that book, they would kill me!"

I put down the New Testament. "Well, if you ever get a chance to read it," I encouraged him, "be sure that you do. It helped me very much."

Ocho simply nodded as he left the room.

◁◁◁◁◁◁◁◁◁◁⌐

HOW WOULD you like something to do?" Fred Rayne asked his pacing, bored associate.

"You must be a mind reader!" replied a startled Juan Ortega.

Fred shrugged and laughed. "In this business, being able to read minds wouldn't hurt!"

"So what do you want me to do?" Juan asked.

"I don't know if you'll want to take this one on!" Fred said seriously. "There's a lot of stress involved. But you're the only one I can really trust with such a delicate job."

Ortega became apprehensive. "Has something else gone wrong?"

"Not yet! But it could if the situation isn't handled right."

"So what is it?" Juan pressed in exasperation.

"I need for you to secure two platters of sandwiches and two bottles of champagne!" ordered the boss. "And there's a critical deadline involved—we need them by sundown. So you'd better get cracking—you only have six hours."

Chagrined Juan knew he had been had. "What's our upper limit?" he responded gamely as he walked toward the door.

"You've had plenty of experience!" Fred replied. "Use your own judgment!"

"That's a pretty heavy responsibility, all right!" Juan rejoined.

"It's heavier than you think! Anything that isn't covered by the insurance comes out of your pocket."

Juan exited laughing.

Fred picked up the telephone and placed a call to the U.S. embassy. When the official he was after came on the line, Fred made one last request. "A Mr. Harvey Hop is en route to San Salvador from Miami in a Learjet to collect our hostages. I was wondering if some steps might be taken to prevail upon Mr. Hop to stay put until the passengers are on board—regardless of when that might be."

His contact understood the message. This plane would not leave prematurely.

I've got the plane, and I've got the food, Fred thought. *Now all I need are the passengers!*

24
Release!

(Wednesday, 7 November, continued)
BY 4:00 P.M. I WAS about convinced that I was really going to be released. The kidnappers brought me several cans of water with which I "showered." They gave me a razor with which to shave—I left the mustache. They brought me the clothes I had been wearing when they abducted me. The clothes and underwear had been washed; the shirt and slacks had been pressed.

"May I keep the briefs that you gave me?" I requested.

"Why would you want them?" said Señor Glasses.

"Oh, as a sort of souvenir," I replied.

The man just shrugged. "O.K., just put the rest of your clothes on over them."

I checked my pockets, looking for the other articles that had been taken from me. They were empty. "Are you going to give me back my other rings and things?" I asked hopefully.

"Don't push your luck!" growled Señor Glasses. "This isn't a charity organization!"

There was no mirror by which to examine my appearance, but I could tell that my clothes no longer fit me properly. I discovered later that I had lost thirty-eight pounds during my captivity.

The leaders left me during supper. In their absence I opened the little New Testament and inscribed a message on the blank first page:

Remember me. With love, Fausto.

If Ocho returned to clean the cell after my departure, he would know it was for him. But if someone else picked it up, it wouldn't get him in trouble, because I hadn't included his name.

I removed the letter from Rita and put it in a pocket in my slacks. As I put down my beloved Bible, I realized that the promise made by the Gideons had been fulfilled—it had given me light and food and comfort. I hoped it would do the same for Ocho. I prayed:

Lord, You gave this Bible to me when I needed it. Now use it in Ocho's life. I would like to meet him again in heaven.

◄◄◄◄◄◄◄◄

IS THERE a Mr. Rayne here?" The proprietor of Hop-A-Jet, Harvey Hop, had been directed to the office that had become the staging area for the airlift of the hostages.

"I'm Fred Rayne!" the negotiator acknowledged, extending his hand.

The aviator shook hands amiably. "Ms. Martin in Miami contracted with me to pick up two Americans here and transport them to Los Angeles."

"You've come to the right place!" Fred said.

"Good!" said Hop. "My plane is being refueled right now. As soon as I grab a cup of coffee and a sandwich we can take off." He glanced hopefully around the room.

"Well, the passengers aren't here yet," Fred said. "So you can eat a whole supper if you want."

"Naw!" replied Harvey. "I'd just as soon get going. These Central American airports give me the jitters! When are the two men going to get here?"

"We're not sure!" Rayne said. "But they should be released any time."

"Released? Hey, who are these guys, anyway?"

"Just a couple of Americans who were kidnapped by Communist guerrillas about a month and a half ago!" Fred replied. "We expect to hear from them any minute now."

The light dawned. "Kidnapped? You mean I'm here to get those hostages they were talking about in the news?"

Fred nodded.

The agitated pilot walked over to a window and began scanning the runway. "My plane . . ."

"Don't worry about it!" Fred assured him. "It's being taken care of."

Harvey spotted the Learjet. "Hey, who are all those guys with the guns around my plane?"

"They are military police. They're on our side! The government deployed them here to protect your jet."

"Protect my . . . excuse me, Mr. Rayne, but I didn't bargain for this! You can keep your money, but I'm getting out of here!"

"I expect you will!" Fred agreed. "But not without the passengers you agreed to carry."

Harvey Hop headed for the door. "Sorry, Mr. Rayne, but your fellows were late for this trip! This flight is taking off!"

"Not just yet!"

"And who's going to stop me?"

Fred walked over to the window and looked out at the jet in front of the presidential hangar. "Those guys with the guns."

† † †

WHEN MY captors returned, they warned me not to reveal their identities or give information about them to anyone. "You are the only man who has seen our faces that we have released alive!" said Señor Glasses. (He and the others continued to wear their pillowcase hoods.) "Do not think that you are ever beyond our reach! Borders mean nothing to us! We have our people everywhere—including the U.S. If anything you say results in harm to the PRTC, you are a dead man—you, your wife, and your children! Do you understand me?"

"I understand," I replied. And I did. His words struck fear into my heart, a fear that would haunt me for months to come.

Then it was time to leave. Señor Skinny took two large wads of cotton and put them behind the lenses of my glasses. They put tape across the front of my glasses and made it adhere to the skin of my face, but they did not wrap it all the way around my head. This time I could not see at all, but the situation was much less painful than the inaugural trip.

Señor Mustache made an attempt at levity. "Fausto, when we establish Independence Day here in El Salvador, after we have taken over the government, we will send you an invitation to come back and help us celebrate!"

I thought, *I should live so long!* But aloud I said simply, "Thanks!"

"All right!" announced Señor Glasses. "Get up! Let's go!"

I tried to stand, but my knees buckled. Even with the weight loss, my legs would not support my body. Two men had to lift me up and hold me on either side as I hobbled blindly from the cell. I was choked with emotion as I took my first steps outside that crypt in forty-seven days.

I was ushered to a small car and made to climb through a rear door into the back seat. Unfamiliar men sat on either side of me. I could tell that the car was small, because the three of us were really cramped in the seat. A woman's voice identified the gender of one of the occupants of the front seat.

Submachine guns were jammed into my ribs from either side, and a man's voice rasped, "Make no noise whatever! If we get stopped by the police, keep your face down. We will tell them that you are sick."

"Please!" I whispered. "The guns are hurting me and I can't breathe!"

The two men eased the pressure of the weapons. "Keep quiet!" hissed the man on my right. "You aren't home free yet!"

How well I knew it. The guns struck terror into my soul. My reactions may not have been totally rational, but I began to doubt whether I was going to survive this ride. Back in the cell I was of late being treated like an honorary comrade in the PRTC—one of the boys. But the people in the car were different. They didn't know me; they probably didn't care if I lived or died. A sharp bump from the road could discharge one of the guns. The line between life and death was excruciatingly thin.

As the engine was started, Salvadoran music blared from the radio. The overloaded vehicle strained to overcome inertia and set out on the journey that would be either the beginning or the end of the road for me.

I prayed,

Dear Lord, if I am to die, I ask that I might be spared from pain.

† † †

IT LOOKS as if we're finally going to pull this thing off! thought Fred Rayne as he rode through the streets of San Salvador in an armored car. The first of the two anticipated calls had come. Bruce Chapman had been released close to a food market near his home. The manager recognized him and gave him immediate access to his telephone.

By the time Fred arrived, Chapman had already consumed most of the contents of a bottle of wine donated by the store manager. "Hey, let's finish the wine first!" were the first words Chapman said to the man who had secured his release. But Fred declined his offer.

"Let's go!" was all he said as he steered Chapman into the armored car. *One down and one to go!* he pondered as they headed toward the airport.

† † †

MY FIRST exact indication of time since I had glanced at my watch forty-seven days before was provided by a radio announcer. At precisely 7:25 P.M., the car came to a stop. I was almost afraid to breathe.

"Listen carefully, *gringo!*" said the man on my right. "When you get out of the car, count to sixty before you remove the tape." Someone pressed a piece of paper and some coins into my hand. "Find a telephone," the man instructed, "and call the number written on that piece of paper. One of your people will come to get you."

The man got out of the car and pulled me out after him. I managed to stand upright on my own. I heard the man get back into the car, the door slam, and the engine rev. I braced myself for the impact of bullets. They didn't come. The car pulled away and left me standing there alone.

"One, two, three," I counted. But I couldn't stand it any more. I pulled the tape off my glasses as quickly as I could without hurting my flesh and eyebrows. It was early evening, so it didn't take my eyes long to adjust to the dim light. On my left was a big field of grass; on my right a cluster of apartments.

Something inside me said, *Don't just stand there—run!* I

tried to flee the imagined danger, but my legs wouldn't work. I took one step and crashed to the ground. I couldn't move.

As I lay there in a state of panic, a little girl, perhaps nine years old, came up to me. "Is something wrong, *señor?*"

"Yes, little girl!" I said. "I am very sick! Could you get me a taxi?"

"Yes, *señor!*" she replied, and she ran away.

In no time at all, she returned, just as a taxi pulled up. I wanted to give her something, but I had no money besides the few coins the kidnappers had given me. I wanted to kiss her, or something! All I could do was say, "Thank you! Oh, thank you so much!" as the taxi driver helped me into the cab.

All I could think about at the moment was getting away from the place where I had been left by my captors. So ignoring their instructions for the moment, I directed the driver to take me to El Camino Real. I was trembling all over. "I am very sick!" I said. "I think I am going to pass out!"

"Don't worry about a thing!" the driver responded. "I will get you to the hotel!" We sped away into the night.

† † †

FRED RAYNE's phone in the airport office rang for a second time that evening. "That ought to be Fausto!" said Juan Ortega as he lifted the receiver.

It wasn't. "This is the PRTC!" said the unfamiliar voice. "Your man Bucheli didn't follow instructions!" Ortega clenched his teeth and waited for the hammer blow. "He called a taxi. We followed him to El Camino Real. You can pick him up there." The line went dead, and Juan expelled the breath he had inhaled at the beginning of the call.

"Come on!" he said to his APLAR chauffeur. "Let's go get him!"

† † †

MY BENEFACTOR in the taxicab delivered me to El Camino Real as promised. He helped me out of the car and supported me as I staggered into the main lobby of the hotel. He eased me into one of the plush velvet chairs, and I heard a commotion stirring in the room as I was recognized by some of the staff.

"It's Señor Bucheli! Señor Bucheli!" Someone brought me a glass of water. Someone else brought a cup of coffee. I don't know who paid the taxi driver. He disappeared and I never saw him again. I never used the coins I was given by the PRTC.

I was unable to drink anything, but I did manage to say, "I need to make a phone call."

In seconds a telephone materialized. I dialed zero and asked for the overseas operator: I had not forgotten my new telephone number back home.

† † †

IT WAS supper time in California. Rita was preparing food in the kitchen and Veronica was setting the table when the phone rang. Veronica answered it.

"Hello!" For a few seconds she couldn't hear anything. There was nothing but static on the line.

"Hello!" she tried again. She almost hung up. But then she heard her name. That voice—she recognized the voice.

"My dad!" she screamed. She put the phone down and shouted at her mother, who was standing just a few feet away: "Mom, get to the other phone!"

Rita felt the blood rush from her head. The closest extension was in the bedroom of Fausto Jr. She walked to the room from the kitchen thinking to herself, *This is it! He's dead! He loved red roses! I'll have to get lots of red roses for the funeral!* She picked up the phone.

"Hello!" Rita said numbly.

"Rita!" It was Fausto's voice.

"Fausto, is that you?" She couldn't understand anything he was saying. He was sobbing. "Fausto, where are you?"

Then she could understand him. "I love you! I love you!" he cried over and over again.

Then there was another voice on the phone, a man speaking English with a Spanish accent. "Mrs. Bucheli, this is Juan Ortega! Fausto is O.K.!"

Rita sat down on the twin bed. "Where is he?" she asked. "Is he in America?"

"No!" replied Juan. "He is still in San Salvador! He has just been released! But we are taking him to the airport right now. He will be home in seven hours."

"Is he all right?" she had the presence of mind to ask.

"He's a little shaky," replied Juan, "but he looks like he's all right. We have to go now! You will be hearing from us soon!"

Veronica and the other children were jubilant. The house couldn't contain them. They exploded out of the doors and were soon all over the neighborhood telling their friends the news of their father's release. For a few minutes Rita remained in a kind of fog. *What shall I do about the flowers?* she wondered.

† † †

TWO MEN entered the lobby of El Camino Real as the phone connection was made with my home in Chino. Though I was not fully aware of them as I talked and wept over the telephone, I dimly recognized one of the men as being from APLAR. The other man—the one I didn't know—gently took the receiver from me and spoke to Rita briefly, putting his arm around me as he talked. Then he hung up the phone.

"Fausto," he said, "I am Juan Ortega. I am Mr. Rayne's associate. We are going to take you to the airport now. The plane is waiting to take you home."

He and the other man helped me out to the little gray car and eased me into the back seat. I was in shock—partly from the physical exertion of just trying to walk after being totally immobilized for forty-eight days; but certainly from the emotional upheaval of being set free.

I was somewhat aware of Juan Ortega's efforts to fill me in on what had been happening. He told me that Bruce Chapman had been released and that Fred Rayne had gone to pick him up in an armored car.

His reference to an armored car raised my hackles. "He went after Chapman in an armored car? Why didn't you come after *me* in an armored car?" It seemed that the disparity in our treatment was being perpetuated.

"We only had one armored car," Juan explained. "And since we heard from Bruce first, we went after him right away. We thought the two of you would be released together. But when we heard that you were at the hotel, we came immediately in the only car that was available." It was a perfectly rational explanation. But I wasn't perfectly rational; I was miffed.

"It might interest you to know that this is the car we used to make the delivery of your ransom," Juan said. That did interest me. So Juan took the remainder of the drive to the airport to narrate the details of the ransom payment. The thing that struck me was that his report coincided perfectly with the information given me by the kidnappers. They had told me the truth, at least about the ransom.

† † †

IT TOOK a while to regather all five Bucheli offspring in the house. Once they returned, they began to discuss what they should do next. Grandma turned off all the appliances in the kitchen—that was one more meal that wouldn't be eaten. Rita attempted to call Hartell, but got no answer. She placed a call to the Pikes, but the line was busy.

"Why don't we just go over there?" suggested Fausto Jr. "John is the one they use to tell us what they want us to know!"

The whole family piled into the car and drove the few blocks to the Pikes' home.

It took Karen a half-minute to answer the doorbell. "Rita!" she exclaimed. "What's going on?"

"Fausto has been released!" Rita announced.

"No, that can't be!"

"Yes, it's true!" Rita insisted.

"How do you know?" Karen asked.

"He called us from El Salvador! I talked to him on the phone! I heard his voice! A man said they were flying him home!"

"Come on in!" said Karen excitedly. "I'm right in the middle of a telephone conversation with Mr. Reynolds at Hartell!"

Karen returned to the phone, and the family listened in on her end of the conversation.

"Rita Bucheli and the children are here, Mr. Reynolds! Rita says that Fausto has been released! . . . He called her and talked to her on the phone. . . . That's right! . . . He is? . . . All right! We'll do that! . . . Good-by!"

Karen Pike put down the receiver and turned to Rita. "Mr. Reynolds said that they haven't received the official word of Fausto's release, but they have been expecting it. My husband is already on his way over to your house. So let's go back over there, and he'll tell us what to do."

"Some things never change!" muttered one of the kids. But they all did as Karen said.

† † †

I HAD made enough trips in and out of Ilopango International Airport to be fairly familiar with it. But I had never seen those parts of it through which Juan drove us. It finally dawned on me that we were not going to check in anywhere. In fact, we would not go inside the terminal at all.

He circumvented the entire public facility and drove straight out onto the tarmac. I saw the familiar outline of a Learjet already in position for takeoff on the runway. It was surrounded by armed soldiers—a sight that sent chills up and down my spine. As we approached the plane, I recognized Bruce Chapman standing next to one wing and another, older man with him.

The car came to a stop, and my two escorts assisted me as I struggled to get out. Bruce and I embraced. Regardless of my negative feelings toward him during the captivity, it was true that we had experienced a terrible ordeal together. "We made it!" Bruce exclaimed. I couldn't say anything. "Are you all right, Fausto?" he asked, showing some genuine concern.

"I'll make it!" I replied.

Bruce turned to the man with whom he had been talking. "Fausto, this is Fred Rayne. He is the man—"

"Yes, I know!" I interrupted him. He came over to greet me, and I gave him a hug as well. I was crying as I said, "Thank you, thank you, thank you, Mr. Rayne! I am so grateful to you for what you have done!"

"As of this moment," he replied, "it is worth it all!" Then motioning to the open door of the plane, he said, "How would you fellows like to go home?"

We needed no further urging, but I did need considerable help boarding the jet. There were six seats on the plane. I occupied the rear right seat, and Bruce sat next to me. Fred Rayne sat in front of me, and next to him were two platters of sandwiches and two bottles of champagne—one with my name on it, and one for Bruce.

Before we took off, Fred handed me two pills and a glass of water. "What are these for?" I asked.

"The company doctor gave them to me for you," he explained. "They are for your nerves. They'll help you relax." I took them.

We were given immediate clearance and, to the great relief of our pilot, the soldiers withdrew from the plane. The powerful little jet raced down the runway, and soon we were airborne. First class all the way.

As I watched the lights of San Salvador diminish beneath us, I said, "Good-by, El Salvador! Never again will I see this sight!"

Bruce liked the idea of becoming relaxed. As soon as we gained cruising altitude, he broke out his bottle of champagne. Fred Rayne celebrated with him a little, but my system couldn't take the beverage. I did eat a few of the sandwiches without getting sick. This was the first food I had eaten—besides bananas and one ice cream cone—in forty-seven days. I have yet to eat another banana.

As we flew over Guatemala, southern Mexico, and the Gulf of Mexico, we compared notes. Fred told us about the first chartered planes from California that came down and flew back without us. He related some of the details of the last couple of days leading to our release. In the meantime I nibbled on sandwiches and Bruce drank champagne.

After a while, Fred asked about our conditions and how we fared during the captivity. It was consistent with our respective temperaments that Bruce should dominate the conversation at this point. I was perfectly willing to let him say whatever he wished. It only disturbed me that he spoke in the first person plural all the time.

But after a while, when Bruce showed no signs of taking a break, Fred interjected, "I would like to hear what was happening with Fausto."

And I said, "Don't say 'we,' Bruce! You can speak for yourself, but it was completely different for me." He remained quiet as I described what had happened to me and the nature of my imprisonment.

When I was done, Bruce said, "Well, at least all of that is behind us now. We can forget about the past and get on with the new life ahead of us."

"Don't say 'we'!" I told him again. "It's not going to be all that easy for me to forget what happened."

I found Fred Rayne to be as compassionate and understanding as Bruce Chapman was insensitive. "When I heard your tapes," he said to me, "I knew that you were suffering severely. I have been more worried about getting you out alive and sane than anything else."

"I appreciate that!" I said sincerely.

"And I truly regret that you weren't prepared as Bruce was for the eventuality of a kidnapping," he added. "It might have made a big difference!"

"I've thought the same thing myself!" I replied. "Many times!" Then I said, "But I did have other provisions that I didn't expect."

Both men looked at me, bewildered.

"Do you know why we are free?" I asked Bruce.

"Yeah!" he replied. "We work for a company that knows the value of good men."

"We are free," I corrected, "because a lot of people were praying—and God answered our prayers."

Both men laughed and I experienced *déja vu*—it was an echo of laughter—nervous laughter—that I had heard in similarly cramped quarters only hours before. "Well, I know that I sure prayed plenty of times!" Fred exclaimed. But it was a statement of jest.

Bruce reached for my bottle of champagne—his was empty—and Fred leaned forward to consult with the pilot as the plane began its descent for a refueling stop in Laredo, Texas. Our conversation was over for the time being, and I was left alone to think about Rita and the children and when I would see them again.

† † †

THE BUCHELI family arrived home with Karen Pike just before John Pike drove up. He was startled to see his wife and dumbfounded by the excited mood of Rita and the kids. "What's going on?"

"Fausto has been released!" declared Rita. John looked at Karen. She nodded her head.

"That's right!" she confirmed. "Fausto called her from the hotel before they took him to the airport."

John looked perturbed. This was not a company-approved scenario. "Well, this means we'll have to move all the faster!" he said. "Rita, pack some clothes for yourself and all of the kids. The media will be descending on this place in nothing flat, and you don't want to be here when that happens."

Rita didn't really care all that much about this. She just wanted to get to wherever Fausto would be coming, but she knew John was the only one who would take her there. So she directed the evacuation.

In the meantime Gert came over to help. Rita took her aside. "The company is taking us away to escape from the media. Nobody is supposed to know where we are, but I'll give you a call and let you know. Just play along with them!"

Gert shook her head in disbelief of the drama unfolding before her. *When are these people going to get to live their own lives?* she wondered.

25
Such Sweet Sorrow

Day 49 *(Thursday, 8 November)*

WHAT WE HAD HOPED would be no more than a pit stop
in Laredo turned out to be more like a layover. Our intention
was to land, refuel, and take off for California. But we were
intercepted by a customs official who came out to the plane to
check our papers. He was not privy to the flow of information
disseminated by the U.S. embassy in San Salvador to government agents who might be processing our arrival. So it took
Harvey Hop and Fred Rayne almost an hour to convince him
that he should clear us on to L.A.

In the meantime Bruce attempted, but failed to persuade
another customs man, a Texan, to donate his beautiful cowboy
hat to the cause.

Eventually we were airborne again on the last leg of our
incredible journey. Our conversation resumed and Fred Rayne
told us what he had learned about our kidnappers. "The PRTC
is a leftist group that was organized about two years ago," he
explained. "By the time of your kidnapping, they had about six
hundred members—though only fifteen of them orchestrated
the abduction and the negotiations. And five of them were
women." I hadn't known that, although I realized that one person in the car from which I was released was a woman. "Basically they were a bunch of highly committed students—mostly

attending law school, I think—who were doing their best to better the lives of their people." Fred Rayne seemed to have a sense of respect for his adversaries.

"They are absolutely committed to their ideology and their cause," he continued. "They simply refuse to tolerate the status quo—and I can't say that I blame them. Their methods, of course, are appalling—there is absolutely no justification for terrorist tactics and their contempt for the rights and lives of others. But I have to admire their competence, from a professional standpoint. They really knew what they were doing." He shook his head. "It could have been much worse."

Harvey Hop called back into the passenger area, "Say, do any of you fellows want to try to call anyone on the phone before we get there?"

"Sure!" replied Bruce. "See if you can get my wife on the line!" He gave him a number. After a couple of minutes, he made the connection and handed the microphone to Bruce. They talked for several minutes. It was a little embarrassing to listen in on such an intimate conversation, especially since Bruce is so uninhibited. But there was little choice. After a while they said good-by, and Linda hung up.

I was anxious to talk to Rita, so Hop tried to patch a call through to our house. The phone rang about twenty times before he finally gave up. Inexplicably no one was home.

† † †

THE DRIVE from the Bucheli home to Disneyland in Anaheim normally takes about thirty-five minutes. But late at night, when the giant amusement park is closed, it takes less time. So it was that about a half-hour after they left the house, John Pike and two carloads of refugees disembarked at the Disneyland Hotel. "The company will tell the news reporters that your family is 'in seclusion,'" he explained to Rita as they unloaded the suitcases. "And this is where your seclusion will be."

Under other circumstances Rita would have been duly impressed. She would have been even more impressed to learn that Hartell had reserved one entire floor of the famous hotel for their family, to completely secure their privacy. But all she could really think about was meeting her husband.

After the family members were installed in their rooms, John suggested, "Why don't we go downstairs to the coffee shop and get a bite to eat? It's going to be a while yet."

An hour later, Rita's patience was running out. "When are we going to go to the airport?" she asked. "This waiting around is really getting to me!"

"We're not going to the airport!" replied John, to Rita's amazement.

"That's crazy!" she protested. "I want to go meet my husband when he lands!"

"We can't!" said John. "We don't even know yet which airport they are coming to. That decision won't be made until they are almost here."

"Why not?" Rita asked, perplexed.

"For security," John explained. "We believe that it would be really difficult for the men if they had to face a battery of reporters as soon as they stepped off the plane. We are taking every step to prevent that from happening. We are assuming that the media know that the men have been released. We are also assuming that reporters will be doing everything possible to cover their arrival. That's their job. But under these circumstances, we want to control how the news is obtained, if we can—for the sake of our men."

"I see!" said Rita. *More control. Maybe it is necessary. Maybe this is the best way. But it takes so long.*

"Rest assured," John said, "as soon as those men deplane, they will be brought here. It won't be long now."

† † †

IT WAS 1:15 in the morning, Thursday, November 8, when Harvey Hop's Learjet touched down at Ontario Airport in Southern California. We had been directed to land on a runway where flight tests are made for the U.S. government. The Federal Aviation Agency has offices there in an enclosed area with tight security.

It was raining lightly as the plane taxied to a stop at the end of a massive hangar. I was the first one out of the plane, and as I felt the cool drizzle sprinkle my face, I breathed a prayer,

Thank you, Lord, for bringing me home!

A dozen men stood about the jet—all executives of Hartell Industries. Two vice-presidents reached up and assisted me as I descended on the short ladder. The company doctor present observed my shaky condition. After checking with Fred Rayne on what medication I had received, he gave me two more pills, which I immediately swallowed.

It was a long walk, perhaps two hundred yards, to the FFA office that would offer protection from the elements. I was shivering from the wet and the cold, so one of the men gave me his coat to cover my bare arms. Then the two vice-presidents came up on either side of me and, with my arms around their necks, they supported me as I hobbled the remaining distance to the office.

As appreciative as I was of the presence of these Hartell executives, especially in the middle of the night, the only people I really wanted to see were Rita and my children. I kept watching for them to appear—and when they didn't, I finally asked where they were.

"We will take you to them very soon" was one man's answer. But it became evident that this man and I were not living in the same time frame.

In the office I was helped into a chair. There I sat and watched as pictures were taken by a professional photographer to provide a permanent record of this great event. I was essentially a spectator to a celebration over the successful accomplishment of a difficult and delicate mission. Bruce Chapman and Fred Rayne were in the middle of it all, laughing, having a drink, answering questions. Bruce had to be somewhat drunk, given the quantity of liquor he had consumed from the time of his release. I marveled that he was still on his feet.

After about a half-hour of rejoicing and photo-taking, Carl Reynolds of Hartell announced, "We'll have plenty of time to talk with you men and get the full story. We should get you on over to the Disneyland Hotel."

"But I don't want to go to the Disneyland Hotel!" I protested. "I want to go home! I want to see my family!"

"Don't worry!" said one of the men as he helped me out of the chair. "You will see them very soon."

This was the second time I had been told that, and it was the second time that "soon" didn't really mean soon.

I have made the drive from Ontario (which is next to Chino) to Anaheim many times. I never covered that distance in less time than we did that night. But it seemed like the longest automobile ride of my life.

Shortly after 2:00 A.M. we pulled up to a side entrance of the Disneyland Hotel. John Pike was there to meet us, and he had a wheelchair. He and Carl Reynolds helped me into my sixth means of conveyance in the last ten hours. They draped a dark blanket over my lap to keep me warm. John provided the manpower to steer me into the hotel.

As we proceeded down the long corridor, I saw three women approach from a stairwell. The first one I recognized was Karen Pike. But the second woman began running toward me. It was Rita! At last I could see her with my own eyes!

Rita ran the length of the hallway and practically dove at me, attempting to hug me. But as she did, the wheelchair yielded to her momentum and rolled backward. "Oh, Fausto!" she cried as she fell across my lap. She lost her balance, toppled to the floor, and passed out.

She was unconscious for only a few moments. She had fainted, I learned later, because of the sight she saw in the wheelchair. Her fantasy of my return had been that I would run to greet her and catch her in a crushing embrace. But the man whom she saw in the wheelchair and recognized to be her husband had no legs! They were hidden by the blanket, but she thought they were gone! The shock was too great for her.

The third woman was my daughter Veronica. Unable to sleep, she had heard Karen's report that I had arrived. So she accompanied her mother down the flight of stairs—the elevator being too slow—to meet me. She provided enough emotion for everyone, and I cried too as we hugged and kissed.

When Rita had more or less recovered and realized I still had my legs, we moved down the corridor together to take the elevator to our second-floor rooms. Rita was holding my hand.

"Fausto, you look so different!" she said softly as she walked along.

"Well, I lost a lot of weight." I said. "And I haven't been able to get a haircut yet."

"No!" she replied. "Your face is different. You are not the same man."

I smiled and said, "We are in the same boat now." By that I meant to inform her that I had become a Christian. But our conversation was interrupted by the arrival of the elevator, and she didn't understand me.

Yet Veronica agreed with her mother. "That mustache, daddy! You have to shave it off. It's not you!"

We reached our floor, and Grandma and the other children were awakened. It was the same scene all over again. I couldn't believe it was happening! They couldn't believe it was happening! There were lots of tears—tears of joy that we had been reunited; and tears of grief as my family saw some effects of my captivity. *What have they done to my husband?* Rita said to herself over and over again.

By this time everyone was exhausted physically and emotionally. Rita tried to get the children to return to their rooms and go back to sleep; but they weren't about to leave their dad. They sat around on the floor and talked. And when talking was done, we were just there, together, enjoying the realization that I was back where I belonged—with my family. One by one the kids fell asleep right there on the floor.

I had been helped into a comfortable chair next to Rita's bed. But I was still so shaken by the events of the past few hours that sleep was out of the question. Finally I suggested to Rita, "Why don't you lie down and get some sleep? We don't know what we will have to do tomorrow."

Sometime between three and four in the morning, Rita fell asleep. And I—with all my practice of remaining still in one place, doing nothing for hours on end—watched my wife sleep for three hours. It was the most entrancing sight in all the world. I wasn't bored for a minute.

It had been forty-nine days since I had last washed with soap and hot water, so when Rita began to stir and then wake up at seven o'clock, I asked her if she would help me take a shower. With gentle hands she helped me undress. Before I stepped into the shower, she got to see the "uniform" of my captivity. (I have not worn any of those clothes since that morning, though we have kept them as a memorial.)

In the shower, with the warm, massaging needlepoints of water cascading over my body, I thought I had gone to heaven without having to die. As she scrubbed my skin from head to toe, Rita made the first of many discoveries that would startle her in the next few hours and days: there was a serious, pervasive rash all over my body that blazed bright red under the scouring and the hot water. It was one of the many nonverbal signs to her of the extent of my ordeal.

Later, after I got dressed in "civilized" clothes, I placed the first of the dozens of calls I would make in the days ahead. This one was to my family in Ecuador. It was almost eleven o'clock in the morning there, and they had already heard news of my release—first from television, then through phone calls from my brother and the American embassy in Quito. But they didn't know how I was. My mother told me that after my kidnapping, because of her bad heart, she had been confined to her bed under the care of professional nurses for the entire time: another hostage. There was probably more crying than talking, but it was a special time for me and my parents. (According to the custom in Latin America, my mother made a large donation to the Catholic Church as an expression of gratitude to God for my release. She sent me a copy of the certificate of acknowledgment in January.)

As we were concluding our conversation on the phone, John and Karen Pike came to take us to breakfast. John offered to push me again in the wheelchair. But I decided that the sooner I could start exercising my atrophied leg muscles, the better. So with considerable effort, and much patience from everyone else, I managed to traverse the plush terrain between our room and the restaurant on foot.

As we waited to be seated, our company of nine milled about behind a family of three. Eleven-year-old Helen noticed that the teen-aged daughter in that threesome was absorbed in some article in the newspaper. Helen caught a glimpse of the picture splashed across the front page—a photo of me embracing Carl Reynolds at the Ontario Airport just hours before. Helen signaled to me to turn away just as the teen-ager said, "Mom, dad, look at the paper! The hostages were released!" I was not recognized, but the close call warned us of the importance of maintaining a low profile in public.

When it came time to order breakfast, I asked if it would be possible to have a T-bone steak and a baked potato. If given the opportunity to select my menu for a final meal on death row, that would certainly be my choice. So why not have it as my first meal after being released from death row?

As it turned out, there was a reason not to: After two bites of the steak, I passed out. So much for the low profile. When I came to, I was soaked with perspiration. Obviously my system was not strong enough for steak and potatoes.

I was immediately taken to nearby Loma Linda Medical Center. That visit had been on the schedule anyway. But my episode in the restaurant accelerated the agenda.

Bruce Chapman and I were taken to the intensive care unit to undergo an extensive physical examination. In the meantime, the children were taken to the home of David and Pauline Solano so they could continue to attend school. (Hilda and Fausto Jr. were in the middle of midterm exams.) Linda Chapman and Rita were registered in a nearby motel.

So far the company had succeeded in shielding us from the media. Our "seclusion" was total. To perpetuate our privacy, they gave us fake identities. Rita and I became "Mr. and Mrs. Harmon." We still have mementos from the hotels inscribed with our assumed name: "The Harmon Party."

At a couple of points, things became comical. Many of the hospital personnel hadn't been informed of our case. Nurses and interns passed through our shared room like a parade, asking us who we were and what we were doing there. I simply said, "Go ask my doctor!"

Rita's experience was even more laughable. Doug Hodges, the missionary who performed our wedding, had returned to the United States. He was living in Sacramento and had planned to visit Rita and the children this weekend to try to encourage them. But with my unexpected arrival, Rita needed to contact him to ask him to postpone his visit.

To do this, she placed a long-distance call through the motel switchboard. When the operator asked her name, Rita forgot about her alias and said, "Mrs. Bucheli."

The call was completed, and Rita made new arrangements with the Hodges family. When the conversation was over, the switchboard operator called her back.

"Who was the person who just made that call?" asked the man.

"Mrs. Bucheli," repeated Rita.

"What are you doing in that room?" inquired the operator. "Mrs. Harmon is supposed to be there!"

Rita gasped. "Oh, I forgot!" she blurted. "I'm Mrs. Harmon too! I just have to get used to this name."

The operator laughed. "Well congratulations, Mrs. Harmon! I won't bother you any more!"

Some honeymoon!

Rita made one more call, a local number, to talk to Gert Verhoeven. She quickly filled her in on the events of the previous few hours. "We're not supposed to tell anyone where we are," she said, "but I need to share this with someone."

"I really appreciate that!" said Gert. "How does Fausto seem to you?"

Rita was slow in answering. "Gert, he's not the same man who left here in September. He is very sensitive." She was close to tears. "In fact, he seems cold to me, almost like a stranger. He is not comfortable touching me, or having me touch him. His homecoming wasn't like I had imagined it would be at all."

"He's been under a lot of stress, Rita!" reminded Gert. "It's going to take some time."

"You are right about that!" Rita said.

† † †

HARTELL
INTER-OFFICE MEMO
CORPORATE

TO: ALL HARTELL EMPLOYEES   DATE: November 8, 1979
FROM: RUSSELL T. SHANNON
SUBJECT: KIDNAPPED HARTELL EMPLOYEES RETURNED SAFELY

Bruce A. Chapman and Fausto R. Bucheli, the Hartell employees kidnapped in San Salvador September 21, returned safely early this morning and are now with their families. Both men appear to be in good condition.

They will be given thorough medical examinations and then spend time resting and relaxing with their wives and children at an undisclosed location.

Mr. Chapman is manager of APLAR, a Hartell subsidiary in San Salvador which manufactures electronic components. Mr. Bucheli, an engineer in the Helipot Division, was on a business assignment at APLAR.

The men were freed after the company met demands of the kidnappers, the Revolutionary Party of Central American Workers (PRTC). The demands included ransom money and the publishing of a PRTC advertisement in newspapers in the United States, Central and South America and Europe.

Needless to say, we are thankful for the safe return of Mr. Chapman and Mr. Bucheli. The company is assisting them and their families in their recovery from a trying ordeal, and we look forward to their return to Hartell in the near future.

APLAR has operated at full capacity throughout this period and will continue to do so unless developments in El Salvador make that impossible. We hope that positive actions will be taken soon to bring political and economic stability to that nation and its people.

(Signed) Russell T. Shannon

† † †

WHEN WE weren't being interrogated by hospital staff, I tried to ask Bruce the questions that had been bothering me about the captivity:

—Why he let the company send me down there;

—Why stronger measures weren't taken to protect me— especially since I had not had counterterrorist training;

—Why he didn't tell the company the true nature of political conditions in El Salvador.

He clearly did not want to discuss these matters. "Look, Fausto!" he said. "What happened down there was very unpleasant. It's too bad that it happened, but I don't want to think about it any more. We have to put the past behind us and get on with life."

I pressed him for answers, but he remained evasive. He acknowledged that he was scheduled to be transferred to Puerto Rico the next October, and he was basically trying to endure until he made the move. I got the impression that he was afraid that sounding an alarm might jeopardize his position with the company. In any event, he certainly had not been frank with me on any of these issues. He was relieved, no doubt, when the doctors arrived to give us our physicals.

The physicians' findings only confirmed the wide differences in the conditions of our respective confinements. Bruce was released immediately with the warning that his lungs were in bad shape from excessive smoking. I was told I would have to stay in the hospital for at least three to four days to begin a regimen of physical therapy. The doctors also wanted to bring in some specialists to diagnose my rash.

The idea of more confinement apart from my family was more than I could stand. I pleaded with the doctors: "Listen, I was in solitary confinement for forty-seven days. I need to get out, to spend some time with my family. I will do whatever you tell me to do, but please don't keep me in here!"

While the doctors huddled to decide my fate, Rita returned. With Bruce discharged, we had the room to ourselves and freedom to talk openly. Rita's increasing awareness of the conditions of my ordeal prompted her question, "How could you stand it! How did you survive?"

"Do you remember last night, when you were walking down the hall with me to our room, I said, 'Now we are in the same boat'?" She only vaguely remembered the comment. "Well, while I was in that cell, I gave my life to God. We are both Christians now!"

In the cell, I had imagined an I-told-you-so expression on Rita's face. Nothing could have been further from reality. Tears of joy welled up in her eyes, and she leaned over and kissed me. "I'm so glad to hear that!" she whispered. "My only hope was that you would turn to the Lord for strength. Can you tell me how it happened?"

This was when our reunion really began. I narrated the events leading up to the day when I prayed placing my faith in Jesus for my eternal salvation. I told her about the Bible and how it had contributed so much to my very survival. So much of what I had to tell about my experiences were negative and painful; but this part brought joy to both of us. The fact that I had become a child of God during my captivity gave meaning to all of the harrowing experiences that by themselves would have been destructive. In time I came to view those painful aspects as spiritual birthpangs.

My doctors returned with their verdict. I could leave Loma Linda for some R & R if I faithfully followed their prescriptions and started a course of exercises they would teach me. Rita immediately signed on as my primary therapist, and I was released.

Hartell transferred us to the Ramada Inn in Palm Springs. To help ease my readjustment to normal life in America, the company invited our neighbors, the Verhoevens, to spend a couple of days with us there. This was a special joy.

When Gert and Gary first arrived, I overheard Gert asking Rita, "How is it going?"

Her cryptic-sounding answer was not difficult to decipher: "The ice cube is beginning to melt."

The children rejoined us at the Palm Springs hotel and, when the Verhoevens had to leave, the Solanos came and took their place. We finally got to have the barbecue that they had been planning the day I was kidnapped—or at least a reasonable facsimile.

The Ramada Inn served as a kind of decompression chamber. It was there that I began to talk with my family and our closest friends about what had happened. It was something that we had all been through together, and even though much of what each of us had to relate was unpleasant, the sharing was therapeutic.

Significantly this was also my first opportunity for fellowship with Christians as one of them. This added a new dimension to our conversations. Even as we relived some of the painful experiences of our mutual ordeal, we invariably ended up rejoicing in the grace of God. Much of what we had to share concerned His provision in our darkest hours. It was both instructive and enriching to hear how each one had wrestled through that most basic question of all: "Why?" At that point we realized that we did not have the complete answer. But for the most part, individual faith was strengthened through the pressure. For this reason alone, the trials were valuable.

I will always be grateful to Hartell Industries for the gift of this Palm Springs reunion. The price tag seemed high: Rita "Harmon" signed John Pike's American Express Card invoice for $1,398.98—the cost for one week's private accommodations. But as far as I was concerned, it was money well spent.

I had hoped that we could go home after our time of rest and relaxation at the Ramada Inn. But Hartell, in the person of John Pike, kept us in protective custody. He did an effective job of convincing me that a confrontation with the press would be a fate worse than death: it was a circumstance to be avoided at all costs. To go home prematurely would be to walk into the jaws of the lion.

So arrangements were made for us to stay in the local residence of a prominent political figure who was in Washington, D.C., at the time. After a few more days, we were invited to visit my good friend Jim Colborn—the professional baseball player—at his home in Solimar Beach. While we were there, I was finally able to make arrangements to have my hair cut. A barber from Ventura made an unusual house call. I had already shaved my mustache, so the last visible reminder of my ordeal, apart from the skin rash and the weight loss, was left on Jim Colborn's dining room floor.

We celebrated Thanksgiving Day 1979 by going home. Being in seclusion in unfamiliar settings for more than two weeks was beginning to feel like captivity again. In my emotional state it never occurred to me that I could just pack up and go home on my own. I may have been frustrated, but I was compliant.

Nevertheless, I was greatly relieved to arrive at last in the driveway of the gold stucco house that was becoming our home. It had taken sixty-eight days to make the round trip. But I was home at last—and there wasn't a camera or microphone in sight.

26
A Grim Fairy Tale

WHEN I WAS THERE [in the cell], I made a promise to God. Since He gave me my life, I know that my life does not belong to me. I said, 'God, whatever You want me to do, that's what I'm going to do. My life is Yours; I owe it to You. Show me the way. Whatever You want me to do, I'm ready to go. That's the way I feel.'"

With these words I concluded my first public statement about my captivity. Pastor Don Crocker had asked me to give my "testimony" to the people at Faith Missionary Church—to tell them how God had answered their prayers. With his assistance, I prepared my first account of the events recorded in this book.

That twenty-minute talk was presented on Sunday, December 2. It represented in many ways the culmination of my homecoming. Present in that service were the people who had done the most to help me and my family through the crisis: Doug Hodges, who had first explained the Gospel to me; Gert and Gary Verhoeven; Pauline and Dave Solano; Linda and Don Crocker, who had supported Rita and the children day by day with their comfort and presence, and me with their prayers.

I meant every word that I said this Sunday, just as I had meant my initial pledge to the Lord on October 12, the day of my conversion. But even as I gave this address on the first

Sunday in December, it was obvious that it would be some time before I was in a position to serve the Lord in any significant way.

I have often thought how nice it would have been to just forget the past and start fresh—to conclude the story of my captivity with that fairy tale ending: ". . . and they lived happily ever after." But life is not a child's fantasy. And while God can and does work miracles, He is not a magician who changes lives with the wave of a wizard's wand. God had given me new life—of that there was no doubt. But that gift, and His presence, did not bring automatic and instantaneous healing to my damaged emotions.

No one was more acutely aware of this fact than Rita. Thinking it would be therapeutic for me to occupy my mind with circuits, designs, and the like, Hartell asked me to return to work on the Monday after Thanksgiving. So Rita chauffeured me to the plant and escorted me into my office.

Awaiting my arrival were Carl Reynolds and my supervisor, Doug Ford. Reynolds smiled warmly when he saw us and greeted my wife politely. "Well, Rita, you must be glad to have your husband back safe and sound."

Rita looked him in the eye and with utmost seriousness replied, "I don't have my husband back! This is not the same man you sent to El Salvador!" With that, she turned abruptly and walked from the room.

Unnoticed in the shadows while the spotlight of attention was focused on me during these days, Rita suffered quietly but continually from the effects of the kidnapping. From time to time, incidents like this one in my office occurred that evoked some expression of her pain. But usually, for my sake she kept her feelings of hurt to herself.

The single incident that revealed the intensity of her anger occurred during the first week I was back on the job. Since there were now no Americans working at APLAR, Hartell brought José, the Salvadoran personnel manager, to the corporate offices in Fullerton to discuss the future of the subsidiary plant. When I heard that he was here, I got in touch with him. He had invited me to his home during my second visit to San Salvador, and I wanted to show him the same hospitality. He appeared happy to see me and was glad to accept my invitation to dinner.

I called Rita and suggested that we go out for steaks—I could eat meat by now without passing out—and she agreed. She met us at the plant, was introduced to José, and drove us to a steak house in Chino.

While we waited for our meal to be served, José told us of Hartell's decision to close down APLAR. His job was to begin phasing out positions and personnel—gradually, so as not to create panic. The Salvadoran workers had a history of violent reactions to foreign businesses closing operations, and Hartell wanted to do everything possible to avoid more trouble.

As we talked, José said, "By the way, Rita, how would you like a souvenir from Fausto's ransom money?"

Rita looked at him, perplexed. "What do you mean?"

"When I get back to San Salvador, I'll send you a one-hundred-dollar bill!" he promised.

I took five twenty-dollar bills from my wallet. "Here!" I held them out to him. "I'll give this in exchange."

Rita looked on, dumbfounded, as José refused my offer. "No!" he said, "I'll just send it to you. It isn't that much."

"How is it that you have some of Fausto's ransom money?" Rita probed.

José shrugged. "That money passed through a lot of hands!" he said. "It wasn't hard to latch on to some of it." He turned to me. "I even got one of the suitcases that the money was delivered in."

"I would be interested in having that!" I said. I still had the twenties in my hand. "Could I buy it from you?"

"Oh no!" he laughed. "I'm keeping that for *my* souvenir!"

Our conversation was interrupted by the arrival of our steaks. As we prepared our baked potatoes, José asked Rita, "Well, Rita, what do you think of El Salvador now that your husband has visited our country?"

José thought he was making polite dinner conversation. Instead he unwittingly popped the cork on a human volcano that had been building pressure for well over two months. Rita errupted. "If I could get an airplane with an atomic bomb, I would fly straight to El Salvador and blow the entire country right off this planet!" She was furious, and she finally had a representative of the enemy on whom to vent her wrath. "The things they did to my husband were inhuman! He never did anything to hurt them!" Tears streamed down her face. "They captured him and tortured him and almost killed him! People that cruel don't deserve to live! That's what I think of your stinking country, *señor!* You can take it and everyone in it and go straight—"

She broke down sobbing.

José looked apoplectic. The blood drained from his face, and he became very agitated. He looked at me, back at Rita, and then at me again. He put down his fork and steak knife and stammered, "Fausto, I think you had better take me back to my hotel—right now!"

None of us had taken so much as one bite of our food. But we left the whole meal untouched and walked out. I paid the bill, and Rita, still trembling with emotion, drove the car as we returned José to his hotel. Not a single word was spoken from the moment we left the table to the instant he got out of the car.

The whole incident was both incredible and inexplicable. José had been in an entirely different state of mind from Rita and me. Rita's outburst took him completely by surprise. After his comments about the ransom money and the suitcase, I remembered the phone call he had made as I was preparing to leave the APLAR plant with Bruce—as well as his aversion to my farewell. The circumstantial evidence seemed to implicate him as an accomplice to my abduction, and Rita referred to José ever after as my "Judas."

José's openness about his possession of ransom money and the suitcase has never made sense to us. He had to be assuming that such a revelation would not startle us. But why he should think so is something we have never been able to fathom. We have formulated several theories, but this is one of many details of this whole affair that remain a mystery.

We did learn later that when José returned to San Salvador, he made public Hartell's intention to close the plant. On December 20, APLAR was temporarily taken over by about twenty employees who interrupted production by shutting off the power. Unable to control the situation from a long distance, Hartell suspended operations in San Salvador, closed down the factory during the Christmas-New Year's holiday, and put more than five hundred people out of work. José disappeared from the country.

In the meantime we learned from television news that in the same week we met with José, leftist revolutionaries in San Salvador kidnapped Gardner Dunn, the ambassador from South Africa. As conditions of his release, they demanded twenty million dollars in ransom and the publication, in international newspapers, of a manifesto denouncing the government of El Salvador.

The conditions of my own release were far less clear—not my release from the terrorists, of course, but my release from the effects of my ordeal. As the final days of 1979 passed into history, it became increasingly evident that I was still in captivity. I remained very much a prisoner to the ongoing experience and consequences of the kidnapping.

Even now it is painful to recall my state of being at the turning of the new decade. But my story would be incomplete if this vital part of my captivity were omitted.

The dominant feature of my life was fear. In psychological terms, I was severely paranoid. I never felt safe. My fear of being recaptured, based largely on the threats made by my captors just before my release, was completely unrealistic, but totally consuming.

I was afraid of being left alone. I never went anywhere unaccompanied, and I did not allow Rita to leave me at home by myself. Even if she simply wanted to go next door to visit Gert (and escape from me, perhaps, if only for a few minutes), I insisted on going along.

Traveling in the car gave me acute anxiety. I suspected terrorists in every vehicle, behind every supermarket display. Freeways were even worse. Congested traffic made me feel trapped and claustrophobic. Seat belts were anathema. A back-firing car could send me diving for cover. After a while, this condition improved so that loud noises merely made me flinch. It was four months before I could drive.

Fear of attack translated into fear of the dark. As the sun went down each evening, I would turn on every light in the house. Except for the lights in the children's bedrooms, they all stayed on all night.

I became a chronic insomniac. Sleeping in the dark was out of the question; yet I didn't do much better in the light. I fell asleep only when exhaustion overcame me. But even when I fell asleep, the "alarm" that invariably awakened me was the recurring nightmare of the kidnapping, or some of the other horrors of my captivity. Consequently I regularly went for days on end with only two hours or so of sleep per night.

I made life miserable for my family. My fear of the unseen enemy provoked me to take extreme measures to protect the safety of my wife and children. I wouldn't let anyone leave the house after dark for any reason. Because loud noises, such as banging cabinet doors or clanging pots and pans, startled me, the children learned to go about the house on tiptoe and avoid whatever part of the house I was in. My nocturnal meanderings, when I couldn't sleep, and my insistence on light not only made it impossible for Rita to sleep in the same room with me, but it disrupted the sleeping patterns of everyone else as well.

In short, my family was once again being held hostage. But this time their captor was none other than their father. Everyone put up with my idiosyncrasies for a remarkably long time. But eventually my tyranny became intolerable. It is just not normal or reasonable to require teen-age children to abandon all nighttime social activities. Fausto Jr. had gone out for basketball, and it was impossible for him to obey my edict and remain on the team.

So the children began to avoid me and went to Rita to gain permission to go out at night. She overruled me and granted release to the prisoners. This not only raised my anxiety level (I was sure they would be abducted), but it made me angry toward Rita. I also felt rejected by the kids. The tension in our home continued to build.

To add to my miseries, attempts to repair the broken bridge in my mouth were never completely successful. For some reason the dentist couldn't match the quality of the original fit, and painful gums were a constant source of irritation and frustration.

My skin rash also defied the best efforts of the most qualified dermatologists. I could more or less control it with external medications, but all efforts to eliminate it failed.

My job at Hartell added to the stress. On the one hand, I still had gainful employment. I was given much significant work to do, and I got along well with my supervisor and my fellow workers. What troubled me was the company's apparent indifference to the problems I was having as a result of my captivity. I never received satisfactory answers from them as to why I was sent to El Salvador without any warnings of danger or any preparation in the event of a terrorist-inspired incident. Their apparent duplicity in hiring me for one job and sending me on another created a resentment in me that only grew in the face of their refusal to talk about it. (I later learned that the president of Hartell told reporters that I was slated for a similar assignment in Puerto Rico as soon as I was finished with APLAR.) Tom Elliott, the only other man at Hartell besides Bruce Chapman who knew first-hand the validity of my complaints, was laid off the first week I was back.

The one bright spot in this dismal picture was provided by Pastor Don Crocker. After New Year's he met with me every Saturday morning for several weeks. I had many, many questions about the Bible based on what I had read in the New Testament. Don was very patient with me and greatly increased my understanding of Scripture. His quiet courage in the face of his deteriorating condition from leukemia was a tremendous encouragement. The ministry of comfort and strength that he had provided for Rita during my absence he now offered to me. Humanly speaking, he was probably the one who kept our family from coming apart during the early months of 1980.

It was Don, in fact, who suggested that I ask Hartell to provide psychiatric treatment for me. To their credit, the company agreed. I began regular visits to the psychiatrist chosen by Hartell and for the first time verbalized many of my real feelings.

Ventilating my feelings helped to relieve some of the internal pressures. I even learned that my condition has a name: Post-traumatic Stress Disorder (a common affliction among Vietnam veterans). But this particular counselor offered little by way of constructive guidance to restructure my perspective or my living patterns. I wasn't getting any better.

As the year progressed, my relationship with Hartell deteriorated. The thorn in the flesh that seemed to poison an already festering situation was the company's reluctance to assume financial responsibility for my post-trauma care. I was seeing a dentist for my bridgework, a dermatologist for my rash, and a psychiatrist for my psyche. Bills were piling up, and I began to get dunning notices.

Dire notices of any sort did not help in my battle with paranoia. They increased my anxiety, aggravated my rash, and irritated Rita.

In fact, it was almost more than Rita could stand. She begged me to quit my job with Hartell and work for some other company—"any other company." When I refused to do this, she insisted that we hire an attorney to secure our rights to have all captivity-related costs covered by Hartell.

We did this, and our lawyer waged a long struggle to define Hartell's responsibility for this particular employee. It was a protracted effort that consumed a great amount of energy.

In the middle of all this, a strange thing happened. I was informed one day in the spring that Robert Hartell, the founder of the company, wanted to see Rita and me. Rita met me at my office, and we were chauffeured by the vice-president of my division to the offices of Mr. Hartell in Irvine.

When we arrived and entered the foyer, everyone working there rose to their feet as if in tribute to some foreign dignitary. The scene was repeated as we walked through the offices. It felt strange to have everyone scrutinizing me—looking to see the man who was held hostage in El Salvador.

In the "inner sanctum," we were greeted by the founder himself. It was a unique experience. Few of the employees of Hartell Industries ever got to see the founder, much less meet him. As he shook my hand, he said, "Fausto, it's a pleasure to meet you! I am so sorry that you had such a terrible experience, especially after only working for my company for seven weeks!"

"I appreciate that, sir!" I replied.

"I've been told," he went on, "that you proved yourself to be very loyal to your company and to your country. And I understand that you have continued to perform your job with a high level of commitment and excellence."

"I've tried to do my best," I said.

"Well, as a token of my appreciation for your loyalty and diligent service, especially in the face of such difficult circumstances, I would like to present you with this check as a token of my appreciation." He handed me a cashier's check, made out to me in the amount of ten thousand dollars. I hardly knew what to make of it.

"Thank you very much, sir!" was all I could think to say. "This is totally unexpected!"

Present in the room with us were the vice-president, Doug Ford, and the employment relations manager from the Fullerton office. As we were leaving, the employment relations man came alongside and whispered, "Be sure that you put that money in the bank. We've made arrangements for you to apply that money toward your house mortgage."

It seemed strange that the company could give me such a gift one minute, and the next minute dictate what I was to do with it. But I was still very much Hartell's property—loyal through and through. So I did what I was told. The result was that my monthly mortgage payments were reduced. But the amount made no significant difference as far as my bills were concerned. If the company was trying to lay the Bucheli file to rest, it didn't succeed.

For her part, Rita was unimpressed with Robert Hartell's generosity. Ten grand represented only a down payment of what the company owed us, as far as she was concerned. Moreover, she was just as unimpressed with the way *I* was handling circumstances. By summertime she had had enough. She was fed up with Hartell, and she was fed up with me. She finally made good on her threat, made before the kidnapping, to take the children and go back to Ecuador.

Actually, she took with her only the three youngest girls. High schoolers Fausto Jr. and Hilda remained in California with me. But her stay with her family in Esmeraldas was an open-ended situation. She didn't say when or even *if* she would return. All she knew was that she had to get away from the insane asylum that our home had become.

Rita, Veronica, Helen, and Tina did return from their sojourn in time for the start of school in the fall, but the situation did not improve. Indeed, I got worse. My inability to come to terms with the company over what I felt were legitimate claims to remuneration, coupled with my psychiatrist's inability to bring about improvement in my emotional state, caused a deepending depression. (I not only felt bad, but I felt bad about feeling bad.)

To my other symptoms were added stomach pains (for which I took antacid three times a day), binges of overeating alternating with long periods of anorexia, loss of motivation at work, and thoughts of suicide. My new faith prevented me from taking any action on such thoughts, but they still came to my mind, especially when driving to or from work on the freeway. One turn of the steering wheel is all it would take to send me into oblivion.

My most acute experiences of anxiety and its attendant symptoms would coincide with news reports of continued violence in El Salvador. There were many of these. If 1980 was a rough year for me, it was even worse for El Salvador.

The violence that was just beginning when I was there in 1979 erupted on a larger scale in 1980. The junta that had come into power during my captivity was able neither to please nor control the extremists of the right or the left. Fighting intensified to a state of virtual civil war. By March more than seven hundred people had been killed—more than the total number of revolution-related deaths in all of 1979. By the end of the year, the list of the dead numbered a staggering ten thousand.

Some of the incidents claimed international attention. On March 24 Roman Catholic Archbishop Oscar Arnulfo Romero was murdered as he celebrated Mass in the chapel of a hospital for terminally ill cancer patients. Formerly a moderate, the archbishop had become increasingly outspoken in his criticism of the government and its violations of human rights. His assassination was blamed on right-wing fanatics. At his funeral, four days later, bomb explosions created panic among the estimated seventy-five thousand mourners, and some forty more people were killed in the stampede.

In July the bodies of thirteen Salvadoran men, women, and children were found in the Arizona desert—refugees who had paid huge sums to smugglers to find freedom from anarchy by coming to the United States.

On December 2 four American women—three nuns and a lay worker—were murdered in rural El Salvador. The government's failure to pursue justice aggressively in this case outraged many in the United States. The unresolved status of this crime and charges of a continuing cover-up on the part of Salvadoran officials continue to keep this atrocity, and the state of disarray in El Salvador, before the American people to this day.

If anyone thought 1981 would be better, this idea was immediately dispelled on January 3. Two American men, employed by the American Institute for Free Labor Development, and the Salvadoran president of the Institute for Agrarian Transformation were gunned down by terrorists in the coffee shop of the Sheraton Hotel—the very place where the negotiations for my life were carried out.

But the news that fell the hardest on me came October 10. On that day, leftist militants calling themselves Popular Liberation Forces announced to the world that they had executed South African Ambassador Gardner Dunn. They had held him for almost eleven months. When their ransom demands were not met, they followed through on their threats.

By the end of 1980, as the disagreement over Hartell's obligations to me was thrashed out before the Workman's Compensation Appeals Board, I found myself trying to cope with the reality that I was in an adversary relationship with the company for which I worked. Hartell Industries was going through some difficult times as a corporation, and there were managerial shake-ups. So I was having to relate to new supervisors while I attempted to do my job with impaired faculties.

Yet I refused to leave the company. My analyst encouraged me to quit, my friends advised me to quit, my wife hounded me to quit. But I just couldn't do it.

So Hartell did. On March 6, 1981, I was given my pink slip by a man I didn't even know. He had nothing else to give me: no reasons, no appreciation. Just the ax: I was fired.

27
The Final Freedom

Upon RECEIVING MY two-weeks notice, the steady, progressive deterioration that marked my emotional health and interpersonal relationships bottomed out. That my psychological profile was on the decline during the winter is substantiated by two reports made by another psychiatrist, who examined me for the Workman's Compensation Appeals Board. On December 23, 1980, he summarized his findings of my condition as follows:

> (1) Psychological. Post-traumatic stress disorder, chronic, with depressive features and insomnia, anxiety about the dark, about driving, about crowded places, increased startle response, constant anxiety about retaliation from his former captors, nightmares, gain and loss of weight, recurrent skin rash, suicidal ideation.
>
> (2) Physical. Recurrent dermatitis beginning at the time of the traumatic event.

In his follow-up report, filed March 11, 1981 (five days after I was fired), the same doctor chronicled the nadir of my descent with this observation:

> Because of the persistence of the above symptoms and the fact that some of the symptoms are actually worse, Mr. Bucheli has a total disability at this time.

The saying goes, It's always darkest before the dawn. Though the dawn was a long time coming, things did begin to turn around for me. What I initially viewed as the ultimate expression of rejection by Hartell turned out to be my Emancipation Proclamation.

To understand why the potentially devastating experience of being laid off proved to be the turning point in my recovery, it is necessary to add one more detail to our record of 1980. It adds one more character to the plot of this story.

One of the lay leaders of Faith Missionary Church, who was also Don Crocker's closest friend, is a man named Bill Trevan. Bill is a clinical psychologist by vocation. But before he ever became my professional counselor, he became my friend.

Through the long months of 1980, Bill exercised great caution in his relationship with me. He could see the struggles I was going through, but he also knew that I was seeing a psychiatrist. So he didn't offer his professional services until I asked if he could help Rita and me with our marriage. He continually encouraged me, prayed for me, and (as I found out later) gave advice to Don Crocker from time to time when Don requested it. All the help he provided along the way was the gift of a concerned friend.

When I saw that my sessions with the psychiatrist were not producing the kinds of changes I needed, even after many months of therapy, I asked Bill to help. My greatest concern was for my marriage. I had severe problems and Rita had significant problems and our marriage just wasn't working.

Toward the end of October, Bill took us on. At first he worked with me alone. I saw him at least once a week, and we explored both the causes of my emotional problems and the defective patterns that governed my relationships with my family.

Later he brought Rita into the therapy process. She unloaded. She told Bill every complaint, every problem with our relationship, every weakness that she perceived in me. I was shell-shocked. Bill had to excuse Rita for a few weeks and work with me alone some more to get me to the place where I could learn to express my feelings. I had always kept feelings inside me. If a supervisor at work upbraided me for some failure in my department, it was expected that I would relay the criticism to my subordinates. But I never did. The wrath stopped with me—and stayed inside. I developed the same pattern with my family.

Eventually Bill was able to help me to recognize and then express what I really felt—about Hartell, the kidnappers, Chapman, Rita, anyone of significance to me. Once I began to do this, I could begin to deal with these relationships constructively.

As productive as our weekly sessions were for me, there was one factor that stymied any significant progress in my condition: my attachment to Hartell. For reasons that I do not fully understand to this day, I could not bring myself to sever my ties to the company. There may have been some psychological bondage related to the kidnapping experience. Whatever it was, I would not quit. Yet Hartell's intransigence over remuneration depressed me greatly. Everyone who counseled me agreed: my employment with Hartell under these circumstances was preventing me from making any therapeutic progress. (Hartell, incidentally, deemed Bill's contribution to be marital therapy for problems unrelated to the kidnapping. They *refused* to pay him; I *could not* pay him. It was indeed a "contribution.")

Though Hartell's powers-that-be never knew it, their initiative in cutting me loose, which I greatly resented, may be the most helpful thing they ever did for me. I was entitled to take off the two weeks following my notification to pursue other jobs, but instead I reported for work every day. In fact, from the day I started back on the job, I worked all day every day. All my medical and psychiatric appointments were arranged so that I could work my full forty hours or more every week.

But finally the cords were cut.

For a month I made no effort at all to find a new job. I just wanted to be at home with my wife and children. I wanted to rest, to enjoy freedom from outside pressures and responsibilities. I continued to see Bill Trevan. I spent more time in church activities.

After a month I began to prepare and send out resumés. As I did this, Bill helped me to recognize how much God had given me in personal assets and experience that I could offer to a company; my sense of self-worth grew. Two months after being laid off from Hartell, I was hired to a better position, with more responsibility and better pay, in a major electronics manufacturing corporation.

Several events were occurring simultaneously during this time to contribute to my overall improvement. One incident was a sermon preached by Don Crocker on the subject of fear.

Once in a while, a person will hear a message from the Bible that seems to be directed straight at him. It was as if I were the only person in the congregation that Sunday. To this day I don't know whether Don prepared the sermon especially for me; but I took it that way.

A key point Don got across to me was that the first step in overcoming fear is to let Jesus Christ rule over our lives. He used an overhead projector to display two large circles on the screen behind him. The circles were like those found in the booklet "Four Spiritual Laws." Both circles represented a person's life. Inside each, Don drew a chair, which he said represents the throne of our lives. Then he asked, "Who is seated on the throne of your life?" On one chair he drew a stick figure of a man. "If you insist on running your own life," Don observed, "then you are going to be more vulnerable to fear—with good reason. You can't control everything!" Then he drew a cross on the other chair to represent Christ. "But if Jesus Christ is the Lord of your life, you can trust Him for all of those things and situations that create anxiety within you."

It was as if someone had turned on a light in my mind. The concept was simple, but for me it was also revolutionary. I realized that I had put my trust in Christ for my eternal salvation. I had given Him my life in general terms—I was committed to being as good a Christian as I knew how to be for the rest of my life. There was no doubt in my mind that God had brought about my release from captivity in El Salvador, but I had not really turned to Him for release from the effects of that captivity.

I paced my bedroom, pondering these thoughts and the rest of Don's sermon. Finally I said to God,

> Lord, you got me out of that hole. Now I'm asking you to take that hole out of me.

My progress from that time onward was remarkable. Bill Trevan was able to build on what Don had said to help me overcome the phobias that plagued me. It would be months yet before my fears returned to a more natural and healthful level; but my ability to function in society was improving rapidly.

Rita returned to therapy, and our marriage began to improve. Bill brought to the surface patterns—some stemming from our personalities, some from our upbringing in Ecuador —that had been harmful from the first years of our marriage. The stress placed on our relationship by the crisis of my kidnapping and its aftermath proved that our former ways of relating to one another were inadequate. We had to unlearn old patterns of communication and replace them with functional ones.

Throughout the process Bill integrated principles from the Bible with sound psychological insights. He explained to me how women are different from men in their make-up because God created them to complement men. I began to learn how to express myself in the relationship as a man and a loving husband.

Ironically, my efforts to accept my place of responsibility in our home initially created new problems. As I gained inner strength and security and attempted to take a more active role in the interworkings of the family, conflicts arose. The children were not used to their father's establishing rules and granting or withholding permission to participate in various activities. I thought this was what I was supposed to do. I wanted them to respect my authority and love me as their father; but it wasn't working out that way. Partly because of my personality and partly because of my trauma, I tended to be more conservative and strict than Rita. We still had the problem of the children avoiding me and going to her for clearance on what they wanted to do.

So the whole family got into the counseling process. We are still working through some areas of tension—we have too many teen-agers to realistically expect an atmosphere of tranquility —and we are learning and growing together.

My new job proved to be as good for me as my former job had been bad. My supervisor is a sensitive man who knows how to correct me and how to affirm me. In the short time I have been with that company, I have been involved in some exciting projects at a high level of performance. My work has been stimulating, challenging, and rewarding.

Two events happening in the summer of 1981 had a positive effect on my return to wholeness. Though the outcome was not what we had hoped for monetarily, we were able to conclude a settlement with Hartell in the Workman's Compensation case. It was more important to us to lay that issue to rest than to gain everything we thought we deserved. I was beginning to establish different priorities in life, and I didn't want that conflict continuing indefinitely. The final tie to Hartell was severed: the hostages were set free, completely free, at last!

The other event was my offer to Don Crocker to become more involved in the life of the church. He and Bill Trevan had agreed that this would be a good step for me to take. In August I was elected to the board of trustees of Faith Missionary Church. For months I had been solely on the receiving end of the ministry. Now I was happy finally to contribute to the work of the church and be of help to others.

As summer gave way to autumn, I learned to my great sorrow that while I was getting better, Don Crocker, my dear friend and pastor, was getting worse. His condition with leukemia degenerated to the point where his doctors decided they should attempt a bone marrow transplant.

The day before Don entered the hospital for his surgery, Rita and I took Don, his wife Linda, and his brother who was visiting from Michigan out to dinner. We rejoiced together in the goodness of the Lord. In the midst of all our pain, God had given us the priceless gift of love for one another—a love that we probably would never have known apart from those trials.

The operation itself appeared to be successful. The doctors were encouraged when Don's blood count rose. But Don himself was just too weak. He contracted pneumonia, and that was the ailment that took his life. He died on October 3, 1981.

Though I did not learn of it until many months later, Fred Rayne succumbed to cancer twenty-three days later.

In the providence of God, I am still alive.